"Enjoy the adventure of this wonderful book and this moving journey. By the end you will be joining me in exhorting Kevin to write another one—about the only challenge more daunting than parenting, viz. life itself."

~ JUDITH LIGHT, Emmy and Tony Award
winning actress and LGBT rights champion

"A deeply personal and humorous memoir about the power of family, courage, commitment and hope: and about the politics of exclusion being triumphed by love. The Montgomery-Duban trio will put a smile on your face. Read it!"

~ AMY MADIGAN and ED HARRIS,
Academy Award nominated actors

"Since the day I met them, I've been inspired by the bond of love and laughter that exists between Kevin, Dennis and their extraordinary daughter Chelsea. Their journey is one that should inspire us all. And their story is one that has compelled me to be a better friend, a better husband and a more generous person to the world around me."

~ JOE SOLMONESE, Former President
of the Human Rights Campaign

"A Dad, a Daddy, and one impeccably dressed little girl. A beautifully told tale about the adventures of parenting and the ever-expanding nature of the human heart. A trio of kind, compassionate, hilarious people you will never forget. Their story is joyful and triumphant!"

~ MELANIE WILSON, "Jennifer" in
the ABC sitcom *Perfect Strangers*

From our family to yours! Blessings Kev

The Family Next Door*

The Adventures of Two Dads and Their Daughter

Kevin Montgomery-Duban

With a foreword by **Judith Light**

If the house next door was really really well decorated!

DEVIN PRESS

*The Family Next Door: The Adventures of Two Dads
and Their Daughter* © Kevin Montgomery-Duban 2015

Published by Devin Press
4250 Wilshire Blvd, Los Angeles, CA 90010

ISBN: 978-0-9962180-4-7   (B&W hardback edition)
ISBN: 978-0-9962180-0-9   (B&W paperback edition)
ISBN: 978-0-9962180-1-6   (Color e-book edition, Kindle/Mobi)
ISBN: 978-0-9962180-2-3   (Color e-book edition, ePub)

Cover and book design by DesignForBooks.com

To Dennis and Chelsea . . . DUH!

Contents

Foreword

*T*here is something that seems awkwardly self-absorbed about contributing a foreword to a book, a memoir, in which one not only plays a role but is also depicted in a flatteringly and potentially over-simplified and positive way.

The truth, however, is that this unique and yet powerfully universal family of Kevin, Dennis, and Chelsea are so embedded in my heart and so fill me with love and awe that there are very few things they could ask me to do that I would be able to say no to.

Additionally, it gives me the opportunity to share their "story" which is to say, share THEM, with a wider audience.

In a way that is reminiscent of my gratitude for being a part of our television series, "Transparent." I love being a part of sharing another example of how a unique human story reveals the reality of our universality. Truly, we are all unique AND we are all the same. When push comes to shove, I deeply believe we are all One.

Like "Transparent," the power of telling one seemingly "unique" and yet inherently and cosmically universal story is to invite if not gently pressure, everyone to reveal their own idiosyncratic distinctiveness.

I love each of the members of this family individually and collectively and it is literally an honor and a privilege to invite everyone to share in knowing the basis for my experience. Each one of them is so special and their life is so blessed and so "gifted" that one would understand those around them having difficulty relating to their "elite" circumstances. Yet their authenticity and depth and humanity make it virtually impossible to relate to anything but their huge hearts, their almost ecstatic love for each other and the world. As a consequence they are inevitably and immediately folded seamlessly and lovingly into every group they join and become part of an ever expanding "family" of like-minded souls.

Just one of the examples of the largely hidden "issues" so powerfully "outed" and brought into the light in this book is the experience and complexities and challenges of surrogacy—for all participants in this idiosyncratic and self-focused and passionate relationship. It has the importance and the potential for an inspiring cultural conversation like the one initiated by the courageously transparent sharing by Caitlyn Jenner of her process of transitioning genders.

And just incidentally this book ends up being one of the best manuals on parenting I have ever read, just as Kevin and Dennis are certainly among the best parents I have ever observed.

It just confirms what I have said for decades, viz. that gay people have always struck me with their gift of being able to demonstrate and model a "way to be in the world" that is not necessarily clear to those of us who have not had to grow up with a spotlight, and an accusatory and condemnatory one, on our "differentness" and, as a result been forced to access the universal principles of making life work as a human being among other human beings many of whom also do not embrace your distinctiveness.

Enjoy the adventure of this wonderful book and this moving journey. By the end you will be joining me in exhorting Kevin to write another one—about the only challenge more daunting than parenting, viz. life itself. And, trust me, he has much to share and much to teach.

〜 Judith Light

Acknowledgments

I firstly have to thank my sweet, brilliant and loving editor Sage Knight who kindly and surgically guided me through this process. You made the journey magical.

To the Jerbeths who loved and support us and with Herb's insistence encouraged me to write him every Chelsea story that would have otherwise been lost . . . that was an incredible gift.

My sweet love, Melanie Wilson who inspired me to keep going and has guided, nurtured and loved me unconditionally through every day since we met.

Justin Pierce, there would not have been a book without you! You made it your mission to make sure I finished. You encouraged, inspired and dedicated your own power to make sure I expressed mine. I'm entirely indebted and humbled.

And of course there are two amazing women that made our dream a reality. Without you this would not have been even a thought.

Sandy you selflessly gave your love, your body and dedicated your life so that we might have the greatest treasure of ours. We are forever grateful.

And dear Helene. You said yes almost before we could ask the question. You gave the most miraculous gift with a smile and your heart. You have been my friend, sister, the best audience and an angel for our entire life together. I love you without bounds. And foremost to the only reason there is a book. The two phenomenal loves of my life Dennis and Chelsea. You are my universe.

DUH!

One afternoon when Chelsea was four and a half, we were playing. I was acting kind of crazy (at least according to Chelsea) and she remarked, "What a whacky family. When I looked down from above I said, 'I want to be in that whacky family!'"

1

e'd had a couple of typical, So-Cal kinda days, except the winds had changed. Temperatures in the 80's with a dry Santa Ana blowing from the East, the opposite trajectory of the Los Angeles basin's usual cool ocean breeze. Normally the direction of the wind wouldn't have mattered, and we may not have paid much attention, but on this day we were having an outdoor wedding—at the beach, and the wind would wreak havoc with flower arrangements and wedding hair-dos.

For weeks leading up to the big day, Dennis and I had watched the weather like hawks.

"Is it going to rain?" we asked.

"Will it be too cold?"

"Will it be too hot?"

And for the last few days, "Will we blow away?"

As you know, weddings require the PERFECT day. Anything short of sublime is a disaster. Well, we'd bought that mentality hook, line, and sinker (and you know I'm stressing if I make a fishing reference; I hate fishing!), but we had more reason than most couples to fret. This wasn't your normal, run-of-the-mill, matrimonial ceremony.

After twenty-six years of living "happily ever before," two guys were about to stand up in front of God, and their families, pledge their love and devotion to one another, seal it with a kiss, and sashay down the aisle as a legally married couple—with their fifteen-year-old daughter. So, in addition to the usual matrimonial stress factors (invitations, family dynamics, choosing a venue, catering, hairdos, flowers, etc.), we had the added spice of societal pressure, right-wing politicians, religious fanatics, and a past fraught with sexual shame (well, I guess straight Catholics have that, too).

Two men legally tying the knot with their teenage daughter in attendance: That's not everyday, people! At least it wasn't in October of 2008. An event of this magnitude deserved a little elemental cooperation, yes? But the wind obviously had not gotten the memo, and we had had enough. So, in a cliff-side house overlooking our beautiful wedding venue, where Dennis and I donned our tuxes, my usually patient husband-to-be called it quits.

"I can't talk about the weather anymore!" he said. "Will it blow away? Won't it blow away? I don't know, and I don't care. I just can't keep worrying about what might be!"

So we stopped. Lo and behold, so did the wind.

Minutes before the ceremony, florists had chased calla lilies across the lawn, but at the moment we needed to take our places, the great God of Gales took a deep inhale, then thought better of it and went to find another place to play. Our guests sat expectantly in the newly tranquil scene, and we took our places with our gorgeous girl, looking like a jubilant angel in shocking pink satin (of course!). Our joy was palpable. Our love overflowed, the three of us ready to walk together, as a family, down the aisle.

Later, we tried to understand why this wedding felt so different than most we had attended—apart from the obvious fact that it was our own. We knew that part of the difference was that we were two gay men, and in California, up until a few short months before, we couldn't legally tie the knot. Part of it was that, even after so many years together, we still adored each other. We hadn't seen that happen on a regular basis, straight or gay. But there was something else. Our big realization was that most weddings signify the true, nuts-and-bolts beginning of a relationship. The couples, their families, and the community share a great expectancy and hope that the marriage will work out, and the couple will be able to create a life together. This was our main difference. We had already created a life and a family together, so our wedding was a celebration, an acknowledgement of what we'd already accomplished. We didn't have to wonder, "Will it work? Are we going to be together forever?" We had a track record. Instead, we prepared ourselves to soak up the love and devotion of everyone in our life and relish the blessings of each other and our baby girl. (Chelsea was fifteen and almost grown, but she'll always be my baby girl; however flamboyant I may appear, I am a typical parent.)

Chelsea had always wanted us to get married. In 2001 when the Netherlands legalized gay marriage, she begged us to get married among the Dutch. Then in 2003, when marriage for gays became legal in Canada in eight of their ten provinces, she wanted to plan nuptials with our neighbors to the north. In 2004, as Massachusetts became the first state in the U.S. to legalize same-sex marriage, Chelsea was hard on our case again. Den and I didn't feel we needed a government to tell us we were bonded. We were already married in our hearts. But marriage was a never-ending mantra with Chelsea. She was on a mission!

Then, on May 15, 2008, an extraordinary event occurred in the California Supreme Court, the In re Marriage Cases, 43 Cal.4th 757 (2008). In this case, the court held that laws treating classes of persons differently based on sexual orientation should be subject to strict judicial scrutiny, and that an existing statute and initiative measure limiting marriage to opposite-sex couples violated the rights of same-sex couples under the California Constitution and may not be used to preclude them from marrying.[1] In plain English, the California Supreme Court ruled it unconstitutional for anyone to deny same-sex couples the right to marry.

Within a month, California started issuing marriage certificates to gay couples. This action was an amazing turn of events. Dennis and I had grown up in a world where we had never even heard the word "gay" until adulthood. In our early lives, bullies (and various other lovely folk) called us "fags" or "queers." The term "gay" was a new development, the beginning of an honest societal effort to humanize the experience of being a homosexual in the modern world. The positive expression, "gay," gave homosexuals a psychological legitimacy we had never experienced.

So much of the shame of being in the closet came from feeling the rejection and hatred from society as a whole. Society's expression of homophobia could be seen on both the mass media level and day-to-day conversation. Direct hate campaigns included the Anita Bryant Crusade in the seventies, which received wide media coverage. In this attack on homosexuality, Bryant fought against any rights for gays, citing her religious views on their deviant lifestyle. More immediate, personal attacks, like simple conversations in the locker room about "fags and queers," scared gays to death and gave us nightmares about how we could end up literally bloodied and broken. Now, with new language, we felt an emerging strength, more support, and an opening to real acceptance.

Immediately after the ruling, the opponents of gay marriage finalized Proposition 8 as a response to the appeal. It asked the voters of California to amend the state constitution to say that

---

1. California Law Review. http://www.jstor.org/discover/10.2307/20441051?uid=3739560&uid=2&uid=4&uid=3739256&sid=21104545020277

only marriage between a man and a woman would be valid or recognized in California. Prop 8 was put on the ballot for the upcoming election on November 4, 2008, and we all held our breath.

Proposition 8 was very simple in it's wording, but huge in its
impact. The future of same-sex marriage in California depended
on the outcome of that vote. There were more than 109,000 same-
sex couples in California, an increase of 19,000 since 2000, according to a Williams Institute analysis of the U.S. Census. Nearly a
quarter of these households had children. Altogether, there were
more than 50,000 children living in same-sex households.[2] But,
no matter how the vote turned out, there was a window from June
until November during which gay couples could legally get a marriage license and wed in California.

Well, this window put Miss Chelsea in high gear, and she
applied full pressure on her dads to tie the knot. We still resisted,
but we agreed to discuss the matter when we returned from
our summer vacation, thinking she might lighten up and forget
about it over time. After fifteen years with the little firecracker,
we should have known better.

We packed up for a magnificent trip to France as my belated
50th birthday celebration. As soon as we got home, our bags still
unpacked, Chelsea started her plea. Now, let me set the record
straight (and the record is the only thing straight here ... well, and
Chelsea ... oh, forget it). We didn't oppose getting married, but we
already felt married. We didn't understand why we needed to go
through a legal or ceremonial process, and a wedding seemed like
a huge undertaking and expense. However, if our daughter wanted
something this much, it was bound to happen. Plus, we realized
an important truth: it is essential for a child to feel their family is
recognized as an equal to every other family.

---

2.   http://articles.latimes.com/2008/oct/07/local/me-gaymarriage7

While raising Chelsea, we had realized that so long as the environment was loving and nurturing, the form or structure of the family unit didn't matter—at all. Single mom, single dad, two dads, two moms, grandparents, adopted, fostered, none of that mattered. What did matter was that the child felt loved. But that was not all. What also mattered was that the family structure be accepted in the outside world. Everyone needs to feel included, to not be discriminated against. We had the inside job down pat. Chelsea felt incredibly loved at home, which gave her the strength to deal with any negativity that came her way from the outside, but she also had the healthy desire to know her family was accepted, acknowledged, and equal in all ways to every other family. So, at the beginning of September 2008, we agreed to go for it, and we started planning our wedding.

Most weddings take at least a year to plan, but our window would be up on November 4th. We didn't have much time, so we went into full matrimonial mode. With the help of our fabulous wedding coordinator, the beautiful, former Broadway veteran and long legged, blonde beauty Charley Isabella King; we found a venue, obtained a marriage license, sent the invitations, and got our outfits together (we'd had the rings for years). Once everything was in place, we started worrying about the weather.

Miss Chelsea was in bliss. She had asked if she could say something at the ceremony, something she'd written herself. So happy that she wanted to express her thoughts and blessings for our union, Den and I said, yes, of course, and she began practicing the speech in her acting class at school. When the day came, she stepped up to the front to address our guests. As she began to speak, Dennis and I glanced at each other with great pride in our girl and held our breath. We had no idea how much emotional impact she would inspire.

Chelsea's speech:

"According to me, marriage is just not a man and a woman, or two people who love each other and promise to be together in sickness and in health. And marriage is not even a beautiful white dress. But what marriage really is, is love blossoming between two individuals and a promise that what they have together can only get better. Marriage is a bond between two people that love each other so much that their hearts are bursting with joy and love and compassion for each other, and no one can tell them that they don't belong together, or that they shouldn't love each other.

My parents are a perfect example of this. Yes, they work hard at their marriage, but they also love each other more than anything in the world. I cannot believe that there would be anyone that thinks that they should not be together, because there are no other human beings in the universe more meant for each other and happier than they are. They are my dads, my role models, and I hope I am one tenth as happy as they are when I find someone to spend the rest of my life with."

Half way through her speech, the emotion of her words took over, and Chelsea broke down and sobbed. As she struggled to finish, the crowd teared up, and we beamed with pride, a perfect moment of pure love.

⁓

The wedding bonded us as a couple, and we were changed forever. The very next day, my sweet Dennis woke up and said, "I don't know, but I really feel different." Hearing this from my non-emotional, logic-oriented mate, I was astounded. It was true. We both realized the difference. We had publicly avowed our love and commitment for each other and were now legally bonded as a couple. (Not to mention the 1,138 spousal rights that are only afforded to legally wed couples in the United States!) We felt wonderful, and we had our beautiful, relentless daughter to thank for our joyous union.

—⁀⁀—

On November 4, 2008, Chelsea, Dennis, and I plunked ourselves down on the couch to witness the progress of this historical election. As the waves of results rolled in, we watched with utter joy. American voters elected the first African-American President of the United States. What an astounding victory, and about time.

Then, the next morning, our hearts plummeted in despair. We woke up to find that same-sex marriage was now deemed illegal in California. Proposition 8 had passed.

However, there was a glitch. Lawmakers didn't yet know what to do with the 18,000 same-sex couples who had gotten married in the brief window between the California Supreme Court Ruling and the passing of Prop 8. For the time being, we were legal. Still, Dennis and I were deeply disappointed. Victory had felt so close. Chelsea was devastated, not only for our family, but for all families who didn't have the same rights afforded straight couples. That night, she vowed to do something to change awareness.

Many of our wedding guests had mentioned that anyone who heard Chelsea's heartfelt speech would understand the importance of allowing everyone to marry the one they loved. With all of this encouragement backing her, Chelsea decided to be proactive. A few months later we posted her speech on YouTube. None of us were prepared for the response.

At first the YouTube post initially found it's way only to those closest to us, as we spread the word to our friends and family, but then an international website picked it up, re-posted it, and wrote an article about Chelsea. We were beyond delighted. Chelsea was determined to change the world, and her determination began to pay off. The speech went viral.[3]

—✼—

Seventeen years earlier, when Dennis and I decided to start a family, we had no idea our future child could have such impact, or that she would be an advocate for us and for all gays. In the beginning, we had no idea we would be parents at all. Starting a family wasn't something gay men could do in 1982. Our main focus had been only to find that one guy to build a life with . . . (okay, at least build a month with). We were totally unaware of the powerful life we would live and the impact we would have in the world, but we received a divine invitation, and we said, "Yes!"

—✼—

3. https://www.youtube.com/watch?v=9aj6cB1pGGg

Dennis and Kevin
Christmas 1982

Washington 1985

Boys night out 1984

On January 6, 1982, my mischief-making roommate, Phoebe, came home from a tax appointment. With her stereotypical short brown hair and piercing blue eyes, Phoebe was a strong, determined, wise, and witty lesbionic wonder. As she sat down at the kitchen table and took a swig of the morning's leftover coffee, she made a confession.

"I gave your number to my CPA," she said. "I don't know why I did it, but I think you and him would get along."

I was taken aback and intrigued at the same time. I'd told myself I wasn't looking for a relationship, but I guess I hadn't listened well, because I also felt a bit excited.

I'd heard of the mysterious "Dennis, the Money Genius" ever since 1979 when my brother took a course from him at U.S.C. and told me (which I certainly did not remember) that Dennis and I should be together. What could my straight brother possibly know about gay relationships? Apparently, a lot.

Dennis graduated from U.S.C. in 1973, and one of his professors immediately asked him to teach Masters Tax classes, so he was a young instuctor, and my brother thought he was great. Dennis subsequently became my brother's, my parent's, my grandparent's, and ultimately my Phoebe's accountant. For three years I'd heard about Dennis from my family.

"I don't know if I should spend that . . . better call Dennis."

"Can we afford that? Don't know; better call Dennis."

And then Phoebe, "Should I buy the expensive toilet paper? Hmm . . . better call Dennis."

By the time Phoebe came home from her combined tax prep/matchmaking appointment three years later and said Dennis might call, I was already curious about Boy Wonder, but I had a dance rehearsal to get to, so I put off drilling her for later.

When I got home that night, our little machine was blinking, and my pulse quickened a bit. Sure enough, there was a message from Dennis. I almost didn't call him back, but on the voicemail he said he'd be up till midnight, and I had five minutes left. I decided this was divine timing and dialed him up.

When Dennis picked up the phone, he sounded like he'd been waiting for the call, and had me cracking up the whole conversation. He'd been asleep for hours, but he has a knack for sounding wide awake while half asleep, a great talent during seminars like "Accounting for Avocado Farms." As he spoke, I couldn't help but notice how different he was from my normal dates. First of all, he was not wanted for car theft in Boston. Plus, he had a job, and, good grief, he was literate . . . intriguing. I think I fell in love on the phone, but that would be so fast, and I'm such a careful, take-my-time kind of guy . . . (yeah, right).

One week later on January 13, 1982, on a chilly Wednesday evening, I stood at the bar of the New York Company Bar and Grill in Los Angeles, and Dennis walked through the door. My heart raced. I knew in that moment that we would be together forever. Let me clarify that statement. I'm not saying I was consciously aware that he was my soul mate, but I felt a deep knowing and trust: This is something different, something I've never felt before.

Still, as the mind will do, I weighed, watched, and assessed every detail about him. Cute as a button; fiery but sweet energy; clever and short (but not an Oompa Loompa) . . . everything looked good to go. Phoebe went to greet him, and for some strange reason, she told him that Kevin couldn't make it, so a friend had filled in for the blind date. For some other strange reason, Dennis bought the lie. Phoebe confessed a few minutes into our conversation, and as we all had a bit of a laugh, I was quietly trying to figure out why she thought the rouse was a good idea. (Dennis later told me it made him relax; because I was not the real Kevin, the pressure was off.)

Once Dennis passed my mental assessment exam (okay . . . quiz), I wanted to grab on and go . . . start picking out china and naming our new pets, but instead I maintained my decorum and asked if he would like a drink.

"Oh no, I don't really drink," he replied. Then a moment later, "Okay, I'll have a Long Island Ice Tea." Too cute . . . in case he didn't already have me.

We sat with Phoebe and her girlfriend, Pam. Pam, with her dry . . . okay, very dry, sense of humor, had moved in with Phoebe and me a few short months before, after they had dated for, hmmmmm, a couple days? But, Pam was from our circle of friends, and I had known her for quite a while, so it was cool.

During dinner, our hands casually resting on the table just adjacent to our silverware, I inched my pinkie to just barely touch Dennis', trying to pretend it was a natural and subtle accident. My hand felt electric. Then, when Dennis slipped off to use the bathroom, the girls were all over me.

"So, what do you think?" they asked in chorus.

"Adorable," I replied, smirking.

The same thing happened in reverse when I took my trip to the powder room, as Dennis and I later discovered when comparing notes. Pam and Phoebe were the Charlie Chans of the Yenta world, pummeling each of us about the other, seeking clues in their matchmaking prowess.

After dinner we went back to the bar and tried to talk over the noise, which was not easy, so I just moved in and planted one on him. The most telling of all romantic tests is the first kiss. This one moment can give you much needed information on compatibility and is rarely wrong. Good kiss. No. Great kiss.

We wandered back to the restaurant section to find a quiet place to talk, snagged a little table near the back, and began a real conversation. We discovered we were in the same place in our lives, not looking for a relationship, but should one come along, these would be the ground rules:

Monogamy (most important for both of us based on our past dating history and resultant heartbreaks.

Monogamy (just can't be too careful or clear on this point).

Fun, laughter, joy, and someone to share the day-to-day, precious details of life with.

Once we cleared that up, Dennis asked me if I wanted to go see his Mercedes.

"Okay, sure," I said.

"Well, I don't have one. I have a Datsun." This guy cracked me up.

Once in the car, more kissing . . . so good! Our kisses carried that tender, sweet radiance with sexual power promising to expose itself at any second. The chemistry could not be denied. Now, let me say something here. Just a few months prior to our date, I had made a pact with myself. I would not just jump in bed right away. I would wait and build a relationship first, and then move into the intimacy department once I felt safe and secure. I never was good with pacts, especially with myself. So, when he asked if I would like to go to his place, I nearly scared him.

"Sure!" I blurted.

Back at his condo, we made ourselves cozy on the couch and really worked on the kissing thing. After about an hour, he invited me to go to his bedroom . . . but with a caveat: this could not be a one-night kind of deal for him. In the gay community, the tendency is to go for the sexual experience first, and then hope it builds into something deeper. At least that had been my approach. Go with what I know will hook 'em, and then pray they call me (or return my call) the next day. But Dennis was different. He said he didn't want a purely sexual relationship or short-term anything. No problem on my end . . . so to speak. I was practically ready to propose. We ended up with a wonderful night together; confirming my intuition that we had something special.

From the moment I kissed him goodbye the next morning, we stayed in contact, talking continuously on the phone throughout the day and meeting for dinner the next night, all of it wonderful!

Dennis had prior plans to go to Palm Springs that weekend. His date couldn't make it (thank God!), but he was still committed to going with his friends, so I settled for phone conversations—every fifteen minutes. On Saturday night, as we talked into the wee hours, I felt an overwhelming sense of love for Den, and I wanted to tell him. I struggled with the fact that it was only a few days into our relationship and thought I should show some restraint and wait a decent amount of time before I said anything, so we hung up our last call without me professing my love. Three minutes seemed like a decent amount of time, so I called him back.

"I love you."

"Thank you," he replied.

I felt disappointed, but it didn't bother me as much as it would have in the past, because, whether he admitted it or not, I felt love from him too. From that moment on, we were inseparable.

Seven days later Dennis called our apartment. When I answered, he asked for Phoebe.

"She's not here," I responded.

"Oh, would you pretend to be her?" he asked.

"Yeah, I can do that," I said.

"Now, you're Phoebe right?"

"Yeah, I'm her."

"Okay, would you care if I spent a lot of time there? . . . Like, a whole lot?"

"Sure, that would be fine," I said.

I was so intrigued that he would resort to role-playing to find out my thinking, or what I thought Phoebe might be thinking, and was totally taken at how adorable he was in his clever little charade.

"You're Phoebe remember?"

"Yes, I'm Phoebe," I repeated, "and that would be fine, I'm sure."

"Okay, bye," he said, and hung up.

A few hours later, Dennis arrived. We had dinner plans, but before we left the house, he asked me to wait by the door while he went to his car to get his wallet.

"I'll walk with you," I said.

"No, you have to wait here."

"Why?"

"Just wait here," he said.

"This is silly. I'll just walk with you," I insisted, and followed him out the door. As we approached his car, I understood. He had packed everything he owned in that little Datsun. The car was so full, there was no way to see out the back window. I was gaining another roommate, and he didn't want to tip me off.

After dinner I went to work. While I worked, he moved in, and we were bonded by a force that we'd never realized could be so powerful so fast.

For Dennis, this was a test. He had never given up his own place and allowed himself to be vulnerable in someone else's abode. He would allow people to share his space and domain, but he never did it in reverse. He always remained in control. Now, he gave up his roots to move in with me.

He was also testing me. In the past, he'd felt he was the provider, and he wanted to make sure I was willing to take care of him or at least participate in our support. So for our first nine and a half months together, we lived with Phoebe and Pam in our apartment, and I paid all of our living expenses. Dennis owned his own firm and a lot of real estate, but he had recently overextended a bit, so when I agreed to support us I believe he felt, perhaps for the first time, that a lover was interested in him for who he was and not what he might bring with him.

Living together felt effortless and wonderful. We quickly fell into a comfortable rhythm, met the families, and immediately designed rings—very gay . . . go for the bling, for heaven's sake; we've been together a month! Gay years are like dog years . . . you get seven for every one; so if a gay relationship gets through a weekend, you're practically an old, married couple.

Everything seemed to click into place.

--\|/--

Dennis had grown up in Skokie, Illinois, a suburb outside of Chicago. Skokie landed on the map in the sixties when the Klu Klux Klan decided to march through the town because of its huge Jewish population. (I'm not sure what they were protesting, perhaps that the Jews got to live in a nice suburb, while they had to wear unattractive sheets and pointy hats?)

Dennis was the oldest of three kids. When he finished high school, the family moved west to the warmer weather and bright lights of LA. Thinking that because he loved math he would be an engineer, he'd started school learning how to make buildings stand up; but there was a glut of engineers on the market at that time so his mom and dad suggested he go for accounting, a much more steady route.

Dennis took his parent's advice and dove into accounting, which he loved. He was a tremendous student, having felt like the nerd growing up, probably partially due to the gay vibe one puts off even as a tyke (not dyke, tyke. Geez). He was subject to a lot of serious bullying, some of it directed and encouraged by the teachers. One day the gym teacher cheered his class on as Dennis was chased down, picked up, and thrown in the mud. Times are changing, but it still hurts my heart to hear the bullying horror stories that go on today and how, in some unimaginable cases, innocent souls lose their lives. Let us not forget Matthew Shepard, who in 1998 was robbed, viciously beaten, and left tied to a fence to die—because he was gay. Progress is slow, and the world being a loving safe place shouldn't require time. In Dennis's case, his persecution led him to feel that the only way to combat the ridicule was to use his brain, and that he did.

While the other kids played, Dennis studied, and, boy, did it pay off! In 1973 when Den was twenty-two, he took the CPA exam with 35,000 other people, he earned the highest score, and won the Forbes Gold Medal. He then put in his obligatory time with a large firm, but after six years realized he would never make partner (hmm, wonder why), and even if he did, partnership was not the ultimate prize it was supposed to be. So, with a couple of clients referred by friends and his sister at his side as a secretary, he bought a little condo in Playa del Rey. He lived in the bedroom, worked in the living room, and started his own firm. When you're good, word travels fast, and when we met a few shorts years later, he had moved the firm to a new location, a building on Wilshire that he owned in partnership. He now had hundreds of clients.

—⁎—

Nine months after we met, Dennis suggested that we look for a house together, and I thought he was crazy. How can we go from living day to day to having enough money to buy a house? Well, when Dennis puts his mind to something and has me supporting us, we can save. I had no idea we'd saved so much. We moved into our first house in the Oaks of Los Feliz ten months after we met. An auspicious year; a wonderful year. I knew exactly how wonderful it was, because I had twenty-five previous ones to compare it to.

—⁎—

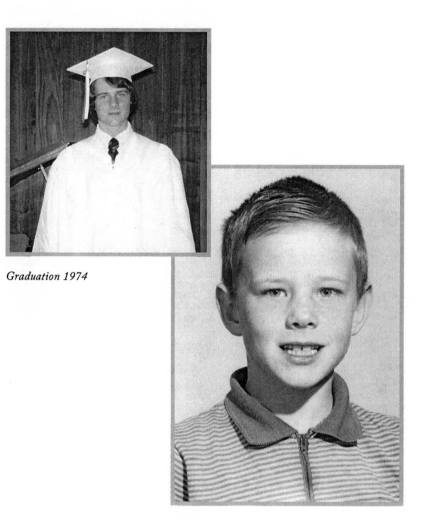

Graduation 1974

Kevin age 8

3

*T*o my parents' credit, I spent the first five years of my life never feeling like I was different or outside of the mainstream. I grew up in Pasadena in the sixties, where the love-child, stop-the-war, bussing era pretty much confused most of the residents. Pasadena is not a bustling borough of change. More like a blue-blood bastion of tradition, and when, in 1961, I entered kindergarten at Audobon Elementary School, I found out I didn't fit the traditional molds.

A few weeks prior to the school's Halloween Parade, I saw the most beautiful ballerina costume in Bullock's toy department, complete with a pink tutu and blonde wig, I knew I'd found the ticket to Halloween happiness. I just had to have it.

At first, my classmates didn't recognize me, and it was kind of fun. I was a pretty little tow-headed boy with bright blue eyes, so I guess when I donned my Halloween drag, I shouldn't have been surprised that they thought I was a new girl at school, but it soon became clear to everyone that it was me. A little bloom fell off my rose that day. I can't extract the exact taunting or name calling that happened, but I became aware that there was something wrong with me and that the other kids did not like me. I never again felt the sheer joy of choosing whatever I fancied to identify or play with; I had to scrutinize every decision.

Kevin so innocent . . . then life happens!

My favorite color magically changed from pink to blue, and from that point on, I dreaded school.

I spent my childhood feeling lost and not fitting in. If I had any friends, they were girls; and when the girls, who seemed less concerned with the fact I was a girly boy, really thought about it, they teased me too. Don't get me wrong, they loved playing house with me, but they would always ask me why I didn't play kickball with the boys. Especially when I beat them at Chinese jump rope. I think they were jealous my troll doll had the best beehive hairdo.

When I was five, my parents watched me dance to anything that had a hint of a musical nature and asked if I wanted dance classes. Are you kidding? I toddled my little kindergartner self right on over to The Amos Dance Academy, where I found I was the only little boy . . . and in tights! But that couldn't dissuade my joy. I loved everything about performing. The dancing, the music, the undivided attention of a rapt audience. It was all perfect.

I celebrated my seventh birthday by staging a production of "Peter Pan" in my backyard, where I played director, producer, and most important, STAR! I enlisted my siblings and our neighborhood friends to be a part of my off-, off-, off-, not-even-close-to-Broadway production, which I will never forget. We had an audience of thirty-two people; a packed house and a rousing success. All of my cast-mates did very well lip-syncing to the Disney record, and my brother played a stellar Tinkerbell. (He didn't once drop the flashlight!) It was just after that, in the church children's choir, where I discovered I could sing.

I was in the church choir, and soon performed Sunday solos on a regular basis. I didn't realize what a gift I had, but I did realize:

Singing came easily to me, and I received great responses from those I made listen.

It was something I got positive attention for—just being who I was, doing something I loved.

Then, when I was seven, I fell in love with Susan Beavers. My Susan had big brown eyes and beautifully wavy hair (that I secretly wanted to put in an up-do). I was taken with her strong personality and sixties-mod sense of style. Through our first kiss and a mock wedding ceremony, I was in heaven, but when she left me for Georgia (the state, not the girl, silly!), I began an intense search for belonging. Even at seven, I wanted a partner to share my life with, and ultimately, to start a family.

When I played house with my neighborhood girlfriends (usually after I begged them), I was always the mom. We never had a dad, and everyone else played my children (who often required great disciplining!). I wanted to cook, clean, and organize. I wanted to have babies, change diapers, and nurture. And I wanted to be in charge. In short, I wanted to be a mom. But then something dawned on me. As I watched TV, played at my friends' houses, and began looking at my surroundings; I realized I was missing one big ingredient: I wasn't a girl. Boys were not moms! I continually heard, "Boys don't play house," and "Boys don't take dance class." I was called a sissy and was always chosen last for any playground sport. P.E. was sheer hell.

Getting picked on by my peers was a powerful motivation to make different decisions. I realized I had to contour my dream not by choice, but by necessity, to survive. I never lost my desire to "mother," but I learned to hide it well—from most people. Old people, dogs, and babies must have sensed my nurturing nature. They were all drawn to me, and I loved it. I was a great babysitter; I listened to older family members with sincere patience; and animals gathered at my feet.

In my twenties, a group of buddies went to Santa Monica to see a friend dance in an old vaudeville-type variety show. There was a chimpanzee act, which was adorable, of course. After the show we went backstage to meet our friend. As I walked on the stage, the baby chimp jumped out of his trainer's arms, hauled it over to me, jumped into my arms, and stuck his tongue in my mouth. After I got over the shock, and the trainer collected his baby boy (a gay chimp?), he explained they do that French-kissing fiasco as a sign of trust. Apparently he felt I was safe. (Privately I welcomed the affection. I hadn't had a date in a long time.)

As I have heard from countless grown gay men, you know your entire life you are gay. But you don't know what "gay" is. You don't know what to call it, and only in retrospect do you realize you were gay from birth. When you're a child, It's not a sexual difference, but an emotional and behavioral one. For instance, other than Susan Beavers I had crushes on boys; I liked to play games that girls played: hopscotch, house, beauty shop. I idolized certain boys and fell in love with male teachers; but I didn't share the same interests as other boys, and I was always afraid they were going to make fun of me. The realization of being gay is a slow process, but the most prevalent characteristic is feeling different and not fitting in. Then, as puberty hits, you realize you are attracted to guys, but the horror of what that means pushes it down in your soul, and you desperately hope no one finds out.

One time in high school, my brother and I were walking across the quad together, and some guy yelled out, "Hey Montgomery . . . you're a fag!" We both kept walking and pretended we didn't hear it, but I knew he meant me, and I was devastated that my brother had to endure my humiliation. Those kinds of experiences do wonders to convince a young man to never reveal his true self.

As I grew through my school years the impact of coming out finally hit. There were no gay parents in the 1970s. A few gay people had kids from past straight relationships, but homosexuals did not start families. Even if I'd had the courage to admit that I wanted to be a parent, I would have never said I wanted to be a mom. That would have been social suicide. So I realized the obvious: I would never have children. I stored the thought of having kids in a little box, locked it up tight, and put it away in the attic of my soul.

I spent my painful middle school years at Wilson Junior High School convincing the druggies I wasn't a narc (though I had no idea what a narc was), and the jocks that I could catch a football; the teachers that I was a good boy, and the girls that I was sperm, loaded and ready to go.

I spent every lunch walking quickly and aimlessly around campus, carrying my books, pretending I had somewhere to be, when in reality I had nowhere to go and no one to be with. When high school hit, my sweet brother, who is two years older, let me eat lunch with him, which was a godsend, because I literally had no friends.

The one saving grace of my teen years came when I joined our church folk singing ensemble. We performed regularly at other churches, and the average age in the group was eighteen, so at thirteen, I was quite the plaything. I felt protected and grown up at the same time, and I seemed to be the perfect mascot, happy to be adored by people happy to adore me. We toured the country for a summer, where I received the one education my parents hoped I would never get an "A" in: drinking, smoking, and sex, if sex can be defined as kissing and touching things quite foreign to me. I did get an "A" and luckily nothing else, at least nothing that required antibiotics, and while I didn't go "all the way," it was still a pretty interesting path. I became a believer!

After that summer I joined the drama club at Pasadena High. The city had begun busing for desegregation and, with two campuses and almost 5,000 kids, my school felt like a small metropolis. Drama fed my love for theatrics, but I didn't find my place until I tried out for the Chamber Singers in the music department. Glory hallelujah, saved at last! All of a sudden, everything fit: the music, the people, and the feeling of coming home. We performed contemporary musicals as well as classical, and it all sang to me and through me.

My close group of friends within the music department became a clique to be reckoned with. We were the most popular contingent in the department and even considered accepting applications, though no one would have made it in. We had all the members we wanted, sharing a safe, family feeling that was fun, comforting, and, I'm sure, off-putting to many; but we had a blast. From that point on, school became a joy.

Our choir director, sporting a blonde pony tail as tightly wound as the woman wearing it, was the antithesis of warm and fuzzy; a force of nature who frightened us all, but we had a deep admiration for her talent and her no-nonsense approach to life. Under her fierce guidance, we learned more about music in a couple of years than a lot of graduate students. She had us perform constantly, and twice yearly we put on a musical that had a reputation all over the San Gabriel Valley. This was a good time, a heady time, and just plain fun. Against the painful contrast of my early high school days, I'd found paradise, and I realized everyone has to find their home, a place where they feel welcome and have mutual interests. I'd found mine.

As my high school years passed, I kept my conscious awareness that I was gay hidden deep in my psyche. I held a picture in my head trying to match society's picket-fence mentality, and I never wavered from the idea that I would someday marry a woman and have a brood of kids. I was still looking for that perfect girl, all the while knowing on some level I was really meant to be—and only desired to be—with a man.

Not being true to my own nature caused a lot of heartache for everyone. Trying to make heterosexuality my reality, I dated tons of girls. Although I went so far as to convince one sweetheart that we should lose our virginity together, even that didn't get me my straight card. I have no idea how it impacted her. As soon as a girl fell in love with me, I ran for the hills, because deep down I knew I couldn't pretend forever. Luckily, I dropped the façade before impregnating anyone. It was cruel enough to have hurt the girlfriends along the way without adding kids into the mix.

For many young gay guys, a lot of the push to have girl-friends and to become sexually active is brought on by trying to prove they are not gay. But in a perfect world, a world of acceptance and love, this idea would be seen as absurd. Instead of a man thinking he has to force himself on women, each man could express his authentic self and be with the person he desires—whomever s/he may be—and eliminate hearts broken by fear-based pseudo machismo.

After high school I experimented my way through both Pasadena City College and The American Academy of Dramatic Arts, sometimes leaving bodies and broken people in the wake of my misunderstanding. When I was twenty, I got engaged. All of our friends, sensing the truth about my sexuality, begged us to reconsider, but we were headstrong and determined we could make it work—until Randy came along.

⁓

Maya, my twenty-seven-year-old fiancé, had moved to New York to pursue her career in the Big Apple. I was too chicken to take on the Great White Way, so I stayed behind to take on the industry in little ol' LA. Before she left, we met a young spark plug at the academy. I was twenty. Randy was twenty-four, pretty, arrogant, and ostracized by everyone at school. He stood only 5'5" but his ego was twice that. A self-proclaimed ladies' man, Randy tried to bed every girl in his path, and usually succeeded. Then he would dump them and move on. By the time I met Randy, most of the girls in school hated him.

Randy came from a little town in the Midwest. When he'd moved to Pasadena, his parents had warned him of the evils of Hollywood and the "fags" that would try and seduce him. So that fear ran him, and a little bit of the chip that comes with being a small man (I mean short . . . good gracious, y'all!) didn't help the recipe. But when Maya, a passionate lost puppy savior, and three or four of our friends got him to lower his guard, he shared his dreams and innermost fears. Turned out he was sensitive, kind, and charming; so we welcomed him into our circle.

When school ended, before Maya had left for NYC, Randy landed a job dancing in a Vegas show, and Maya and I went to check him out. When we arrived, he was gambling all his money away and seemed desperate. We felt he needed love, support, and understanding. Plus, he really wanted to bed Maya. Maya, being the free sex kitten that she was, said that she would only participate if we all three could be together; and Randy, who was much randier than even his name would suggest, agreed.

We started with a threesome, hoping the love, support, and understanding would follow; but after that night, Randy felt depressed and disgusted that he had been with a man. Because of society, I still couldn't openly accept being gay, but I sure loved our sexual encounter. My woman had given me what I'd wanted all along—a man. But now he didn't like it, she was on her way to New York, and I was confused.

When the show ended, Randy returned to LA. Since he had no home, I invited him to live with my family (yes, I still lived at home). He and I never really talked about our encounter, and all I knew was it gave me feelings I didn't know how to handle. I was in love with him.

We both got cast in a production of "Oklahoma" together, and as I watched him sleep his way through the girls in the company, my feelings grew to a boiling point. During one rehearsal a piece of flying stage equipment (theater is a dangerous place!) hit him. He went to the hospital, and I was left crying with no one who understood my distress. Who could I tell? At the cast party, Randy, not too hurt to screw, ended up having sex with both his co-star and the director, and I flipped

Randy and Kevin in Oklahoma '78

out. I felt he was cheating on one of them. I knew I couldn't have him, but, however freaky it sounds, if he could not be loyal to someone, anyone, I felt like he was cheating on me.

The night of the cast party, Randy came home and found me crying in my room. He held me and explained that the girls knew about each other and were a-okay with his partying ways.

He was so tender that I decided everything was alright—until the next night.

As I got ready for bed, Randy came into my room and asked me to sit down. He looked into my eyes and began speaking in a calm, loving voice.

"Kevin, I believe I know why you're struggling so much."

"What do you mean?" I asked.

"I love you," he said sweetly, "but I'm concerned. I believe I know the root of the problem. You're a homosexual, and you need to deal with it."

There it was, point-blank, the one thing I vowed I would never reveal to anyone. I sat there, glazed over, and went numb. His next words, that he cared about me and that nothing would ever change our friendship, sounded distant and thin. My internal fear had come true. My sexuality was obvious to everyone, and I could no longer deny it. I felt like a lion in a cage, trapped and exposed at the same time.

I promptly went to my mom's room where I found her sitting in bed with a Harlequin romance. As I walked in, she slowly put down her book, and I told her I was leaving; I didn't know where I was going; and no, I didn't want to talk about it. I then jumped in my car and started driving, trying to see the road through tears and fear. I'm not sure how, but I ended up at my brother and sister-in-law's apartment a hundred miles away in San Diego. I must have had a mini breakdown, because I don't remember getting there. My brother and his wife welcomed me with no questions asked, and as I sat stunned in the living room of their San Diego apartment, they sweetly made up the sofa bed. Without talking I climbed into my lumpy retreat, my world in turmoil, and fell fitfully asleep.

⁓⁂⁓

The next morning I called my mom to let her know I was alright, and she informed me that she knew what I was dealing with.

"Have you talked to Randy?" I asked.

"No," she said.

"Then how do you know?"

"I'm your mom."

She then proceeded to tell me that I was dealing with homosexuality. Great. I guess the whole world knows.

One of my greatest fears was my parent's disappointment, but my mom said although she didn't understand, she loved me and would support me no matter what. That was half the equation. What about Dad? Well, mom had told him, and he was just as accepting. He said I was his son and he loved me.

I was blown away. All of my worst fears alleviated, I could start anew and be true to myself, whoever that was. My mom suggested therapy, which I jumped on. I wanted to understand. Plus, I never passed up an opportunity to talk about myself.

At my first session, the therapist suggested I explore and experiment. So, armed with the permission of a professional, I immediately ran out and got in the back of a truck with some guy. When it was over, I felt grossed out and confused. I practically jumped out of the car with this poor dude telling me he thought he loved me. Oh, dear gay people, we so want to be loved. Now, because I found the sex gross and thought maybe I was straight after all, I went back to the therapist, more troubled than ever, to sort it out. Time, she said. I needed time. So I vowed to take some time, to go slowly, to think before acting. But then Eddie came along, and I embarked upon a torturous year and a half, one day filled with passion, and the next, heated arguments and pain.

Smitten by his dark good looks, wit, and strong personality; I'd fallen for a gay Don Juan. Although he had no malicious intent, Eddie was shut down emotionally and unable to meet my relational needs, which only caused them to escalate—to the point of an attempted suicide.

My recovery from the Eddie drama took a few years, but I will always be grateful to him for what I learned: loving another man was not only a possibility; it was my destiny.

I also received another gift. In my obsession with Eddie, I'd lost my own identity. The pain and the determination to heal put me on the long and arduous path of becoming a complete, strong, and secure person, and made me ask some million dollar questions:

1. What is my life about?

Is there a God out there with a better idea and some answers?

I began a quest for a new spirituality, a fresh destiny. From that pit, I began a journey to find myself and to discover what a loving deity might have in store for me.

—)|(—

Festive Dennis & Kevin

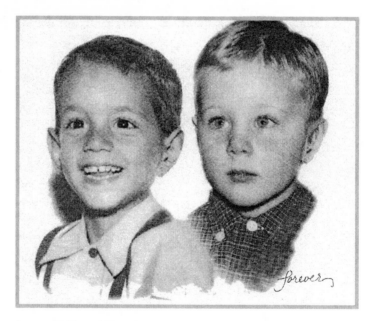

Dennis & Kevin before they met

4

*T*o who (or what) was this loving deity? My upbringing told me Christianity was the only path, and I'd
bought the idea as a child, mostly to assuage my fear of "that
burning place." Eternal fire can be quite the motivator. However,
at this point in my life, I'd buy a brimstone condo rather than
endure the pain of self deception. No more lies, denials, or
excuses. Besides, what kind of deity would punish His children
to the point of hell? It didn't make sense, and I started shopping
for a God untainted by fear.

I began reading about other philosophies and found ideas
I resonated with. I discovered a God who loves His children,
gives us the opportunity to make our life what it is, and immediately reveals karmic consequences when we act less than loving.
My spiritual transformation didn't happen over night and wasn't
always easy, but it was rewarding, fulfilling, and educational; and
I learned how to apply what I learned to the problems of living.
Well, at least I practiced, and what better place to practice than
on other people! In my relationships I sometimes succeeded in
bringing a whole me, acting with kindness, detachment, and
honesty; but I sometimes failed, and my worst demons (usually
the ones I was sure I'd exorcised!) reared their ugly heads. In life
in general, I sometimes felt confident and comfortable in my

skin, and other times felt like I had to apologize for being gay. Through it all, my spiritual base held me, helped me through, and kept me moving toward happiness.

In my search for a partner to share this spiritual life with, I went to the only place I thought gay people congregated . . . gay bars. Out I was every night looking for love, sometimes finding sex, sometimes thinking it was love, and then feeling unsatisfied. Then I made a shift. After flying to Oklahoma to attend my cousin's wedding (and drinking for a week straight), I felt like crap; and on the plane home, I knew something had to change.

I decided I didn't need a relationship after all. I would be just fine on my own. I stopped looking for someone to fill me up and decided to get to know myself. So instead of going out to gay bars, I stayed in and read inspiring biographies. I ate alone; I went to the movies alone; I went to the beach alone; all things that had previously scared me. To my surprise, I didn't need anyone to validate me, and my own company was plenty. I concentrated on my performing career, allowed my friends to fulfill my desire to love and be loved, and became happy being me. I had never felt so secure and content. When I let go of the desperation to have a partner, my fears dissipated. The bottomless hole must have transformed into a welcoming space, a space for a relationship to be possible, because that is when the door opened and Dennis walked in.

Just about the time I was letting go of my codependent tendencies, Dennis was clearing a path of his own. He had never come out to his parents, and because he thought it would be easier in business to play the old-world, patriarchal game, had even married (a woman). Then, when the marriage went south, and he knew for certain he only wanted to date boys, he came clean. So, when he walked into that bar, we were both ready. If we had met any sooner, who knows if our relationship would have survived? All I know is there is magic in every move, and both the pain and triumphs were stepping stones to our shared destiny. Apparently, prayer is being answered, even when we can't see it.

～⋅ノ⋅～

After diving head first into the jeans-at-the-foot-of-the-bed pool, and realizing the water was warm and relaxing, Dennis and I spent the next few years discovering who we'd jumped into the water with. We traveled abroad and nested at home. We spent time bonding, working out our differences, and having a blast.

We also nurtured Dennis' firm and watched with joy as it grew. Like a child, it sustained bumps and bruises, but mostly triumphs and success. Early on Dennis realized that whatever money I brought in was not even enough to cover my job-related parking tickets. Plus, every time I got a job, it took me away, and Den liked having me around. With relief I turned over the financial baton, took classes, and occasionally worked in my profession; but never found the drive to make earning a priority, so he graciously agreed to let me pursue my performing career without sharing the bread-winning burden.

Unfortunately, the financial "free ride" had a downside, as any house-husband will tell you. I struggled with the cultural belief that to participate in life you have to bring in cash. Although Dennis never asked for more than my love and support, it was hard to let go of the societal beliefs and the pressure to measure my worth by the size of my wallet.

Dennis and I worked out our snags by accepting our complementary strengths and weaknesses. We had opposite personality types. Den is type A+. Okay, A++. If he were homeless, he'd organize all the carts and trash can schedules. I, on the other hand, inspired by my parent's southern roots, am more of a type

Z, content to sit on the porch with a cold lemonade and observe life as it glides on by. Like oil and vinegar, we don't mix into one, but if you shake us up a bit, we make a delicious salad. We clarified what we expected of each other and made sure both of us received what we needed to feel satisfied. With good communication and determination, it worked, and each day, we pinched ourselves, recognizing the blessings of our rare and beautiful life together. It seems I'd found someone not only to practice on, but to practice with, and Den was the perfect practice partner.

Although Dennis is Jewish and I was raised Christian, we ultimately had the same spiritual philosophy: God created us in His/Her likeness, out of love; and we were on a journey to realize our oneness with God, and to remove any fears that got in the way of that truth. Easier said than done, but we sought to do our best, and the eighties offered a plethora of options on the path. Each self realization organization I tried gave me new awareness, and I tried many, from the Advocate Experience, geared to the gay market, to Lifespring, which in 1984, Den and I tried together. We dove in wholeheartedly, signing up for not only one weekend, but an advanced intensive and then a three-month-long, very in-depth program.

I loved Lifespring. In this group, I found help in letting go of many judgments about myself and others, and I realized how and where I resisted my full potential. We met some very dynamic teachers and guides and some folks who would become life-long friends.

Unfortunately, no organization is perfect, and one of the possible pitfalls of groups like Lifespring, especially groups with charismatic leaders, is that either:

You leave what you learned at the weekend and don't take it into your life, or

You get addicted to the process and just keep doing seminars
to avoid your life.

There is also a third potential trap. When a sincere student is seeking a spiritual path and finds one this powerful, it is easy to walk in with a healthy respect for the process, admiring the teaching and the teacher; but then lose yourself and give away your power. I chose option number three.

While in Lifespring, and through what I am certain was a divine appointment, I drew into my life the perfect, powerful, charismatic person to remind me (by allowing me to do just the opposite), to never, never give up my power. That was one of the greatest lessons I've ever learned. Whatever the spiritual path, each individual, and only each individual, knows what is ultimately right for themselves. Teachers are wonderful guides, and I will be forever grateful for mine, but no one can replace God or the way God speaks through our own quiet intuitive process.

―⁄ı∖―

Helene and
Dennis 1992

Helene and Dennis 1983

5

I'd met Dennis' sister, Helene, in the first week of our relationship. Despite their ten year age difference, Helene and Dennis could have been twins. She was a petite, curly brown haired mini Denny, whose big brown eyes mirrored his impish glint. Over lunch, and in front of me (?), Dennis had her size me up, kind of a like a new tie.

"So, what do you think?" he asked.

"I like him." Well, what's she going to say?

This little scene made it clear to me that they had an unusually close and comfy relationship, and in the pecking order, I may not be top dog. Hmm.

Dennis had a protective bond with his little sis. Growing up, Helene had been a rebellious young woman, and when she'd finished high school Den had asked her to work for him as his secretary, the first employee in his new firm. When I came on the scene, Helene was about to leave LA to move in with her drywalling boyfriend in northern California. Even with her gone, they talked daily, and I felt a profound jealousy, always competing for his attention. Coming from a family who almost never called when someone was hospitalized (eg. "I wanted to see how your father did first. We didn't want to incur unnecessary tolls."), I thought their constant contact a bit odd. It was like their family was a nucleus, and I, a lowly orbiting electron, was never allowed in the center.

One day, particularly peeved, I went too far and blurted out, "Why don't you just marry her," at which point a close friend took me aside. He, also coming from a very tight-knit, Jewish family, told me I had to accept Den's family's closeness, or I would be the one on the sidelines, so I did my best to keep my cool. However, this dynamic remained a point of friction for Den and me, and we kept working on how we would all fit together in harmony, or at least without emotional bloodshed.

After a few years, when Dennis and I joined the Lifespring movement, our enthusiasm attracted Helene, who, after being away with a cheating boyfriend and suffering financial struggles, needed little convincing for a spiritual solution. After her trip through Lifespring, she felt to me like a changed person. Some of her guarded nature fell away, and a new woman emerged. (It may have helped a little that I'd dropped the jealousy.) She left her dry-waller, moved back to LA, and returned to work at Dennis' firm; which had grown to a boutique accounting firm with a dozen employees and a building of it's own on Wilshire Blvd. In no time at all Den, Helene, and I became like the "Three Musketeers," doing everything together, from hanging around the house to traveling the world.

Helene and I formed a relationship outside of the typical "brother/sister-in-law" thing. We became very close friends, and in the dead of winter, 1991, Helene and I decided to go to Great Britain to recuperate from a grueling gig I had just ended in Las Vegas. Although Den loves to travel, he loves his work more, so he was relieved when Helene jumped in to satisfy my need to get away and play. I had always wanted to go to Jolly Ole . . . ya know; and we had friends there, as well as Helene's ex-boyfriend, so off we went. We had a blast! Theater in London, friends to visit, sightseeing, the whole kit and kaboodle. Despite the dismal London fog, we were warm, toasty, and on an adventure; and I had the time of my life—until we had to come home.

As we flew over the Big Pond and then the continental US toward sunny So-Cal, the serenity of the trip began to fade, and the moment the plane touched ground at LAX, reality hit. What am I going to do with my life?

Over the next several months, I auditioned for a few shows but had no success. I pondered daily what path to take; what would give my life meaning and purpose. I put a prayer in the air, and by April, the answer began to trickle in.

It all started with one miraculous week. One Monday during a conversation with a friend, he mentioned what a wonderful relationship Dennis and I had.

"Have you ever considered having a child?" he said innocently.

"Well, no," I said. "That's so sweet, but no, not really."

The truth is, I had always wanted a child, but when I came out, I let that dream go the way of Santa and the Easter Bunny. Gay men don't have children. Plus, Den was not a kid person. I'd watched him with our nephew, and he seemed out of sorts with him, not sure what to do with a small child. Then again, when he'd read John Irving's "Cider House Rules," the wonderful novel about orphans and abortion, it moved him tremendously and inspired him to think about being a father and taking care of some little being. So who knew? But, that had been about three years before. Best to leave it alone.

Later that week, while Den and I ate lunch with another friend, I happily munched my chicken Caesar, and out of the blue he commented that Den and I should be parents. Now that was weird . . . but we shrugged off the universe's second message. A few days passed.

Then, that weekend, we sat on our deck having brunch with two of Den's longtime clients: Clive, a sweet, articulate sixty-ish screenwriter, and his dear wife Barbara, many years his junior, with her adamant refusal to wear make-up (or a bra for that matter). Barbara grew up in South Africa, had traveled the world, been a writer, editor, and eventually earned her doctorate in Women's Studies. With an opinion about everything, she was a force to be reckoned with and a character Auntie Mame would have found adventurous.

Clive and Den walked into the house leaving Barbara and me alone outside. As soon as they'd left, Barbara turned to me and began speaking in her lovely British-raised-in-South-Africa accent.

"Dahling, this house needs a child."

Well, I nearly fell off my seat. Three times in one week, and the final blow from such an unlikely source! I was struck dumbfounded, unable to respond for what seemed like minutes. When I recovered my senses, I explained to her that this was a miracle, she was the third on the list, and the icing at that. I agreed that Den and I should talk about it.

After Barbara and Clive left, I told Den, who was just as amazed as I was. He mentioned reading "Cider House Rules" and how that had planted a seed about being a parent, but that he'd never thought about it in reality. Both shaken with the serendipity of the moment, we thought we should have a discussion. We'd agreed on the importance of having a spiritual path, and this smacked of a holy wake-up call. Raising a child would be a heck of a way to get on board with a divine plan. We decided to talk during an upcoming car trip to our house in Washington, right after Dennis finished tax season.

I couldn't stop thinking about the possibility of being a father, or having a child, or that my childhood game of playing mom could be a reality. The more I pondered, the more excited I became, until the idea gained critical mass. Three days later, half an hour into our road trip, my seams burst.

"So, Dennis, what do you think?"

"About what?" Like anything else existed.

"Having a baby," I said, barely able to contain myself.

"Oh," he said with perfect calm. "I think we should try it."

I don't think he believed it would ever happen. However, we proceeded to "act as if" and decided that if we were going to do it, we wanted the closest thing possible to birthing the child ourselves. We wanted family. That meant Den's sis.

꧁

When we arrived at our house in Anacortes, Washington, we immediately called Helene. Just as the sun was beginning to journey below the horizon, we each huddled at our phone extension, took a deep breath of anticipation, and listened to the phone ring at the other end. When she answered, we nervously explained that we wanted to have a baby genetically linked to us, and would she help make our dream come true? Helene barely took a breath before agreeing to donate her eggs. Wow. Okay, we've got the egg. Now all we need is a hen to lay it.

We had to find someone else to carry the baby. Helene was still single and didn't have a child of her own, and we didn't want her to give up her first born, so whom could we get to carry the little rascal? Den, ever the organizer and practical man, decided we should go to separate rooms and each write a list of everyone we were willing to consider. We agreed on two things:

1. We needed a woman who already had children, and

2. She had to be someone who was giving and kind, but strong and non-emotional enough to carry a baby who she would ultimately hand over to two gay guys.

After half an hour we reconvened, holding our papers.
"Okay, Den, who's on your list?" I asked.
"Nobody," he said.
"Who's on yours?"
"Sandy."

⁓/ı\⁓

6

y cousin, Sandy, had lived in Oklahoma her whole life. Sandy, a pretty and very soft-spoken Miss Clairol blonde, was quick to laugh and very easy going. As kids, I visited every summer with my family, but it's tough to forge a solid relationship on a week-long summer vacation, so we weren't particularly close. Then in 1967, when, at twenty-one, Sandy married Tom, they decided to move to California, and rented a tiny cottage about 20 blocks away from us.

Tom was the type of man who made me very uncomfortable: a quiet type, but a big bruiser of a guy with an engineering degree and a passion for rebuilding cars. I didn't know how to relate to a macho car mechanic, and he had no idea what to do with a skinny, effeminate boy who liked to knit. Though we had nothing in common, we tolerated each other, and Sandy seemed to be a good buffer.

Once they'd settled into the neighborhood, Sandy and I immediately became best friends. A little odd, as I was only eleven, but we had a blast. I didn't get along with my peers, and I was thrilled and relieved to find someone I could laugh and hang out with. I felt loved and accepted. I didn't care what we did, which was often washing clothes at the laundromat. I just wanted to be with her.

Tom mostly wanted to converse on carburetor problem solving, so you can imagine how much buddy time we shared, but he let me hang around. Then when I was thirteen, they invited me on a family car trip to Oklahoma. I was on cloud nine! I had the time of my life, and in my diary (I was gay, but not out, so of course I had a diary), I professed how in love with them I was and didn't know how to handle my crush on my cousin (not in that way, people . . . for Heaven's sake, we weren't from Appalachia).

Sandy and Tom lived in California for quite a few years, but then they had some marital issues and decided to head back to Oklahoma and have a couple of kids. This didn't save their marriage, but it did give them a two amazing girls, and Sandy and I had already bonded for life. Over the years, we sometimes went long stretches without talking, but when we did connect, it always felt like old times.

I visited once in awhile, and when I graduated high school I spent a summer with them in Oklahoma. One time, after I came out, Eddie and I went to Oklahoma City and had a blast with Sandy, partying in "country gay-land." What a hoot! They had these amazing gay country and western bars where you could two step backwards around the dance floor with your boyfriend while wearing a cowboy hat. This gave me a lot of mixed signals: boots and hats with queens in jeans; and all of it good, clean, American fun!

Sandy was always soft spoken, fiercely honest, quietly determined, and not too forthcoming with her emotions. She was very strong, and when she committed to something, she always followed through. That's the main reason she was the only person I would ask to carry our child. If she agreed to do it, she would never back peddle. Plus, I knew she wouldn't do it just to appease me. So I called her.

When I presented the idea, Sandy didn't say anything, and as was her way, she didn't even seem surprised to hear from me out of the blue. She simply listened while I, talking a mile a minute, pleaded my case.

"We want what every other couple wants, to have a child. We think we could be wonderful parents. We know each other really well. This seems like the perfect logical step."

On and on I went, rattling off every convincing argument I could think of. Dennis sat near by not saying anything. I couldn't tell if he was anxious or curious or what. So far he'd let me be the sole spokesman for our endeavor, and he definitely took a passive role in our little parenting passion play. The more I talked, the more it became clear to me how much I wanted a baby.

When I ran out of words, there was a pregnant (haha) silence. Sandy paused, saying nothing, then said she would have to think about it. That was it. No comment. No questions. We hung up, and Dennis and I looked at each other.

"Well, let's see what happens," he said.

Although I wanted what I wanted, I knew this was a huge decision for a woman. So that I could let it go and think straight while I waited, I decided that any struggle or conflict from Sandy would be my sign that this wasn't supposed to happen. Den and I decided to go to a movie, and on the way, we bought baby-naming books. I felt pretty optimistic about our prospects, so why not think of names? When we got back to the house, our answering machine was blinking.

Sandy's soft voice floated through the speaker.

"Okay, we better get started, I'm not getting any younger."

We were astounded. I thought Sandy might say yes, but I had no idea it would be so quick and effortless. Here was my sign from God! We had all the players. Now we had to find a way to make it happen.

⸻

One of Den's clients was an In Vitro Fertilization (IVF) doctor, but he was out of the country, and now that I had everyone lined up, I wanted a baby today, if not yesterday. I didn't have the patience to wait for the doc, so I started looking at other options and thought a big university must have a program, so I cold called UCLA. I was in luck. They had an IVF program all right, so I left a message for the nurse in charge.

"My name is Kevin Montgomery and I have been in a gay relationship for ten years and we want to have a child . . ." I rattled off the spiel.

Within minutes I received a return call.

Barbara, the IVF nurse's "voice of the program," explained that they had done IVF for a lesbian couple, but never for a couple of gay men, and it might be a possibility, but they would have to run it by their Board. She sounded like a no nonsense, non-judgmental kind of gal, and I didn't feel like she dismissed us as non-viable candidates. Although Barbara didn't sound shocked, she did seem unsure of how this would work. She simply stated the facts as she saw them, and I got from her hesitant manner and stilted conversation that we were in uncharted territory.

I over-explained our situation with a nervous and excited dialogue that could only be described as frantically passionate. When I gave her the chance to get in a word, she told me that we would have to find an egg donor.

"Done," I said, just a little smugly.

"Really?" she said.

Also, she let me know that if the donor was not going to be the surrogate, we would need one of those too.

"Done," I told her for the second time.

She took a pause.

"You are really serious about this, aren't you?" Well, duh, Nurse Barbara! How could we embark on a journey of this magnitude and not be serious?

Barbara thought the most difficult part would be finding a doctor to do the procedure as UCLA would only provide the facility not the doctor, so I asked for any suggestions; and she gave me names of doctors that she thought might do it, and I proceeded to leave several messages on each of the various message machines from the list:

"My name is Kevin Montgomery and I have been in a gay relationship for ten years and we want to have a child . . ."

I can't tell you how many times I left that message or on how many machines throughout this process. The psychologist, the lab for the sperm tests, lawyers, doctors, Indian chiefs . . . Every time there was a new person to add to our team, and there I was, each time, telling my story. I would leave a message, look at Den, and then talk about the possibilities.

"So do you think they'll call back? Do you think they will do it?" I would wonder.

"I don't know, honey. We'll just have to wait and see." My sweet man would answer.

"But, I'm so nervous and excited I can't wait."

Dennis would take a breath and soothe me, "Well, honey there is probably going to be a lot of waiting in this process, so you might want to take a walk and think of where we should go to dinner."

Amazingly the first doctor I'd called had her nurse call me back and say that they would be willing to do the procedure for us. We were dumbfounded. The whole thing, from calling Helene to choosing our doctor, was settled in twenty-four hours.

We'd barely had time to think about the woods we'd entered. Everything moved so fast, it's a wonder Den and I didn't get whiplash. Egg . . . check! Surrogate . . . check! Doctor . . . . Check! We were having a child, a new life entrusted into our care. This wasn't like buying a new car or refrigerator.

Thank goodness we didn't have time to process the gravity of what we were trying to accomplish. Had we really thought about what it would mean, the work involved, and the changes we would have to make, we may not have moved ahead; but here we were, all of our ducks in row, happily quacking away. Before our brains had the time to engage in questions, everything had fallen into place like magic—or a divine appointment.

⚬⚬⚬

UCLA agreed to do the procedure under the condition that we agree not to seek publicity. If the religious right got wind that they were doing this for "these kinds of families," they could cause great trouble for the whole program. We assured the staff that we only wanted a child and didn't want to carry the kid on any floats in the rainbow parade. They consented, and we were off and running.

⚬⚬⚬

The next day, I called Sandy and made arrangements for her to come to California. She arrived on May 11th, two hours before our first scheduled appointment with the doctor. Helene already lived here, and the four of us convened in three cars— this is California, people . . . we'll make a baby together, but we require personal space in our vehicles—at the Woman's Health Clinic in Santa Monica. The clinic was in a rather chic, modern building that gave the impression that women's issues were definitely the trending topic in hip-and-happenin' Santa Monica, CA.

Helene, in her casual work attire of khakis and a floral blouse, arrived as I walked in with dear Sandy, who probably would have preferred to change out of her flight-rumpled jeans and white blouse, but this was no time for fashion police. Den came on his own from the office.

Den and I had no idea if the ladies would relate, connect, or bond; so when they connected immediately, joking with each other about being the egg and the oven, our shoulders dropped an inch or so, and we breathed a little easier. Sandy seemed calm and matter of fact . . . well, Sandy-esque, while Helene was prone to nervous giggles and a bit of knee shaking. Nevertheless we knew we were all on board and engaged in this caper, and "Team Baby" was born.

We signed in and met Dr. Carolyn's staff. Cathy, the nurse, said she couldn't believe we'd put it all together so fast. When I told her I'd received the doctor's return call ten minutes after my message, she couldn't figure out how that had happened, saying it usually took weeks for the doctor to answer her calls. She seemed dazed and confused at her office's unusual response time, but I told her it was divine intervention.

In the waiting room, we scanned the patients and analyzed the bevy of heterosexual couples waiting to meet with the fertility doc. The couples varied from nervous and excited, to some whom we thought must have been going through the horrors of not being able to conceive for a very long time. These folks looked drawn and dejected, poised on the verge of tears. I felt unnerved to see such emotional upheaval while we felt like we were on an exciting trip to Babyland.

Dr. Carolyn entered the room, looking to be no more than thirty and skinny as a rail. I would have sworn she was a lesbian with her short cropped hair, plain style, and lack of anything girly about her. She was definitely a "woman of sensible shoes" with Levis peeked out below her stark, white lab coat. Come to find out she was happily married with a couple of kids. Just goes to show, you can't judge a book . . . you know.

Dr. Carolyn couldn't have been nicer or more willing to help us with our case, but she said she would have certain requirements. We all had to have psychological screening to confirm we weren't all psycho and, Sandy would have to have a physical to make sure that, at forty-five, she was in good enough shape to go through with this. Did I forget to mention Sandy was forty-five? Crazy, right? Crazy wonderful!

With my usual level of patience, I wanted everything to happen stat! This time my push was not all about me; Sandy lived in Oklahoma City, and I didn't want her to have to go back and forth, so we hustled to make all the appointments before she flew home. We got our psychological evaluations and her physical out of the way immediately. According to the professionals, we all seemed (key word: seemed) sane, so that was a go. Sandy had a bit of a blood pressure issue, but they thought that would not be a factor. Bottom line, we were good to go.

Now, let me just say, throughout this little escapade, I learned more about a woman's anatomy and inner workings than I ever wanted to know. I'm gay, for Pete's sake, so mastering the clitoris-vagina-ovarian world was not on my top-ten Things to Do list. It wasn't even on my radar, and I liked it that way, thank you very much; but the process was under way, and we weren't turning back.

Among other things I care not to mention, we learned about the process of coordinating Helene's and Sandy's menstrual cycles, so that when the womb was ready, the embryos would be too. In order to manipulate their cycles, both Sandy and Helene had to start hormone shots. We were all a bit surprised by the amount of shots and medications that this would entail, but neither one of these women flinched. Don't get me wrong; we looked at each other with that, "Really?" kind of look, but there was never a question of anyone's commitment, regardless of the pain or procedure that it might entail.

Sandy's shots were like insulin injections which she could do on her own. This was a good thing, because her plane left in three days. But Helene's shots were big ol' monsters, and as it was a pain in the keister to travel to the office daily to receive the injections (also in the keister), someone had to administer them for her. Well, it sure as hell wasn't going to be Dennis. He couldn't even look at a Band-Aid without seizing up. So, guess who drew that short straw?

Amazingly enough neither Helene or Sandy had a moment where they thought they might bolt. Even when it entailed painful, long, and uncomfortable procedures. They each just took a deep breath and said, "Let's go!"

The first time I had to inject the hormones into Helene, I was petrified. I started to prepare the shot, afraid at every step I would get something wrong. Would I be able to load the syringe? Would I get the measure of medicine right? It was all in millisomethings, for heaven's sake, and they don't even teach that measurement in America. Then the ultimate question: Would I be able to actually stick a needle in someone's body?

It seemed to take hours to get the damn thing loaded with meds, and after I gave it the instructed flick, flick, flick with my finger to get any unwanted bubbles out, I paced around her condo, nervously pointing the syringe in the air like a crazy addict, till Helene couldn't take it any more.

"So, Kevin, whaddaya think? Do you want to give me that shot or just walk around with it?"

"Oh, okay," I said.

She slowly lowered her pants to expose her hip, leaned over the kitchen counter, and waited for me to give it to her. I took a deep breath . . . and let her have it. It was so frightening. Everything moved in slow motion. The first time I took a stab at her (literally), the needle bounced back and didn't even think about going into her tushy.

"I'm sorry, I'm so sorry . . . oh, I'm sorry," I rattled at her as I took another trip around the dining table. The failed attempt really jarred me, but Helene, the epitome of calm, told me she didn't even feel it. So back we were to her bent over and me with my syringe poised and ready to fire. I decided I would have to really stab it in this time, because I didn't think I could take another failed attempt. I took a deep breath, aimed again, and . . . bulls-eye! This time we penetrated. Helene didn't flinch. I slowly and carefully pushed the plunger forward, emptying the syringe, then pulled that puppy out as fast as I thought I could get away with.

Helene turned to me, smiled, and said, "That didn't even hurt." I was both in shock and grateful it was over and giddy that I was successful without causing pain.

That day, with a very stiff drink, I celebrated my 68th career as a Fertility Injectionist. Sandy went back to Oklahoma City to work while their cycles were uniting on a path of synchronized fertilization, and Dennis and I started getting excited about the possibility of being parents.

*L*ike any good fairytale, the magical road to Daddyhood came with many tests and obstacles. Our next hurdle: the legal world, was every bit as exciting for me and Den as shots in the rump were for Helene. We had to clarify the foundational questions:

1. What is our contract and commitment with all the parties?

2. Who is responsible for what?

3. Who pays the medical bills?

4. What if the child is born with Downs?

What if the surrogate changes her mind midstream?

We had details upon details and soon became articulate in the Language of The Law.

We soon located a surrogacy center that dealt with these issues, but they only served straight couples. Of course. I gave my perfected spiel to yet another message machine.

"My name is Kevin Montgomery. I have been in a gay relationship for ten years . . ."

One more opportunity to wait in faith. One more opportunity to ask the universe for help and trust that it would come.

One more opportunity to breathe while waiting to see if the help we needed would come through.

We found throughout this process that each player we engaged, whether Dr. Carolyn, the IVF doc, the UCLA team willing to do the transfer, or the lawyer we needed to make sure that everything was legal, was enchanted by both the idea of our having a baby and the amazing loving kindness of Helene and Sandy to make our idea a reality. We'd started out unsure about what our own sister's and cousin's responses would be, let alone the public at large, but one thing was certain: we'd thought there would have been a lot more resistance. With each step Den and I mulled over all the possible road blocks and negative responses. The worry kept us up nights; our excitement about the process offset by our discomfort with, and lack of control over, the unknown.

"Do you think UCLA will really give us a green light?"

"Do you think the fertility doc will get spooked about doing this for a couple of queens?"

"What if Sandy is too old for a pregnancy?"

On and on we went, but the resistance and fears were in our heads, and in our heads only. They definitely were not in the heads of the people we met. Or, if they were, we did not see it. Our story seemed to warm their hearts and give them the idea that with love (and enough hormones!) anything is possible.

The next day, we received a call back and an appointment, and then met with the surrogacy lawyer there, who was more than willing to help us. He drew up for Helene and Sandy the standard contracts the company used for straight couples, with a few minor adjustments.

Both contracts had to clarify that the girls were doing a service and had no parental rights to the baby. For Sandy, we agreed to a fee for her part and also to take care of all of her expenses incurred with the process. That included maternity clothes, health insurance for doctor visits and labor and delivery, travel and boarding, and literally everything else that would come up during the process. With Helene we, of course, paid for all the medical expenses, but there was no payment to her for her part.

After we got all of that in writing, signed, and notarized we were then on to the next phase.

⸻

Every egg needs a sperm, and we of course had to use mine, because we'd asked Dennis' sister for the egg, and a brother/sister baby would just make everything too confusing:

"Hi, this is my father/uncle . . ." Not gonna happen folks! Although I hear in Alabama they save on inheritance tax to this day!!

I had a sister too, but she was of a religious ilk that would have precluded us from even approaching the subject. So my sperm it was.

Dr. Carolyn needed to test my little guys for viability to make sure they could fertilize an egg, so a few days after our initial appointment, she sent me off to a little room at UCLA— where, unknown to me then, I would soon spend a lot of time. My little room had all the accoutrements of a tryst for one: a lovely recliner and a library of porn. Straight porn of course. Hmm. Well, it'll work; there are naked men in it. I completed my task, placed my cup in the unmarked bag provided, and left it on the counter for the nurse.

Within two days, my test results came back saying that my little soldiers were shy and lonely. They were so low enough in number that, a few weeks later, I had to go to UCLA for The Hamster Test. A hamster test is where they take your sperm and fertilize a hamster's egg with it to ensure that the little guys can penetrate an egg. You don't have to tell me how weird that is.

Trying not to dwell too long on the strange genetic pictures invading my mind (eg. So, I may become a hamster daddy?), off I went.

I checked in with the receptionist and handed her a little bag with a tiny box of chocolates and a miniature silk rose.

"This is for the hamster," I said with a charming smile. "I like to treat my partners with respect!"

She looked at me deadpan. No reaction whatsoever. Like THAT happens every day! Geez. So, off I went to another little room with more straight porn. My little swimmers were strong enough, just not very many, but lucky for us, I only needed one . . . so . . . HIP, HIP, HOORAY! I impregnated a hamster! I hope she liked the chocolate.

_ \ ' / _

Den and I didn't want our child to be illegitimate, so we decided to get married on my birthday, June 25th and the day before our first transfer. We had a tiny ceremony on our deck at the beach witnessed by my brother and his wife; their son, my nephew and godson; Helene; and Sandy. Our officiant was our lovely, longtime psychic who did an excellent job. We walked out onto our deck with beautiful flower arrangements framing the picture and started our ceremony; onlookers watching from the beach.

"Oh look, a wedding," we imagined them saying, "but where's the bride? Oh, there is no bride . . . oh dear . . . it's two men! Put your head down and keep on walking. Pretend it's not happening, and maybe it will go away."

Despite my imagination, we had a lovely time and a great little celebration, and we'd made it official . . . well, as official as could be, seeing that we couldn't legally marry.

_ \ ' / _

The next day we were off to the hospital for the egg retrieval/ embryo fertilization/transfer. First it was Helene's turn. After several weeks of coordinating Sandy's and Helene's female cycles through the injections, the staff determined that the timing was right, and Helene was ready to produce some teeny tiny eggs.

On all of these occasions I was the chosen companion in our family, because there is no way that Den could endure any medical procedure, even as an observer. He fainted at spilt milk and was nauseated from dust bunnies swept from under the fridge! So off Helene and I went to UCLA to dive into yet another mile of unknown terrain. And Dennis went where? To work, of course! His comfort zone.

After we checked in at the IFV desk, they gowned Helene up and explained that was a simple and painless event. It was in a normal examining room with the required stirrup-ed table and fabulous crinkly white butcher like paper we all love so dearly. They sedated her until she was very drowsy, then took a long needle and inserted it through her uterus and into her ovary to suck out her little ova. I KNOW! I can't even imagine! She grabbed my hand as they started the extraction, squeezed her eyes tightly shut, and prepared for the worst; but then she seemed to not be in any pain at all. The only problem was that the anesthetic made her nauseous. So, I held the little bucket, she spewed, and the doctor retrieved. Minutes later we learned, through the miracle of science and good microscopes, that we'd gotten a lot of eggs. Yay, team!

⁓᠊

Now, my turn. Back to my little room with no one to hold my hand, just a cup and a lot of nervous energy. No more rehearsals. This was showtime. I settled into my porno matinee feeling conspicuous and alone, but charged with a mission to create life.

I felt so self consciousness walking down a hall at a major hospital, passing UCLA college students, and ducking into a room to perform an act that everyone knew was going on but didn't want to admit was happening. It was unnerving to say the least.

Each donor is required to be alone, but that did not stop one college student from slipping a girlfriend into his lair. Aw, youth. I was too nervous to break any rules. I wanted a child. What if I got banned from my little cubicle of delight? I wasn't just donating; I was creating a baby. This was serious! I made my deposit, slipped the plastic cup into the unmarked brown paper bag (as though no one knew its contents), conspicuously carried my pseudo lunch sack down the long hall to the reception room full of possible donors, and placed my swimmers quietly on the receptionist's desk. They then took all the ingredients to the lab and I went home. On they way, I got a call on my cell phone.

"Mr. Montgomery?"

"Yes?"

"We need more sperm."

My heart sank to my toes. I felt nauseated, and for the very first time, I felt as if maybe this wasn't going to happen. What if my sperm was never going to produce? I called Den at the office, and he so wonderfully calmed me down in his sweet way, said it was probably nothing, and that he was sure everything would be okay. I made a u-turn with my heart still racing and my head in a fog, clear in that moment of one thing: I wanted this more than anything.

You don't know how much something means to you until the possibility is taken away. I wanted a child. This was going to happen. It had to happen. But, my fear raged on as I careened down Sunset wondering if I would be able to make another donation. I hadn't tried repeat performance since my early twenties. Now thirty-six, I thought that ship of wild libido had sailed off into the horizon. Thoughts bombarded my brain. What if I can't? What if the sperm won't work? What if this is never going to happen? On and on again.

When I got there, the tech explained that something had tainted the first batch, some kind of bacteria in the sample. The technician wasn't sure exactly why. Maybe I had touched the edge of the cup and my hand hadn't been clean. For them, theories. For me, guilt that I had screwed up the process. So back once again to my little cubicle away from home where I washed my hands—four times. Tried to hit the cup without it making contact with any body part, a trick that is not easily accomplished and not worth the visual (oops, too late!).

They accepted my second sample in a matter of an hour and told me they would let me know asap. I took my butterflied stomach, headed for home, and within half an hour I got the call. This time everything seemed on target.

We had been informed by the staff at the hospital that the fertilization process takes three days to start. At that point we would know how many eggs took my sperm, and thus, how many embryos we ended up with. We waited. Two days later we got the call: ten viable embryos! Barbara the IVF nurse said ten was wonderful. The average was four.

꘎

Now, just over a month from our very first visit to Dr. Carolyn, it was Sandy's turn. She had taken another leave from her job, and had flown back, amazingly and graciously prepared to take on our embryos. Back to UCLA and ready for implantation, our excitement was palpable. We were on our way to having a child!

Dr. Carolyn and nurse Barbara brought in the embryos on a cart with a microscope. It was surreal to think that our possible future baby was on a wheeled table that looked like the movie projector carts we had back in elementary school classrooms.

Sandy lay in her hospital-type bed that had a removable foot to access . . . well, you know what part of her they needed to access. I sat next to her in my fold-able bedside chair, trans-fixed. Dr. Carolyn asked if I wanted to see the embryos before we implanted them. Are you kidding? I looked through the micro-scope and saw four embryos that had divided into four or six cells. It was amazing. When they start out, it takes two days for them to divide into four to six cells. After that, all bets are off. This was a moment I'll never forget. The miracle of life had never been so clear to me. One of those group of round circles could become a person. My person. Miraculous!

The transfer process appeared to be easy and painless. The doc simply took a plain plastic syringe, and, while looking through the microscope, guided the nozzle to the small glass slide and carefully pulled back the plunger to suck up those pup-pies. Barbara had Sandy ready, laying back with the speculum positioned to give the doctor access to the cervix. I observed from my over the Sandy shoulder position. From my view I just saw the doctor move the syringe of life down between the legs and very carefully position and push the plunger. Dr. Carolyn pulled back with an empty tube.

"Done," she said. "Now we wait."

The crucial part was that Sandy had to stay in bed for a few days and be still. They'd implanted four embryos into her uterus and frozen the remaining six in case we needed them later. But we were so confident that this was going to work, we couldn't imagine we would need them. Sandy came home with us, and we waited on her hand and foot. She didn't have to get up except to go to the bath-room. After three days she had permission to be mobile again and left to go home to Oklahoma City to work and be with her family.

Sometimes the embryos "take" and sometimes they don't. We would not know anything for two weeks. Once in Oklahoma City,

Sandy needed to find a clinic that would give her a daily progesterone shot, which was needed to keep the body in pregnant mode.

Finding a willing clinic wasn't easy. Oklahoma had no surrogacy laws and was a very conservative state. If Oklahoma authorities got wind she was carrying a baby for a gay couple, we would be out of luck. Fortunately, she found a clinic that didn't require a lot of explanation and began the necessary injections.

The next few weeks were very exciting and anxious. IVF was an evolving field, and although the percentages of successful implantations were much better than just a few years earlier, we were still left with a 30 percent chance of success. The hardest part was getting the embryos to stick. Once they were secure and growing, the percentages of miscarriage went down, but were still greater than with regular pregnancies.

Despite the odds, we were certain we were pregnant, and we planned away. We imagined how we would decorate the baby's room, dreamed about life would after we were dads, and walked around in pregnancy bliss. Sure of a good result, we waited anxiously like kids watching for Santa.

The day that Sandy went in for the blood test to find out if we were actually pregnant, Den and I decided to take our nephews and niece to Universal Studios. It seemed like a lovely distraction and would feel like a great celebration once we got the call. We toured around the Studios, seeing shows and the sites and called Sandy at around 2:00 pm for the results. I found a pay phone (at that time, we didn't all have cell phones on our hip) and made the call.

We weren't pregnant.

The shock hit both of us like a ton of bricks. We'd felt so certain it had worked, and that we were on our way to parenthood, so the remainder of the day was painful. We didn't tell our niece and nephews anything, pretending everything was fine, but inside we were devastated. I will never forget the anguish of trying to smile mixed with the torture in my gut. I don't think I realized until that moment how attached I was to the process and to the idea of having my own child.

As soon as we got the kids home, I called our Dr. Carolyn and asked her what we do now. She told me we could try another transfer with the embryos we had frozen, but that the odds go way down with frozen embryos. I wasn't giving up that quickly. I talked to Sandy and asked if she was willing. She agreed to try again, so we scheduled the transfer for September.

In this process we had met many couples that were working through in vitro-fertilization to have their own children. After our first attempt failed, I had such respect and empathy for these couples. They only came to this method after every other avenue had been exhausted. I could tell they felt like there was something wrong with them. They couldn't produce their own children and the pain and stress it put on their relationships to have to work so hard was devastating to watch. I remember one couple who had tried three times. I will never forget the pain when even their last attempt came up negative. They felt that something was wrong with them, because they weren't fertile or couldn't carry their own child. We were just an alternative situation. After our first attempt didn't work, I looked at every parent with children crossing the street or at the store with envy and jealousy. Why couldn't I have that? I could only imagine what straight couples must go through . . . heart-wrenching.

Take two: The doctor put Sandy back on the hormones to get her uterus ready for transfer, and we waited the several months it took, though not quite as optimistically as we had the first attempt. Helene had nothing more to do, so we only had to get Sandy's cycle ready to receive (more shots and more shots).

Plus, we had to coordinate our attempts with her work schedule, so it wouldn't interfere with her life too much. Of course if it worked she would be having a baby, so I'm not sure how that couldn't interfere with everything.

By the time September rolled around, we were excited again. We flew Sandy out, three months after our first attempt, in readiness to make our second try.

The frozen embryos thawed and looked good, and the transfer went off without a hitch. The doctor decided, because the chances go down with the frozen ones, to put in all six. There is a risk of multiple births the more embryos you use. I wasn't ready for six kids, but that was a very outside chance in this process. If we were lucky enough to have this high-quality problem, we elected "selective reduction." Selective reduction is a procedure where they take out embryos in multiple births, but only down to twins. So, six embryos went in, we prayed for only one to take. I don't think I was ready for dos bambinos! Sandy went back on bed rest, and we went back on baby watch. After three days, Sandy flew home to Oklahoma City again, and this time I went with her.

I thought that rather than sitting at home waiting, it might be more of a distraction to hang out with Sandy in Oklahoma to at least be closer to the womb. So I sat in Oklahoma City, knitted a sweater for our dear Sandy (I am a screaming stereotype), and waited with her daughters, Christy and Alex, for the time to pass. Christy was twenty-one and lived with her dad, but Alex, still in middle school, lived at home with her mom. Being there was a great distraction and felt like a bit of a vacation. Now an expert with needles, knitting as well as hypodermic, I was able to give Sandy the painful Progesterone injections (like a thick penicillin shot) necessary to save her from going to the clinic every day. She and her second husband at the time had separated, so he was basically out of the picture, and she appreciated having me around the house. It was a long two weeks, but I prayed and waited until the date arrived for the test.

Sandy went to the clinic in the morning, but we knew we wouldn't have the results until the afternoon. Time slowed to a halt, while I knitted my fingers into a bloody stub, all the while finding out what Oprah was up to. Eventually the clinic called. Negative. Dennis, Sandy, and I went into shock again. This couldn't be true. I felt a depressed, out-of-control feeling that I had never felt before. Why negative? Why is this happening? The process taught me the meaning of desire. I thought I had desired my entertainment career, but looking back, when the going got tough, I went missing. I didn't push through the hard parts. I realized now that I must not have desired it enough. If I had, nothing would have stopped me or stood in my way. Now I felt that desire. I wanted a child like I had never wanted anything in my life. I feared Sandy and Dennis were feeling like they couldn't handle much more. They seemed tired and emotionally spent, and both told me how difficult the process was. For Sandy, the physical toll of shots and hormones was intense, and although she didn't say it to my face, there was an obvious sense of failure on her part to help us have our wish fulfilled. For Den, the stress of not being in control and then being emotionally let down time and again was simply not what my boy was used to. Both told me separately that maybe we should stop. I said to each of them just one more time; knowing in my heart that if one more time didn't work, I would figure out how to make it just one more time . . . again.

⸺⸙⸺

Helene lovingly agreed to do another egg retrieval, and just a few days after our negative result, as I was about to board the plane back to LA, Sandy said the unthinkable.

"I don't think this is going to work, unless I move to California." Well, that's interesting. With Sandy in California, it would be a lot easier. If she got pregnant and lived in Oklahoma, she couldn't have the baby in Oklahoma, because they didn't recognize surrogacy, and the baby would be Sandy's and her husband's. Oklahoma also didn't allow gay couples or single men to adopt, so she would have had to have the baby in California anyway. If she moved, she also would be closer to monitor, and I could give her the shots. To make this move, Sandy would have to give up her job and sell her house. This was huge. However, she worked as an accountant, and since we had an accounting firm, that seemed like it might be the perfect opportunity. Her daughter would have to move to a new state with no friends and start over in high school. A daunting task for any child. Sandy talked to Alex and she, amazingly enough, was ready.

I talked to Den, and in his usual fabulously giving nature, said he would give Sandy a job. They could live with us until they got settled, and they would start on a new life. Once again we were off on a whole new adventure, and we had no idea if the next time would work, or we would have to go back to the drawing board (or, for some of us, the little room with the straight porn).

We started the relocation process. Sandy put her house on the market, and they started packing and readying themselves for California. Because they wanted to get Alex into school as soon as possible in the new school year, they moved before the house sold. Once again we started the shots, and the cycles of two wonderful women began to merge in preparation for pregnancy.

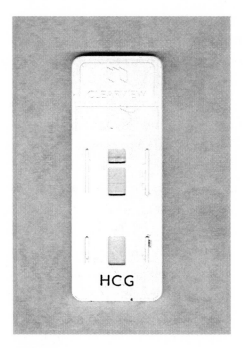

We're pregnant!!!!

8

I found it a bit shocking that Sandy's daughter, Alex, was so willing to move. Aside from her divine new accommodations, of course, why would a kid want to uproot themselves from the only home they'd ever known and start over in the middle of high school? Believe me, we were grateful, but I wondered what might be happening behind the scenes.

Back in the fall of '81, a few months before I'd met Dennis when the girls were still young, Sandy called me to say she had met a wonderful guy and she was going to remarry. Bob, a tall, brown headed, neatly groomed, and handsome adjacent kind o' guy, came at you with his hand out for a shake. His over eager demeanor drew my suspicion. He was so emphatically okay with Sandy's gay cousin that I looked for homophobic pamphlets hanging out his back pocket. In other words, he didn't quite pass the smell test. Not that I wanted to smell him, but I'd promised Sandy years before that if she got married again, I would be there, so when they announced their wedding was imminent, off I went to Oklahoma City.

A few nights before the wedding, Sandy, Bob, and I had a heart to heart. It was the '80s and everyone was into group shares and brutal honesty. So we got plowed and sat in a mini circle declaring we were going to bond and welcome my new cousin-in-law. I told him straight up that if he hurt her, I would personally take him out . . . (I know; not a chance in hell I would follow through, but it sounded so butch, and I really wanted to take care of her). Once I'd extracted his promise of fidelity, trust, love, and good down home husbanding, I gave my blessing and the wedding went off without a hitch. I did the flowers, hair, and make-up; and I sang and played the piano . . . (helloooo! I'm GAY!).

Sandy and I didn't talk much for the next few years, which was not unusual for us. She never let on that she wasn't happy. But, when we started the baby process, I began to piece together what was really going down. Sandy said nothing to me directly, but from what I could surmise as a mouse in the wall (and from listening to other mice informants), Bob had been abusive not only to Sandy, but to her girls too. By the time I had gone back to Oklahoma City to await the results of the second implant, Bob was gone. Long story short, I believe that was what made it easier for Sandy and Alex to jump ship and start over in California. Whatever it took, we were grateful.

Alex was a little cranky at first, which was understandable given the major life change she was undertaking, but other than that everything seemed to be moving along wonderfully.

On October 15, 1992, we implanted six more embryos in Sandy's uterus. We hadn't gotten as many from this extraction, so we decided to just put them all in and wish for the best. (I have no idea what we would have done if six had taken hold . . . yikes! I guess I would have been known as Sexto Mom.) We all sat back, held our collective breath for two weeks, and tried to move on with our lives. Alex started school at Santa Monica High, Sandy started working at Dennis' firm, Dennis worked like always, and I followed everyone around . . . like always. We weren't quite as tense this go around. After a few failures, you begin to stop hoping so hard, because, when you are unsuccessful the fall is so tough. We all prayed quietly, meditated, and sent so much white light to Sandy's womb, I'm surprised she wasn't glowing.

I had an amazing experience during this last attempt. This might be a bit TMI (too much info), so if you get squeamish from the mushy stuff, I suggest you skim and move on.

One night Dennis and I were making love (told you!), and I felt filled with light. I had never felt so close to him and God at the same time. Although I believe this is the true purpose of lovemaking, I had never experienced this intense feeling before. I told Den afterward.

"I think we just conceived our baby," I said.

Den replied, "Well thank the Lord because I'm exhausted!"

I believe to this day that this is when the embryo implanted.

Two weeks passed, and the day came when we, well, Sandy, got to take the pregnancy test. She went in for the blood test, and I felt like we were all numb, afraid of getting our hopes up. I was in my car at about 10 in the morning, driving furiously down the Santa Monica freeway, when my cell rang (hands free, everyone!). I will never forget the call.

"We're pregnant!"

I can only describe my reaction as a lightness of joy I had never felt before sweeping through my body. Never! The car, the freeway, and the urban sprawl around me melted away and I just floated through space (albeit at 65 miles an hour, in a 2,000 pound metal machine). Dr. Carolyn explained that they measured the level of Human Growth Hormone through the blood. A reading of 25 U/ml determines that there is a new little being embedded in the uterine wall. Sandy's reading was somewhere in the tens of thousands! I felt beyond joyful. That day was the most extraordinary day of my life, so far. Sandy was excited.

Alex was excited. Helene was excited. The doctor and nurse were excited. Dennis was stunned. I'm not sure he really believed we would get to this point, and for the first time he saw the glimmer of reality that we were going to be parents. I, on the other hand, was on cloud nineteen, trying to imagine how we could possibly be so blessed.

We decided not to tell anyone until we'd completed the first trimester, the most likely time for a miscarriage to occur. We wanted to be confident that the baby was healthy and on it's way and avoid the possibility of going back, while in the midst of our own disappointment, to tell the multitudes that it hadn't worked.

To keep myself busy, I went into planning mode:

1. Schedule Lamaze classes.

2. Plan for a baby room.

3. Learn how to parent. Hmmm . . .

4. Buy copious amounts of baby literature. And, finally,

Make sure that I keep giving Sandy her progesterone shots.

Sandy had to have shots every day until the end of the first trimester. This after she had received them through the first two unsuccessful attempts. Progesterone shots are horrible, with a thick-like-glue medicine. You have to use a two-inch-long needle with a hole so big at the end you could see the angle of the razor-sharp opening. The shots left Sandy's backside a bruised, bumpy mess. Despite the obvious discomfort, I kept comin' at her, and she took it. An amazing trooper, she never complained. While Sandy endured, I floated. Because I had so many things to do to prepare, I felt purposeful and was carried on a wave of euphoria.

We were prepared with a name no matter which way the Y and X chromosomes fell. That was the easy part. The day we confirmed that Sandy and Helene were both on board, we'd headed right on over to the bookstore for a baby naming book, remember? On the way there, I had asked, "What about 'Chelsea' for a girl?"

Done deal. We both loved the name, so that was a piece of cake. But what if we had a boy? We originally thought about Nathaniel, but we didn't like Nat or Nate, so we settled on Nicholas. We tried to think of every possibility to make sure the initials didn't spell "CRAP" or something equally open to child-hood derision. We searched out every hidden element we could think of that might lead to teasing in the schoolyard. Neither of us were willing to let go of our last name, so we decided the child would get the whole ball of wax. If s/he wanted to convert it to a shorter name, s/he could do that later. The one question was, "Whose comes first?"

We decided on "Montgomery-Duban," based on the audi-tory rhythm. "Duban-Montgomery" sounds like an uphill climb. Say it with me, "Duban-Montgomery." Now say, "Montgomery-Duban." Awwwwww, nice! Hear it? Did you really say it out loud? Try again . . . see?

Next, the middle name. The boy's name was easy: Chace. I don't know why; it just came to us. However, a girl's middle name eluded us for several weeks until one Saturday morning, on a weekend adventure, we were walking through an artist's co-op and noticed someone working on a name plate: "Austin." Perfect! Chelsea Austin Montgomery-Duban. If she wanted to alter it, she could be:

1. Chelsea

2. Chelsea Austin

3. Chelsea Austin Montgomery

4. Chelsea Austin Duban, or CAMD

It all worked. We even called the Social Security Department to make sure that there was enough room on the social security card for the whole name. (I told you we tried to think of everything.) Naming the baby was the easiest part of the whole deal.

Two months into the pregnancy, we went to our first ultrasound appointment. Sandy, because she was the star, and Helene, Dennis, and I to see the heartbeat. It was a'beatin'! What a surreal moment, witnessing the impossible on a little monitor. All four parents stood there enthralled. We left the office proudly carrying our pictures of the little kidney bean with a heartbeat home and put them on the fridge.

The first three months were riddled with excitement, anticipation, and a bit of drama. Alex became increasingly miserable. She hated school. She hated LA. She hated traffic. She even hated Sunset Boulevard. When I asked if she'd ever been on it and why she hated it, she replied, "No, I haven't been on it, but it's so long!" I don't know how she knew it was too long. Perhaps high school gossip? Concerned for our youngest trooper, Dennis and I had a conversation and decided we would need to talk to Sandy and Alex to find out if we could help with Alex's misery.

Although we wanted a baby more than anything, we called a family meeting in our living room, and I told the girls that this wasn't an interesting proposition if it destroyed their lives. We felt terrible that Alex was so unhappy. We never wanted our dream of being parents to adversely affect anyone, and I suggested that maybe they should move back to Oklahoma. Well, Sandy nearly went through the roof. Her eyes grew as big as saucers, and her face flushed to the point that I thought she was going to blow a blood vessel in her neck. I had never seen her so furious, and she made her preference quite clear indeed. Going back to Oklahoma was never going to be an option for them. They had nothing to go back to. I thought if Alex could go back to her friends at home, she would be happier. Sandy got more and more upset, and when I told her that maybe we should terminate, because our having a baby wasn't worth the pain and heartbreak of wrecking people's lives, she stormed out of the house.

Alex, on the other hand, broke down, and I hugged her. She was so sorry that she was so miserable, and she was willing to change her attitude. From that day forward Alex was a different person, and we had an amazing relationship. It was like night and day; she flipped the switch, and everything turned around for her.

Sandy was a harder nut. I had truly believed they would both be ecstatic with my idea of going home, so I was floored by Sandy's response. The willingness for Sandy to have our baby will forever be a mind-boggling gesture of love and selfless giving. Den and I will be grateful for lifetimes to come. But, as life seems to play out it's never a clean, linear road to the finish line. There are always multiple issues to contend with, and not all of them are visible, and I was in the dark on this one. However, the storm soon blew over, and as Alex settled in and started to see a light at the end of a tunnel of darkness, we concentrated on the baby at hand.

᠆ᜠ᠆

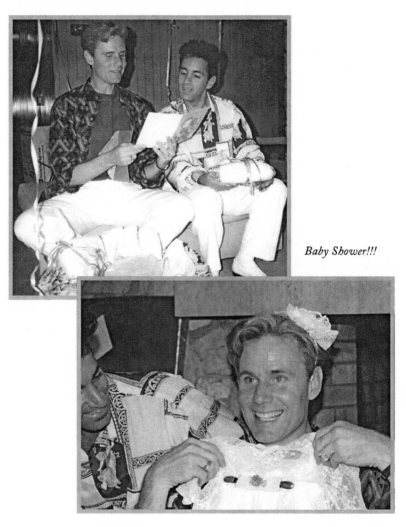

Baby Shower!!!

I wish it fit!

9

*S*andy would turn forty-six before giving birth—quite an amazing endeavor at any age, let alone with menopause barkin' at the door. But science is a wonderful thing, and every day new procedures and options come to light that astound and provide new hope for, not only infertile couples, but society at large. I learned so much through this process that I had no idea was possible. Through the use of hormones, doctors can coordinate two women's cycles for the purpose of implanting embryos, which is what we did. Doctors can also, through the use of hormones, recreate a woman's menses with hormones— after she has reached menopause. Who knew? I was shocked . . . and appalled! What self-respecting gay man wants to visualize a woman's private areas? I much prefer lollipops and puppies.

Even with all the scientific miracles, pregnancy is still a life and death event, and problems can and do occur, especially in middle-aged women. Sandy developed gestational diabetes, which is very common. Gestational diabetes in early pregnancy can lead to birth defects and after the first trimester, the blood sugar transferred to the fetus can cause an unusually large baby, which creates a risk to both the child and the mother at birth. So we became a high risk pregnancy requiring lots of monitoring, and off we went to the nutritionist and weekly ultrasounds at the OB/GYN department of Cedar Sinai Hospital, where the doctors told us that with monitoring it shouldn't be a problem. Gestational Diabetes can be controlled with diet, and usually goes away after the delivery; we just had to keep watch and make sure Sandy's diet was immaculate. The good news is that, usually parents only get two ultrasounds during the entire gestation, but we watched every finger, toe, and ear develop on our beautiful baby; more proof of the miracle of life! And not just any ol' life, the life of our little wonder.

Sandy cracked me up. She had a very limited palette and decided that the nutritionist's orders of balanced protein and carbs provided by vegetables, meat, and grains could be found in a taco at Taco Bell. Not exactly my idea of the perfect food group combo but hey, she was having my baby; so if it kept her happy, all her tests results stayed in line, and the baby continued to grow in sweet divine perfection, let's hear it for the taco!

In the middle of January 1993, we passed into the all important second trimester, reached critical mass, and decided we could announce to the world that we were going to be parents. Our excitement was electric, but we were also aware that perhaps not everyone would receive this news with joy.

When Den and I first considered the idea of being parents, we'd thought long and hard about the impact our decision would have on our lives and on the world. We wondered whether it would be too much of a hardship on the child to grow up in a world where the mainstream did not accept gays. There had been much progress since our youth of the fifties and sixties when we never even saw an example of any man who was identified as gay, but the road to change can be slow and arduous, so we had much to consider. There were still many instances of hate crimes on homosexuals, including cruel beatings and death. Not an environment to bring a child into lightly.

Ultimately we decided society would not dictate our future. Instead, we would write our own place in the world, and this child could very well help to move our world toward more love and acceptance. We also realized that every child has obstacles and challenges in their life and this would be our child's unique set. So we moved forward, but thought at least half of the people we encountered might have an issue. However, as we began our public acknowledgement of our situation, we were filled with joy. Similar to our experience with people during the impregnation process, as we announced our situation, the love and support was astounding.

Our closest family members floated on air, especially my dad. When he'd accepted that my sexual identity was not a passing fancy, he was heartbroken that I wouldn't be able to experience the joy of parenthood, which was his greatest love. So when he found out about his imminent grandpa-hood, you would have thought we'd found a cure for cancer or ended world poverty. Almost everyone we told was as ecstatic as my dad.

Now, if you remember, the person that tipped the scales toward us being parents was our friend and Dennis' client, Barbara. We thought we'd better give her the good news that we were on our way to diaper changes and spit-up, and we wanted to make this announcement special, so we took her out to a beautiful restaurant for lunch warning her we had news. We sat down, and ordered a round of iced teas.

"Now, dahlings, what is your news?"

"Well," I said. "Remember when you said that we should be parents? We're pregnant, and are expecting in July."

"Hold on, dahling," she said with perfect calm. Then she yelled across the restaurant.

"Waiter! I need a martini." Some moments are forever molded into your mind's eye. That brilliant picture of Auntie

Barbara in her casual but crisp white blouse and navy slacks, topped with a look of deadpan disbelief, etched itself in my brain. Barbara was beside herself with excitement and immediately started her lifelong mission: making sure we raised the next Dalai Lama, Pulitzer Prize winning journalist, or at the very least, Secretary General of the U.N.

While most of the reactions were wonderful, some, like Barbara's, blew me away. Many years before our choice to become parents, we had purchased property in the San Juan Island's area of Washington State. When we'd landed in the real estate office in Anacortes, we were greeted by Phyllis, a perky and energetic character with a short haircut blown dry to a style that was as perfectly in place as a Marine's uniform in bootcamp. She had a Christian fundamentalist radio station casually playing in her car as she drove us around house hunting. We'd bought our beautiful property through her, and eventually her husband, Harold became our caretaker.

Now, Den and I held the philosophy that you can change the world in different ways. While we need placard-carrying, protesting activists to bring awareness, you can also quietly change hearts by living your truth, but not necessarily announcing your arrival. We never shied away from being honest about our sexuality when asked, but we didn't start our conversations with, "Hi, we're Gay!" Instead, we trusted that as people got to know us, they'd like us before they had a chance to judge our sexual identity, and by the time they realized it, they'd be hooked on us as people and maybe change their whole idea about "Gay" as a stereotype.

We never mentioned our relationship to Phyllis or Harold. Over the years we had dinners with them, and Phyllis would give us a bible for Christmas or a well-placed reference to "our

Lord" in conversation. We loved them dearly and were loved in return. The first time we realized Phyllis might have had a clue was when she announced, "I think you would get along with this artist fellow who moved onto Edith Point." Hmm.

Now, as we planned a visit to our San Juan haven, we realized we couldn't just show up with an unexplained child, so we decided that we should take them both to lunch (always over lunch??) and break the news. When we shared the news about our imminent bundle of joy, Phyllis didn't even breathe before responding.

"This is going to be the luckiest child on the planet."

We were stunned and moved by her unconditional joy about a situation that I thought would be impossible for most fundamental Christians to accept. She not only did not judge the situation, but was thrilled at the prospect of us being parents. I cannot tell you how that opened my eyes about my own preconceived ideas. Two days later, Phyllis called. She'd been thinking about our child ever since we'd talked, and she couldn't imagine a more blessed child. We'd expected a lot of Ricky Ricardo "splainin" to be done, but Phyllis's response was more the norm than anything negative. Although one of Dennis' clients left the firm, because he couldn't support such an "un-Christian idea," there were many more cheers and hurrahs than jeers and boos. We were shocked and relieved with the amount of love and support we received. While we'd prepared ourselves for the worst, it was the best that surprised us.

We received cards and gifts during the entire pregnancy and beyond, many from Dennis' fifteen hundred clients. You'd think we were heralding the "second coming."

With preparations in full swing, we tried to absorb our new destiny, body, mind, and soul. As with all great efforts, there were some challenges. One of them was, what flavor of little being were we going to have? There were only two options, and I didn't realize that, to one of us, one was much scarier than the other.

─∕⟨∖─

10

*T*he moment we were pregnant, Dennis went into shock. Not that he didn't want to have the baby, but his type-A, need-to-plan-every-moment, I-don't-want-to-be-out-of-control, nervous Nelly brain went into high gear. The reality of raising a child was hard to grasp, and to him, the responsibility felt overwhelming. He wasn't obvious or vocal about it, because let's face it, then he would have been me. Instead he surrounded himself with a mysterious and compelling quietude.

When we started this whole baby spectacle, perhaps he thought, "Nice exercise, but we won't ultimately end up with a child . . . that would be too bizarre." But the bizarre had become the real deal, so now he had to wrap his mind around the fact that there was going to be a third person in our home, and that person might dictate our lives in a way he couldn't clearly determine in advance. Den didn't appear depressed, angry, or upset, just out of sorts. He listened to my baby ramblings with a smile that hovered just over a flat line. When we talked of baby rooms and cute cribs, he didn't jump in right away, instead offering a non-committal, "That's nice." As best I can describe it, he simply wasn't totally adjusted to the thought of becoming a father.

However, one thing's for sure. If Dennis was going to have a baby it was going to be an heir apparent—and a boy. He always referred to our growing little one as "he," and if I asked for an opinion about baby furnishings, his choice always had cowboys and baseballs. I know . . . so stereotypical, but we are all a product of our culture. We're all influenced by the same straight society when it comes to gender identity, and let's face it, Den grew up a Cubs fan.

Den had always gotten what he wanted in life. In his mind, God was on his side, man-ning his vessel, and there was no way that there could be another outcome than the picture running in his mental screening room. What he didn't realize was that God was not only the director, but the screenwriter as well, so if they should have a creative difference of opinion on the plot (and the actors), we all know who gets the last word.

At five months into the process, Dennis, Sandy, and I went for our fifteenth ultrasound, the one that would reveal once and for all whether a little mister or a little miss was making themselves cozy in Sandy's belly. Although our OB/GYN, Dr. Leong, kept looking, moving the instrument this way and that to get the best view, there was not a penis to be found. This new information took Dennis down a profoundly defeated path and was the closest I have ever seen him to being depressed. He turned dark and inward. He got very quiet and lost the bubbly, fun-guy nature that defined him. He became cold and withdrawn, and I missed my manic busy boy with his witty come backs.

On the way back from the ultrasound, Dennis told me the gender determination had to be a mistake. There was no way that it was going to be a girl. He didn't know how he would relate and it frightened him that he could mess up a girl with his ignorance and unfamiliarity of women. He became detached and not inter-ested from March through May, our seventh month while he tried to process the information. He felt betrayed by his Maker and couldn't see how the rest of the story would play out in a way that he would want to be a player.

As gay people, our interplay of male/female is fascinating and complex. While in most instances, my mind set would be considered a woman's point of view, and Den's more male, we each flip-flopped from being more male oriented to more female oriented, based on the situation. In the business world, he was definitely "da Man!" and this masculine mindset included a desire for a boy. He'd had a clear picture of little Nicholas growing up and becoming an accountant, so that one day he would take over the firm, and the sign would read: Duban and Son Accountancy. He wanted a son to carry on his name, his firm, and his legacy.

As we dream about our life and it's future, we each have a picture. As part of the American dream, we picture a white fence around a lovely home and a luxury car to drive off in each morning to our own company of happy employees. That's just one scenario, but you know what I'm sayin'! When I was younger, the picture of what I thought I "should be" made it so hard to come out, because "gay" didn't fit the perfect picture in my head. "Gay" was coloring outside the lines.

Dennis faced the same difficulty about the gender of our baby, a particularly hard painting in his mind to release. He held out for quite a while hoping for an emerging penis that we hadn't yet seen (of course, if it were that small, our kid would have other issues!). Maybe one other test would help us to clarify that our child really was a boy after all. But, alas, after multiple ultrasounds, amnio tests, and grief; there was no more room for doubt. We had a girl on-board the Sandy train, and Dennis would have to adjust. As I gloried in the process, from day-to-day planning, doctor's appointments, and readying the baby's room; Den quietly smiled beside me and tried to understand what it would mean to have a daughter.

Whatever the gender, there was much to do. Dennis' huge clientele combined with our unique situation resulted in multiple offers of showers, and the gifts started rolling in at a staggering pace. We registered at baby stores, had one huge shower with over a hundred guests and one smaller, family gathering. The car seats, pacifiers, and jumpers started arriving, and I started to accept on a deeper level what was going to be a reality. We turned our guest room into a baby palace, and I spent long hours sitting in the room, trying to wrap my brain around the upcoming event.

⸻

At around our sixth month, we registered for Lamaze classes. Dennis, Sandy, and I walked into the first session at Santa Monica Hospital, a little pillow-carrying birth trio. We were the last to arrive, and it felt like the first day at a new school. Everyone went silent and had their tight, "I'm trying not to judge you, but why in the hell are there three of you here when this is a two person job" smiles on. Even the teacher gave us a polite, "What the hell?" look as she pointed out a good place on the floor for the odd party of three. We awkwardly took our places at the end of the semi-circle and listened as everyone introduced themselves and told their story.

One couple had just relocated from the South, and the husband, Budge, was in the military. Clinton had recently started the "Don't Ask, Don't Tell" fiasco, and Budge's testosterone gave me wind burns. The rest of the intros mostly consisted of, "This is my husband, Bob, and we're due in May." Then they reached our gang, and Sandy was up first.

"Hi, my name is Sandy," she said, then looked at Den.

"Hi, my name is Dennis," he said and looked at me. How do I always draw the short straw?

"Hi, my name is Kevin, and Dennis and I have been in a gay relationship for ten years . . ."

As my tale wound down, you could have heard a pin drop, so for emphasis, I turned to Budge.

"Oh, and by the way," I said. "We have no desire to enlist in the Army, Navy, or Marines."

That broke the tension, and I have to say that after that, everyone was lovely and couldn't have been more supportive. I noticed that all of the couples were over thirty. People were waiting to have babies these days, which I can't say is a bad thing. Having a baby is the biggest undertaking anyone can pursue, and any scrap of maturity is a welcome addition to the pot. In six weeks, we graduated Lamaze with our pillows and a new way to breathe . . . fabulous!

As we approached our eighth month, Dennis' perky, happy, self resurfaced. His fast as lightning comebacks reappeared, and his busy bee planner side mapped out furniture layouts for the baby's room. He still didn't know how he was going to handle being a father to a girl, but he seemed to be much more open to the thought. His mood lifted and returned to "Dennis normal." I even sensed a twinge of excitement brewing in his chest. He brought up baby subjects and questions of birthing logistics. However, as any dad can attest, no amount of acceptance or mind alteration could have prepared him for the real story about to occur.

—)(—

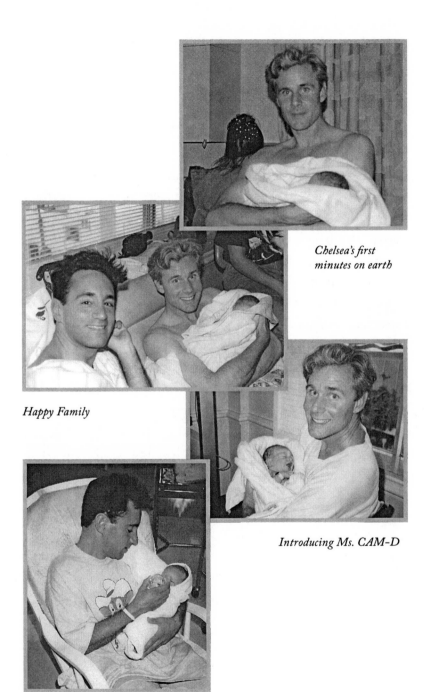

*Chelsea's first
minutes on earth*

Happy Family

Introducing Ms. CAM-D

Dennis gives Chelsea her 1st bottle

11

As we neared our eighth month, everything progressed swimmingly, with many ultrasounds and tacos. The baby was healthy and seemed to be happy in her cousin's womb. With every detail we learned, the excitement built. At one ultrasound appointment, the technician said, "What a beautiful ear she has." I'd never thought of an ear as beautiful, but you know what? Hers were stunning!

At this stage, we felt that Sandy and Alex needed their own space and privacy, and Dennis' parents generously offered a townhouse they were not using. I think this helped to settle Alex into the transition from Oklahoma City and helped to boost their happiness quotient.

The doctor put Sandy on bed rest and told her to stay home and grow that belly. Den, Sandy, and I began to talk about the birth process and how we saw the birth scenario. This is where my naiveté and ignorant male mind took hold. I wanted *nothing* foreign or impure to affect my baby, so I asked Sandy if we could do natural childbirth and not use any drugs. Sandy, the astounding trooper that she was, agreed. Silly girl! I'd done some research and learned that mother's milk contained antibodies which help the baby deal with immunities in the first part of their young life, so I asked Sandy to pump her breast milk for the first month after the baby was born. Now, the breast milk thing was a huge commitment. She'd have to pump every two hours day and night, and Sandy agreed, proving yet again what an angel she was.

The three musketeers, Sandy, Den, and myself, got beepers; and I tracked the quickest path to the hospital. The mounting excitement was surreal. We talked about whom Sandy wanted in the delivery room, and she chose Den and me (of course), plus Helene, and Sandy's daughters, Christy and Alex. The hospital said we could have as many people as we could fit in the room, but I wanted to make sure Sandy felt comfortable.

We arrived at the thirty-eighth week of our forty-week extravaganza, and our doctor said that the baby looked great and that any time after the beginning of the thirty-ninth week, we could induce labor. I believe Sandy's response was (now let me get this exactly): "Let's get this thing out of me." So even though our daughter was due on July 8th, my niece, Shannon's, birthday, Sandy and I checked into the hospital on the evening of July 1st and got ready for the big event. I was allowed to sleep with her in the delivery room, and they planned to start the induction of labor early on the 2nd. We laughed and slept as well as could be expected. Sandy's older daughter Christy had flown in from Oklahoma City, so all the players were ready to go, and at 7:00 am they hooked Sandy up to a fetal monitor and the Pitocin IV drip, and we were off!

All the girls arrived early, but Den said he would work (how unusual!) and that we should let him know how it was going and when he should arrive. Christy was designated as the official videographer (only over-the-shoulder shots, and Sandy must have lipstick). I was the main coach, and Helene, Alex, and Den would be the cheerleaders (sans jumps, yells, and pom-poms).

The contractions started slowly at about 8am, an hour after the drip, and they gradually increased the meds to get the party rolling. At around 10:00 am, Sandy's water broke bringing on yet another of the many "Oprah, ah ha moments" that had followed me through this quest. The surreal very quickly became real with water on the floor and Sandy standing in front of me, in her very non-emotional, matter of fact way, quietly declaring, "This is it!" I called Den and told him he'd better get down here, because the little girl was on the move . . . or so I thought.

After Dennis arrived the day passed slowly. We didn't seem to be making much progress, so they upped the Pitocin, and Sandy's pain increased. By late afternoon she said she needed something for the pain. Based on her face, I realized my misogynistic, arrogant error of "no pain meds." They gave her a shot. However, about fifteen minutes later, she spoke up again.

"This isn't doing shit," she said, so I pulled my best Shirley Maclaine, "Terms of Endearment" moment and yelled at them to, "Get her some medicine!" Thank God we hadn't gone so far into the process that she would be denied an epidural. Having observed the miracle of birth, my advice to any woman is this: the moment you check in at the reception desk, ask for the epidural to be administered—before you reach the elevator. The process becomes so much easier (if you can use a word like "easier" to describe anything about the birth), or at least it became easier for me to watch.

Sandy had appropriately dilated, but the baby wasn't moving down the birth canal very fast. At about 5:00 pm, Dr. Leong, our very confident and non-emotional OB-GYN thought that Chelsea had progressed enough for Sandy to start pushing as a way to help the baby to make more progress. Pushing is usually the very last of the effort and doesn't last that long, but not for us! Sandy pushed forever. We were right there with her, breathing, holding our breath, bearing down; so not only Sandy, but the entire room, felt weary. My family had arrived and was waiting in the lounge, and we kept going to them to give them uneventful updates. The little one would make headway (literally) on each push, but then, just as quickly, slip back to the recesses of Sandy's womb. Finally, after almost two hours of pushing, the doctor said that she thought we are going to have to help the little bugger out by attaching a vacuum device to her head.

There was our little group with Christy filming only over-the-shoulder shots (and Sandy wearing the requisite lipstick), I'm holding up one leg, Den is (reluctantly) holding the other, Helene and Alex are at the side of the bed, and the anesthesiologist hovering with a bird's-eye view of Sandy's baby-birthing parts. There were two nurses helping with equipment, and the doctor was at the foot of the bed with a vacuum ready to attach to Chelsea's head the next time she made an appearance. It was a production.

In all my birthing studies, I had read that the newborn would respond to skin-to-skin contact, so I had removed my shirt and was wearing a lovely pair of whimsical parachute pants that had just barely gone out of style ten years prior. The lengths one will go to in trying to do the best thing for a child.

After almost two hours of pushing Sandy was exhausted, and we all watched as the doctor quickly attached the vacuum, and with two huge pushes and one M.D. pulling, Chelsea Austin Montgomery-Duban came rushing out—and then lay limp on the doctor's lap. The first words I heard from the doctor were, "She needs oxygen." My heart did a flip flop, and the nurse scooped Chelsea up, took her to a waiting table, and placed a little mask over her face. In a moment, Chelsea took her first breath, began to cry, and the room celebrated. And breathed!

Christy, Alex, and Helene were in tears; Sandy smiled; I was ecstatic, enthralled, and floating; and Den was in shock again. He stood behind everyone in the room with a look of surprise and "I really don't know what to do with myself right now" stare. The nurse wrapped Chelsea in a warm blanket and handed her to me, and I recited a Baha'I prayer of welcome given to me by some friends. My heart melted as I brought her to Sandy to see how beautiful she was. I'll never forget Sandy's words.

"I'm surprised," she said. "I don't feel like she's mine at all. I feel like she's yours."

We passed Chelsea around, until the doctor noticed Dennis looking on from a distance.

"Dennis," she said, "you can hold her." Dennis quietly took Chelsea, and a light came over him, a real-life Grinch-like event (not that he was ever like a Grinch!). His heart grew several sizes to bursting, and the second half of his life began. Then he looked at me.

"Can I feed her?" he asked.

"Of course."

The room glowed with indescribable joy and love. We invited my folks and my brother's family into the room so they could meet our newest member. As the euphoria settled and people got tired and left, Dennis sat in the hospital nursery and gave Chelsea her first bottle of formula until Sandy had time and energy to pump. We took a picture of the new father and daughter that still steals my heart every time I look at it.

⁓

We'd reserved a suite at the hospital because we wanted to room with the baby. After we'd worked so hard to get the genes right, we didn't want to end up with the wrong baby and we wanted to be with her every single second. I guess we thought we were at the Ritz Carlton, and Sandy, Dennis, Chelsea, and I started to settle in. Before we could retire though, they had to give Chelsea a bath and get some blood. The bath was cute, but the blood thing nearly killed me and Den. A new nurse took her and proceeded to prick Chelsea's heel, and she screamed. As Den and I flinched, the nurse said, "I hate when the parents act like you are torturing their child!" I wanted to slap her. She *was* torturing my child, and my protective-mother gene had kicked in at 6:55pm on July 2, 1993 and was not going anywhere fast! I have often thought that the only relationship with the opportunity for instant unconditional love is from a parent to a child. We don't instantly have that with our own parents, our siblings, our spouses or our friends; in those relationships we have to work at unconditional love. With a child, if you are open and ready to receive, it is there like a lightning bolt. The love overtakes you, envelopes you, and is the most incredible feeling that I have ever experienced. So, Miss Nurse thing, YES! I am going to react when you torture my child, so get used to it!

Chelsea was pronounced perfectly healthy, and I deemed her incredibly beautiful. I know I'm biased, but I've got the pictures to prove it. Our dear friend, Anne, from Washington, responded when I told her how beautiful she was, "Well, that's what every parent thinks," but several weeks later when she met Chels for the first time, she relented.

"Wow, you were right," she said. "She is beautiful!" So, we took our *beautiful* daughter and our exhausted cousin to our suite and tried to get some rest.

I promised myself I wouldn't be one of those neurotic parents that worries about every little burp, but I got up every twenty minutes trying to get in the bassinet to check if she was breathing. Some behaviors will not be avoided.

-\|/-

As best I can describe it, I wanted to somehow put her inside of me, so she could sit next to the heart that she had emboldened with joy. I couldn't get enough and couldn't stop staring at her, and how Dennis reacted . . . that's another story. He was so quietly taken with her. He morphed into a man I hadn't met before, so totally overwhelmed with love and joy, that he glowed. His daughter was his light and his life, his original picture of a son now a blurry memory. I could see that Chelsea was definitely going to be Daddy's little girl.

To this day my sweetheart doesn't know how to place the joy Chels brings to his life. Dennis is over the top in love with his daughter, displaying a joy worthy of the finest fairy tale. We now have a trust for God and our incredible predestined path. If Dennis could have thought he wanted a son to the point of depression and then be filled with the joy he now experienced, then we obviously have no clue what the best plan for us is.

—)|(—

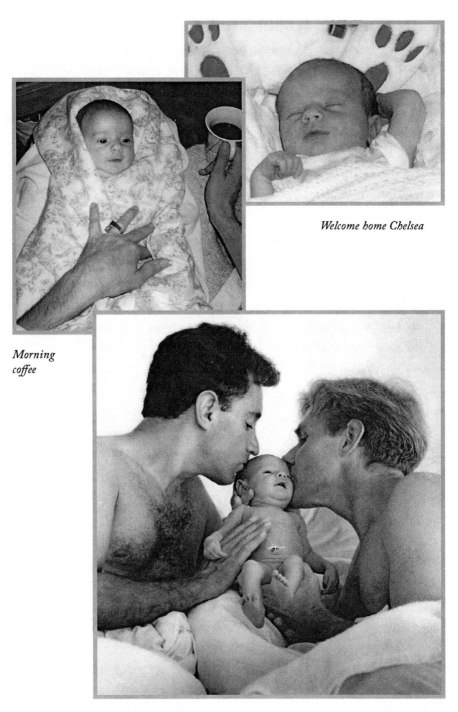

Welcome home Chelsea

Morning
coffee

So much lovin'

12

*D*ennis, Sandy, and I spent a sleepless night in our suite at the hospital trying to crawl in the bassinet to make sure she was breathing. Okay, only I did that, but no one really slept well because of the excitement of the evening of July 2nd. We were all exhausted and exhilarated. After our doctor declared Chelsea a perfect specimen of the human race, a nurse handed us a check list of instructions and said we could take our baby home. Take her home!!? Does she realize what she's saying? We now had an actual little being, our daughter, entrusted to our safe-keeping forever, the most exciting prospect I could have imagined, but a daunting thought as well.

We said goodbye to Sandy, and sent her on home to recover and rest—and pump breast milk. Then we, the Busby Berkeley logistical team of clowns, tried to figure out how the rest of the transport should work.

"I'll get my car . . . No, you get your car . . . No, my car's better."

"Okay, your car," Den said.

"Where's the car seat? Does it go in the back seat facing front or in the front seat facing back?"

"Okay, front seat facing back." (Back in the Jurassic Age car seats could be in front.)

"Okay, I'll put her in and try not to break her."

"Okay, we'll caravan home"

And finally, "She's in . . . Let's go!"

I got in the car, as nervous as I'd ever felt, Chelsea's seat strapped in next to me. I'd never had this level of responsibility for anything or anyone. I pulled away and . . . Oh, geez! Chelsea was crumpled over like a ninety-year-old woman with osteoporosis. The car seat was too upright. With my left hand on the wheel, I placed my right hand on her forehead and tilted her head up, so she could at least look at the sights as we sped down Pacific Coast Highway. I had my first realization that all the little details of raising a child could be quite intricate and not necessarily easy. To calm my nerves, I began to chant a mantra.

"Just let me get home . . . just let me get home."

My stomach was in knots. But, as I would come to experience with many Nervous Nelly moments, Chelsea was perfectly fine. I was a wreck for nothing.

Once home, Dennis and I settled her into her bassinet, sat for a moment of awe and wonder, and allowed the joy to wash over us. Our dream had come true. Against all odds, we'd become parents. It didn't matter what anyone said or did, whether they showered their approval or condemned us to hell. Chelsea Austin was our daughter. At last.

All we wanted to do was stare at her. Unlike a Christmas gift, whose thrill could fade in minutes, a baby kept us fascinated and enthralled 24/7. Every finger and toe, each little gurgle and eye flutter, filled us with love, admiration, and wonder. I didn't want to leave her side for a second. But I did need to clear my head and settle my brain, so, with Den's encouragement, I went for a run.

I take great stock in signs—not road signs, but spiritual signs, and as I ran I saw a penny on the ground. I'd always thought

Tell me your secrets!

a lucky penny was simply that: a lucky penny, but a friend had recently informed me of a rule that a penny is only lucky if it's head's up. What? Now, whenever I found a penny with Lincoln on his face, I turned it over and leave it for the next lucky soul. The penny I saw in front of me now had Lincoln's face staring right up at me, so I picked it up. What a wonderful, simple sign that all was right in the world. Then, just a few feet past the first, I saw another head's-up penny. Okay, now God is telling me that everything is on our side. When I spotted the third penny shining face up ahead, that was it. My eyes teared, and I felt a peace

and contentment I hadn't felt before. My heart filled with gratitude for my amazing spouse and our incredible baby. We three
were totally and completely blessed.

‑‑⁄⁄‑

Back at the house, I ran through the hospital check-list. If
this should happen, if that should happen, yadda, yadda. One
item stated if the baby didn't eat for eight hours, we should call
our doctor and take her back to the hospital. Chelsea seemed
content, but she wouldn't take a bottle. At first we weren't concerned, but as the hours wore on, we became increasingly upset
and worried. I had visions of taking her back to the hospital and
them screwing a fetal monitor into the top of her head with
tubes coming out of every orifice. That just couldn't happen.

Six hours, no bottle. Six and a half hours, no bottle. Seven
hours, no bottle. Then, just as my blood pressure was about to burst
a vein in my forehead, Dennis' brother came to visit the baby.

"Let me try," said Mr. Confident Father of Three.

Sure enough, Chelsea latched on, and away we went. Whew.
First crisis averted. I felt so relieved, but nervous with a new
awareness. What other issues were we going to encounter that
we had no idea how to handle? I called my mother.

"Hey, Mom. Whatcha doin?"

"Well," she replied, "We're giving you some space."

"Well," I replied. "Can you stop doing that and come stay
over? I'm too nervous we won't know what to do."

"Of course!"

So mom and dad toodled on over to spend Chelsea's first
night with us. Now I felt sure that everything would be fine. I
figured Mom had raised three children and would have every

answer, but every time I asked a question, she told me she had no idea or couldn't remember.

"What?" I said. "You raised three kids!"

"Oh, that was so long ago," she said. So much for generations of knowledge, but at least we had four of us trying to figure out the best move instead of two.

Chillin' with Daddy

On the go Miss Hollywood

Her first Halloween

Chelsea's bassinet stood by our bed. After our oh-my-god-the-baby's-not-eating freak out, we easily fell into a routine. Den took time off. Well, for him time off. He doesn't take time off, but he didn't go into the office for a couple of weeks. Instead he worked at home. For Dennis, that was good! Through milk, poop, and sleep, the three of us bonded. At first, I was afraid the sleepless nights would be too overwhelming, but then I remembered it would pass. Babies eventually sleep through the night, and I can survive almost anything for a limited amount of time. For the most part, I had no trouble waking up. Deeply in love with Chels, I relished every moment together.

We enjoyed a glorious time of bonding and, after a week of home time, complete with a constant stream of family and visitors coming to meet the new Montgomery-Duban, we decided to try our hand at going public. We clumsily put together our first diaper bag, stashed the stroller in the trunk, and headed out to the mall. It felt like we were packing for a six week vacation. Babies certainly require a lot of accoutrements! We thought the trendy Beverly Center would be the perfect indoor foray into public. A little shopping, a little showing off our baby girl. We had so much fun pushing the stroller and watching people "oooh" and "ahh." Some lovely elderly women (who had to be nearing one hundred) just couldn't get over how adorable she was. With their tightly curled blue tinted coifs, they peered expectantly into the stroller and cooed over the beautiful little wisp of a girl riding in style.

"How old is she?" they inquired.

"She's a week old," we responded.

"A WEEK OLD?" they wheezed at us. "Take that baby home. She shouldn't be out in public. She'll get sick!"

Now we knew we were parents. We'd received the first of a million bits of unsolicited advice from the public at large. Everyone had an opinion, especially when they found out she had two dads. We obviously needed help in our child rearing.

We didn't take her home that day. I believe that we live in a germ-phobic society and that most of us don't let our immune systems protect us as they are designed to do. We went with our instincts and trusted that she would not contract any dreaded disease. We also didn't fret about falling pacifiers, sterilized nipples, or sand on the beach. Somehow Chelsea not only survived, but is the healthiest child I know. All the kids we've encountered who've had overprotective parents seemed to contract a different illness every week, while Chelsea just sailed through infancy, toddler-hood, and her youth as a specimen of good health. Don't get me wrong . . . we baby proofed our entire house and watched her like a hawk to make sure she didn't befall any harm, but we didn't worry over many of the little things that seem to concern other parents.

When Chelsea was six weeks old, we decided to make a trek to our house in Washington, the perfect place to play house, parent, and relish our daughter. I was petrified the plane ride would be awful, but Chelsea flew without a peep and received her first wings from the flight attendant who spent every break coming back to admire our little one.

First bath of many

On the plane I realized how fun our new adventure could be. As we told our story (it's hard not to with two guys and a baby), our listeners' hearts warmed. People couldn't seem to get enough of her. Because there really weren't many gay men having babies at that time—and none that had used their own genetics, we had achieved a sort of celebrity status. Everywhere we went, we told our story and received rave reviews. As I said before, I thought at least half of the public would have some sort of issue with our unique family arrangement, but I was dumbfounded. We encountered zero resistance. Which just goes to show, perhaps I was stereotyping the public?

~✶~

With a new baby comes a profound lifestyle change. However, we did not have to revolve around her, and I don't think it would have been healthy if we did. We realized we could either let Chelsea transform our lifestyle, or we could incorporate her into it. We chose the latter, so off we still went on our many adventures—with baby trappings in tow. On one flight to San Francisco, we sat in the three-seater side of the plane. Den by the window, me in the middle, and a very serious businessman on the aisle. He barely looked up from his laptop the whole flight and seemed to be making the world go round with spreadsheets and emails galore. Well, our darling daughter nestled in my arms was uncomfortable on the descent, and for the last five minutes (which felt like five hours) of the flight, she screamed. We tried milk, pacifiers, fingers, anything to alleviate the pressure in her ears and on our brains, but nothing worked. I was sure that this guy would give us the "get that baby out of here" attitude. When it was time to deplane, he turned to us, and I braced myself.

"You guys are doing a great job!" he said.

My heart leaped. Even in situations where I was sure we would have problems, not just because we were gay, but because we had a screaming kid, people were kind and understanding.

I think the most significant thing about the whole process was how natural it felt to the two of us—well, after the first week. I felt confident as a parent and quite at home with the whole baby thing. As we moved through the early months, I didn't think of us as a gay family. If we were at the market buying toilet paper, it would take someone asking about the two of us with a baby to remind me that were doing something unusual. This has never ceased to amaze me. We were so much like the average American family, that I would have to be reminded we were different. I didn't feel different. After a lifetime of feeling like an outsider, this shook me, in a good way. Sometimes, when someone would mention that we were gay fathers with a daughter, it would jar me. Really? I had forgotten.

Now, I must say that while I stayed calm about germs, my serenity did not transfer to all areas. Nope. I had the same angst and crazy thoughts of any parent. If she sleeps in our bed or uses a pacifier, will she end up a serial killer? Every decision seemed critical and important. After the first month of Sandy's milk (God love her!), we changed to formula, and Chelsea cried every afternoon for more than a hour. We changed formula. We tried every calming technique we could think of. Nothing seemed to help her—or us. Perhaps crying was her way of letting off steam, but who knows; it was torture, and she wasn't even as bad as I've heard infants can be.

Now that I've survived and even garnered some wisdom from those infancy months, I realize every baby is different. There is no one-size-fits-all perfect solution. If there were one way to parent, there would be one book and one answer for everything, but this is not the case. There are too many variables. Each child is unique, and so is each parent, and that leads to endless possibilities.

You can find back up for whatever direction you want to take with any given issue. Some say let them sleep in your bed; some say every issue they have from failing algebra to serial dating comes from the fact that they slept in your bed. Some say they should have no sugar, some say some sugar, and some say let 'em suck on sugar cane to calm their nerves. There is no lack of opinions when it comes to child rearing. Bottom line, every baby will have some issue. One of Chelsea's issues was sleeping.

As we reached the six-month mark, Chelsea woke up more and more during the night and was not getting the rest she (or I) needed. We decided it was time for her to move to her own room and start the never ending "white knuckle" process of growing into independence. Den and I discussed it and realized we needed an intervention. We first decided that we would let her cry in her crib, but just for an hour. Big mistake. We lay tortured in our bed, as our angel screamed, and the minutes wore on. I felt tormented for our little darling, but it was worse for Den. He was beside himself with pain. At forty-five minutes, he broke.

"Can't we go get her?" he said. "She's obviously going to cry the full hour."

He sped off to her room, and as I caught up to them, he had lifted her out of the crib, and they were both crying. Now I had two crying souls to contend with. We needed another plan.

We had heard of the famous "Ferber Method" that teaches children self comforting by letting them cry in small increments. The parents go into the child's bedroom to assure them, but don't pick them up. You let them cry five minutes, then go in to tell them you love them and it's bed time. Then you let them cry ten minutes and give them the same spiel. You keep increasing the length of time until they fall asleep. Okay, we'd try it. There was no way Dennis could survive such a night, so he packed up his bags and headed out of the house, while I hunkered down for the duel.

Chelsea cried the first five minutes, and I went to the bedroom to assure her that I loved her and I was there. She then cried the next ten minutes, and I once again went in and played my part. That was it. Somewhere in the second ten minutes it was all over. She was sound asleep, and I felt elated. I believe the success hinged on the fact that

1. I had a plan (so I knew exactly what to do), and

2. Because I had a plan, Chelsea felt my conviction and realized it was useless to keep crying.

I think the first time we'd tried letting her cry, she sensed our insecurity and lack of confidence, and that kept her feeling

out of sorts and insecure, but when we were concrete in our conviction, there was no wiggle room for anything less than success.
That has been my experience throughout our child rearing; if we
stayed a united front with a fixed plan, and we didn't veer from
our intention, success was usually not far behind.

Three months later, as we neared our ninth month of parenthood, we needed a new plan.

-⁊ɪ⟍-

Our sweet Angel Amparo

I look to the hills whence cometh my help

You can never say enough about outfit coordination

14

The success of Dennis' firm provided us with the option of a Mr. Mom, and the part time nature of my entertainment career allowed me freedom to take a break (no big sacrifice at this point). I chose to retire, at least for the moment, and be a stay-at-home dad. Happy and grateful for the opportunity to do so, we fell into the typical "husband and wife from suburbia" scenario.

Now, this "two men and a genetically linked baby" thing was uncharted territory, and we didn't know exactly how it would work or what the response from the outside world would be. As I said before, we'd had no responses we could call negative per se, but people either weren't sure how to categorize us, or they put us in a box. Conversations went something like this:

"Who is the mom?" says Joe Public.

"She has two dads," I say.

"Are you (meaning me) taking the role of the mom?"

"Most definitely—sans breasts."

"How is she going to feel about having two dads?"

"Who knows?"

"Who's going to do her hair?"

"We're gay, remember? Like gay people have never done hair before? Hello?!!" (For heaven's sake I had a cosmetology license.)

However, much to our surprise, the number-one, most asked question was . . . are you ready for this?

"What is she going to call you?"

It was shocking that this was the most frequent query we received. I thought, "How'd you get her?" maybe, or, "Is your cousin going to be a mom to her?" or, "What are you going to do when she gets her period!?" These are the questions I thought I would have had, but "What is she going to call you?" ruled supreme. I didn't care what she called me, as long as it wasn't my first name. I was her parent, not her teacher.

We never wanted Chelsea to think she lacked anything, so we presented everything in the positive. When anyone asked about her parentage, we never said she didn't have a mom. We said she had two dads. Sometimes they would rephrase the question.

"Where is her mom?"

"She has two dads."

"Who is the mom?"

"She has two dads." If they kept asking, we were always more than happy to let them know she was genetically connected to both of us, and we freely gave the whole biology lesson, but we refused to make this about lack. Maybe it was to make themselves feel better about their issues, or perhaps we all share a basic human frailty, a belief that things can't be perfect. Whatever it was, I began to believe that people have a need for problems. I saw a lot of people who seemed happy we had a baby, but who were also dying to find the weak link, and we were not going there.

~\'⁄~

On January 17, 1994, when Chelsea was six months old, the Northridge earthquake struck Los Angeles. Interstate 10, the major artery connecting the beaches with downtown, collapsed near La Cienega Blvd., cutting off Dennis' usual and most effi-cient commute to the office. Lucky for our family one of his clients owned a rental condo a few blocks away from the office, and with a little tax-return bartering, graciously offered the space to us while Caltrans repaired the freeway. So we stayed in town during the week and went home to the beach on the weekends.

Being so close to the office was heavenly. Dennis could walk to work, and I could bundle up our little dear at a moment's notice and go visit Daddy in the middle of the day. There were also parks nearby and all the modern conveniences within walk-ing distance, certainly less isolating than being on a highway at the beach.

In our "condo away from home," we encountered some wonderful neighbors. An elderly Jewish couple, Esther and Barry Goldstein, who seemed to be close to 100 years old lived across the courtyard and upstairs from us. Even bent over like gnarled trees, they seemed to beam happiness through every crevice and wrinkle. The first time Esther saw Chelsea and me about to begin our daily morning stroller outing, she yelled from upstairs and across the courtyard, as if she were a mother calling her petulant child.

"What a cute baby . . . where's the mother?"

From my door, I looked up and returned the volley.

"She has two dads," I screamed back. "We're a gay couple," I added, then continued with the Reader's Digest version:

"I took my sperm and my partner's sister's egg . . ." Yadda, yadda . . .

I yelled the whole scenario, delving into our story for about fifteen times, Chels bouncing happily on my hip.

"That's nice she responded, "But, where's her mother?"

Perhaps it just wasn't part of Esther's vocabulary, so it didn't compute. She was a doll though, and she wanted to hold the baby. With her adorable shuffle-and-step way of travel-ing, it took twenty minutes for her to come downstairs, and I, always very happy to share our girl, relinquished Chelsea. After a minute Esther strained under the weight of my healthy ten-pound baby, and Chelsea started to slowly slide down her stom-ach. As Chelsea reached her hip, just shy of her slipping out of grasp and to the concrete Esther calmly said, "Okay, you can take her now." Life in the big city was fun and full of delightful characters wanting to share in our parenthood adventure.

Soon after CalTrans completed the freeway repairs, we moved our little threesome home. How lovely to be back in idyllic Malibu—until the floods hit. This time Chelsea and I were cut off from the world, and Den was stranded in town. At first I thought it would be fun, a bit like camping with indoor plumbing. Plus the situation presented odd perks, e.g. Chelsea and I could take the stroller for walks down the middle of PCH—an impossible feat in the absence of citywide catastro-phe. But, after the second day, I realized I had no way to get to the store, and we were running low on milk, so I threw Chelsea in the backpack, and off we went, hiking through the wilds of Malibu to Ralph's Supermarket.

As we approached the bridge at Cross Creek, damaged by the rising water, I noticed a lot of action. Governor Wilson stood in a crowd of locals, closing out a speech, letting us know that the powers that be would soon open one lane on PCH and fast track the construction. Yay! We would soon be free again; Den could come home; and I could drive. (When locusts swarm Malibu, we will consider it a sign from the universe to leave, but not a moment sooner.)

─᠃─

Despite the occasional natural catastrophe and our unusual family structure, our daily parenting issues weren't much different from what every couple faces. I was with Chelsea all day, and Dennis worked full time at the office, then drove home, often in traffic. So, by the time he came home in the evening, we both felt tense, fatigued, and ready for a break. Dream come true or not, being with an infant is a 24/7, intense scenario. Den and I both loved our girl beyond measure. At the same time, we were exhausted and beat, and might I say I was just a touch frazzled. Okay, a lot frazzled. As we got close to Chelsea's ninth month, Dennis, with all the love he could muster, made it plain.

"Kevin, either you are going to get some help, or I am going to kill you."

Not the homicidal type, Den suggested we hire someone part time, so I could take a break during the day a couple of times a week. We agreed that we were not going to compromise when it came to our baby, so we contacted several employment agencies; Den saying that if we had to go through one thousand applicants to find the right person, then that is what we would do. I started by setting up three interviews.

The first interview was scheduled for a beautiful Monday evening at our little Casa de Oceano. When we opened the door, this beautiful Colombian woman entered with gorgeous black hair past her waist and a smile that lit up the room. Enter Amparo, apparently an angel. She swept past us and immediately sat down on the floor with Chelsea, cooing and talking to her like she had been her nanny forever. We watched in awe as they played. Sophisticated, elegant, intelligent, and loving; she seemed to be the perfect fit.

Luz Amparo Montealegre de Parra, one of thirteen children born in a rural area outside of Bogata, Colombia, traveled at sixteen years of age to live with her aunt and began work in a

Amparo and Chelsea

local hotel. But this girl wanted to see the world, and in the early '80s she flew off to London to be an au pair. She then worked in Italy and many exotic places, eventually ending up in America, on our doorstep. Amparo ('Paro, according to Chelsea, after she learned to talk) was the kind of person who always lived well no matter what her funds. She looked elegant and was incredibly worldly, energetic, and positive. She saw nothing as a problem or road block. Instead she made everything easy, fun, and inventive; nothing like the standard nanny we had seen, just getting by and

Amparo's wedding

hoping to move on to something better when they had a chance. Amparo, having found her mission in life, wanted, needed, and adored children.

That first evening we asked her all the pertinent questions. We tried as much as we could to seem calm and not too excited, but as she swept out of our house, leaving a trail of light and joy, Dennis turned to me with desperation in his eyes.

"I hope she takes us!"

We went through the other two interviews half interested, then asked Amparo if she wanted the job. To our delight, she agreed. We'd passed the interview!

Now, Amparo had her work cut out for her. Chelsea had become very attached to us and was not the kind of child who would go to anybody in the room. Other than a sleepover at my brother's house at six months, which went okay, she made a scene of epic proportions every time I left. But, I felt it was important to give her the opportunity to know she was safe with others and could thrive when her dads weren't present.

Each time Amparo loaded up the stroller to exit the house, Chelsea would start in, but Amparo, always calm and reassuring, never wavered in her kind demeanor. I would hear Chelsea's wails and Amparo's gentle voice reassuring her that she was there and remind her of how much fun they would have together. Usually, when I returned home, Amparo would report that soon after they had left, Chelsea was happy as a clam.

As we traversed the baby minefield, Amparo brought wonderful knowledge and suggestions that helped us immensely. One day during the first week when Den came home from work and I returned from my various errands, Amparo called us over.

"I want to show you something," she said. She put Chelsea down on the floor, and we watched our little bundle crawl to a ball across the room.

"How did you do that?" Dennis asked.

"Well," Amparo responded, "First I put her on the floor." Oh, in order for her to crawl, you have to put her down to crawl. What a novel idea!

From the moment 'Paro started, she made constant contributions to Chelsea's upbringing. She suggested the perfect starter foods (peas and carrots), made a new friend every time they went to the park, and planned a plethora of play-dates. Amparo always interacted and engaged with Chelsea no matter what fun activity they chose. I can't tell you how many times I saw other children in the park while their nannies grouped over to the side deep in conversation, as though unaware they were taking care of children. Sometimes our paths would coincidentally cross while Amparo and Chels were at the park, and 'Paro was always in the sand, on the slide, or swinging with Chelsea. When they played in Chelsea's room, Amparo always had music or a learning tape in the background. To this day I still hear, "Apple, apple, ah, ah, ah . . . Baby, baby, buh, buh, buh . . ."

Dennis and I constantly thanked our Maker for the gift that was Amparo. She also created stability for Chels. We had a deal that we would have a regular weekly schedule, so when we went out of town, Amparo stayed with Chelsea. This way she didn't have to go through lots of different sitters, and our leaving was less traumatic.

Our life was full and rich beyond measure in love and joy, but it wasn't always easy. Chelsea confounded us when it came to separation anxiety. Even with Amparo, getting Chelsea to be comfortable with us leaving was a mountain to conquer, and we needed some serious help.

─◂╎▸─

My playmates

Will someone get me outta here?

15

*B*efore Chelsea was born we'd had a session with a channel. For those of you not in the metaphysical know, a channel is someone who goes into a trance state and then allows a spirit or soul that is not presently incarnate to speak through their body.

I'm a firm believer in an eternal soul and our present life as one mile on an infinite path, one that could never be defined by one lifetime. I've received amazing insight and information through many seers, psychics, and intuitive folks; and I'm always searching for more information to explain and increase our joy in this lifetime.

This channel was a middle aged, bearded man. At first glance, he looked like your average truck driver, but once we were introduced I saw that he was a very soft spoken and kind gentleman. He lived in Arizona and would come periodically to LA to do readings, and we had heard about him through a friend and gotten on his list for a reading this trip.

When the date arrived he came to our home, and after we got him a bit of water, he sat quietly and told us it would be a few minutes before the spirit guide would start to speak. We waited patiently, and after just a brief few moments, his face scrunched up, and a very high pitched voice with a slight British lilt began to speak.

We asked this spirit guide if there was a particular soul that was wanting to incarnate into our family.

"Yes, a Judeo-Christian soul who will be a bridge for humanity." Dennis and I looked at each other and smiled. Any kind of confirmation that there was a baby coming was wonderful, but this sounded like a beautiful soul with a mission to make the world a better place. We were on Cloud Nine again.

A bridge she might be, but once she was born, this incarnated darling didn't want to cross over into any other humanity unless we were coming with her. Chelsea was sweet and wonderful, but there were few people with whom she wanted to spend time alone. She felt no real connection to Sandy, her cousin and our surrogate. We'd picked Sandy because of her non-emotional nature, which seemed perfect when giving birth and releasing the child to waiting parents, but we were surprised that Chelsea didn't seem to recognize her at all. However, Helene, her aunt and egg donor, was another matter.

When Chelsea was born, she came out looking just like Dennis and her Auntie Helene. She had a lot of dark hair and their big eyes. I believe from the beginning of the embryo stage, their genes looked at my genes and told them to "Back up, Jack"! Aside from looking like her aunt, from the time Chelsea was able to make a noise, she squealed whenever Auntie Helene entered the room. This always fascinated me, because I felt that Chelsea recognized her connection to her aunt intuitively. Auntie Helene was her "fave." But few others garnered that response.

While Chelsea may not have taken easily to anyone, there was a plethora of people in our life who adored her and were so grateful that we had a child. She may not have made it easy to

I should have worn sunscreen

make a connection, but they wanted to be connected none the less, so Chelsea had numerous honorary Auntie's and Uncle's.

One day when Chelsea was about 5 months old, I had an appointment in the San Fernando Valley, and I dropped Chelsea off at dear, sweet Auntie Melanie's house. I was gone for about two hours, and when I returned I saw no blood in Melanie's face and a far off look in her eyes.

"I walked her. I showed her everything in the house. I sang. I talked. Nothing worked."

Melanie was one of our dearest friends and an amazing "kid person," so she was dumbfounded, and I was sad and sorry I'd put our friend through such an ordeal. I realized that I was going to have to be very careful about whom, how, and when I asked anyone to take care of my daughter.

As if Melanie hadn't suffered enough, she and her husband invited us to join them at their house in Carmel. We were thrilled to go. Den had a business trip to San Francisco that week, so we flew to San Fran first and then we arranged to meet them in Carmel on Friday and make the five hour drive home with Mel and her hubby on Sunday.

We had a wonderful trip. Chelsea was a dreamboat the entire time with everyone she met. She was quiet, sweet, and smiley—until the drive home. As we started out it seemed like everything would be okay. But, to steal a phrase from our favorite and departed comedian John Pinette: "Oh, nay nay!" Chelsea never liked the car seat. Airplanes were fine, because we could move around and wander the aisles, but car seats were her nemesis. Even if I was just going to the store, ten minutes away, using the car seat was screaming time in the O.K. Corral. As we started out from Carmel, the crying began . . . and continued for five straight hours. I took her out of the car seat. I put her on the floor. I laid her on the seat. I think I even threw her in the back of the SUV. Nothing helped. Finally at about hour four, sweet Auntie Melanie turned to us in the back seat and announced that her ovaries were tying themselves in knots. Not that Mel ever thought she would be a mom, but if she had, our little princess put a nail in that coffin. Five hours of a crying child. I think we all upped our therapy sessions after we returned to LA.

As long as Dennis and I were with Chelsea (and there was no car seat in sight), she was wonderful, and everyone fell in love with her. She had such a sweet and wonderful disposition and loved all the people and places she went; but we could not leave her with anyone. We both worried that something was seriously wrong. Had we done something to harm her? Was there some terrible physical issue that was making her uncomfortable? We sought out professional help, which calmed us, but didn't make the situation any easier. We had a session with another channel who gave us amazing insight into some past lives the three of us shared and a horrible existence where Chelsea was left at an orphanage and tried daily to claw her way out. Again, the session gave us great insight, but it didn't make our lives any easier.

Then, when she was just over a year old, we started putting the pieces together. I came upon a wonderful book called, "The Highly Sensitive Child." Ding! Ding! Ding! Inside this book, the author described Chelsea to a "T." For the highly sensitive child, everything is heightened. Loud noises, uncomfortable fabrics, very bright lights; all of these things contributed to her sensitivity and discomfort. And, they become very attached to their parents.

The great news is this type of child forms strong, lifelong bonds, but the pitfalls can be trying for all parties involved. Knowing she wasn't the only one in the world with this issue helped tremendously, and the book gave us some fabulous suggestions. We culled her wardrobe to include only soft fabrics for her clothes, took the tags out of her shirts, and kept her away from loud music. She could never wear pants because they bunched at the crotch. All her socks had to have the line at the toe in the perfect place, and for three years during preschool she wore the same thing, because it was the most comfortable. When "The Puffy Sleeve Dress" started to fall apart from all the washings, I sadly had to find other dresses. I plan to give her that dress in a Lucite box when she has her first born. Not sure if this is a gift or payback. Hmm. Besides her attachment issues, dressing her was my least favorite activity.

Don't get me wrong; the first years were glorious, but they were also some of the hardest times Den and I had ever experienced. I tell new parents that having a child is both the greatest joy and the hardest thing in life. Even with gobs of advice from so many well-meaning people, we were never positive that we were doing the right thing for our child, especially when it seemed like our baby was suffering. We constantly second guessed our decisions and worried about everything from diet to socialization. We didn't give her sugar for the first year of her life, but then realized for us we would rather teach moderation than abstinence. We also felt angst about her pacifier. She was obsessed and usually had three; one for her mouth, one to rub on her nose and one for a spare. We worried this might make her anti-social and not want to interact; something to hide behind. It was a mine field of concerns and questions.

We talked to child psychologists, read many books, and did our best. Chelsea's anxiety was not the only thing on which we concentrated. That was only half the coin. The other half, when she didn't feel abandoned or uncomfortable, was how wonderful, sweet, and engaging she was—with adults. Since she was an only child, we felt preschool would be the perfect opportunity to engage with other children, so at nine months we began our research.

Right at the beginning, I felt nursery-school panic: If she doesn't get into Kenter Canyon Pre-School, she will never get into Harvard. When a dear friend said Chelsea needed to be at Kenter Canyon, I ran off with my nine-month-old daughter in tow to interview for a spot some two years hence. When we showed up for the tour, my anxiety grew. There were many other parents with faces just as determined as mine busily filling out waiting-list paperwork.

Now, Kenter Canyon was a wonderful school, and at first I agreed that Chelsea HAD to attend. But, as I drove down the hill, I had a "Wait-a-Minute!" moment. I realized we lived forty-five minutes away, too far to drive home each day, so I would have to sit somewhere and return in a few hours to pick up my daughter. I decided then and there that I was not going to play the desperate, childhood-school game. A calm came over me as I chose instead to trust that the perfect place for Chelsea would present itself—when the time came. I mean, come on, she just started crawling!

August '94 The Honorable Judge Henning

She does like a good ensemble

$\mathcal{W}$e were in an unusual situation (no kidding). Therefore, we had unusual legal issues, or at least the possibility of unusual legal issues. While other families run the risk of divorce and child custody battles, at least the identity of each parent is clear to all parties. However, Chelsea's birth certificate listed Sandy as mother (for some reason, it had no line entry for "oven") and yours truly as father. But what if, God forbid, something should happen to me, or if, Lord help us all, Dennis and I broke up? That could leave Dennis with no parental rights. So, as Chelsea approached her first birthday in order to plan for every legal issue that might cause grief down the road, we sought out legal advice on how to give Dennis every right that I had.

We first went to Bill Handle, an attorney connected with the Center for Surrogate Parenting, where we had done all of our contracts with Sandy before we got pregnant. Attorney Bill, who had a weekly radio show for legal issues, God love him, saw an opportunity to go public with a landmark case, but that didn't sit well with us.

1. We weren't interested in going public and

2. We had also promised UCLA that we wouldn't go

public to protect their IVF clinic from the religious right backlash.

Fortunately, we ran into an attorney friend of ours, Roberta Bennett, at a local restaurant. Thrilled that we had a daughter, she listened as we told her about our desire to draft up a legal adoption for Dennis.

"This is part of what I do," she said. "I help gay people adopt children." Although, as far as any one of us knew, there had never been a case with all family players like ours, but Roberta wasn't interested in the publicity. She just wanted to help us. Roberta Bennett was a strong, tall, very confident, lesbian lawyer whom we'd met years before through mutual friends in the gay rights movement. She was very connected with the family court and could help us with the whole process—still an unusual case for the court, but without an attorney vying for the spotlight.

Our mission was simply to secure Dennis and I equal parental rights. In order to do this, Dennis applied for a second parent adoption which allows an unmarried, cohabitating couple to let the non-biological partner adopt the child while the legal partner doesn't give up any parental rights. This would entail an entire adoption process including a social worker, home visits, and evaluation. As we started down that road, we met in Roberta's office and got the low down on just what we could expect. Roberta very calmly and clearly stated what we were about to try to accomplish. We were excited and nervous at the same time. We didn't know how this would work and based on the fact that no one that any of us had spoken to in the legal realm had ever heard of a case like ours; we didn't know if it would work at all. California recognized single parent adoptions, but not for gay parents.

The first order of business was to lay out the process so we knew the road we were on. The social worker would have to make a home inspection and then write up the paperwork stating that, though they thought we would make fit parents, they had to regretfully deny our adoption, because their agency didn't allow single gay parent adoptions. Then, with their "regretful denial," a judge could overrule that finding. This had been done before, so our job was clear: lay out a convincing case for the social worker that Dennis and I would be great parents; because before they could regretfully deny that finding, we had to get them to discover that they wanted to regretfully deny it.

All of the power was in the social worker's hands. We needed a report from her claiming that we would be fit parents, that we had a safe and loving environment for a child to grow up in, and that a baby would thrive in our care.

Before the scheduled inspection, we cleaned and prepped the house to make sure that everything was perfect. We had gate guards at the staircase, locks on every cupboard, plug protectors in every wall socket, and rubber bumpers on the corner every piece of furniture that a child might bump into. Once our house was ready to be used as a set for a Spic n' Span commercial; we sat our little scrubbed faces down, held the adorable Chelsea at an attractive angle on our laps, and waited for the doorbell to ring. When the doorbell sounded, I glided to the front door and put on my sweetest smile then gently opened the door to find the Wicked Witch of the West looking back at me. She had long stringy hair that looked like it hadn't been cut since the late seventies. There was not a hint of Maybelline or L'Oreal or even Rite Aid make up anywhere near her face. Her mouth turned down, and I swear she seemed to growl at me as she introduced herself.

"My name is Miss Brown. I'm from Social Services."

I begged my stomach to keep it's food in place and my face to hide my terror as Miss Brown walked in, refusing water, wine, a hot towel, or any kind of social grace I thought would soften her up a bit. She didn't seem to notice how cute we were let alone the fact that we had a baby. I tried to make light conversation as we walked into the living room.

"Isn't the weather just peachy?"

Scowl.

"Don't you think traveling is a great way to open up your horizons?"

Smirk.

And my last ditch effort, " How about those Dodgers?"

Nothing. She abruptly sat down on the edge of our sofa, pulled out her clipboard, and started into her litany of the most ridiculous questions: Where and how did we sleep? Did we have a lot of arguments? And my personal favorite: Would we ever have sex in front of our child? That, my friend, is when I thought I was going to have to restrain Dennis from kicking her ass. As I held Chelsea in my arms and threw my leg over Dennis to keep him in his seat, I lovingly answered all her queries with a Miss America smile and a wink. When she finally left, Dennis was fuming. But then we both shifted into panic that she would not only regretfully deny our adoption, but give us a bad review in the process. There were a few weeks of mucho anxiety around our casa. Based on our interview with the ever charming Miss Brown, we were sure that she would never recommend that we could be anything other than child molesters. We were destined to not have Dennis approved as a parent, and our anxiety was palpable. Chelsea was our great distraction from the waiting and wondering.

A few weeks later I plucked a big envelope from Social Services from the mailbox and beckoned Dennis to the living room. Bad or good, we had news. I tore open the envelope, and to our shock and surprise she gave us not only a glowing report, but you would have thought that we were a couple of gay Dalai Lamas. We couldn't imagine that the Miss Brown we had met had written one word of this. Then, as was expected, at the very end of the report we found our, funnily enough, perfect answer: the agency regretfully denied our adoption. Hurrah! Let the games begin.

Our lawyer scheduled a hearing in family court with a judge she knew well and thought would be sympathetic to our case. So Den, Chelsea, Sandy, Helene, and I all gathered at the family courthouse about an hour from our home and talked nervously in the hall with Roberta, who tried to lay out how it might go. On one hand, the judge could just accept the denial of Social Services, and then we'd be screwed. However, he could just as easily grant a petition to overrule their finding and allow Dennis to adopt, but Roberta wasn't positive because this was uncharted territory. We all nervously walked into the courtroom and sat down behind the defendant table feeling very much like Perry Mason would come out soon. The judge arrived looking very official in his black robes but with a sweet, crooked smile and a very easy, relaxed manner about him. When we saw him, our little tribe took a collective breath, then waited for his ruling. He took a few minutes to look over our case, then looked up at us. Then he looked down at the papers and, with a very quizzical look on his face, looked up at us again. I returned his look with my best "I'm-a-great-dad" smile.

"This is a first for me," he said, "so I think all of the parties need to find lawyers to represent you and protect your individual interests."

He told both Helene and Sandy that they would have to officially give up any parental rights to Chelsea, and that there was no going back; meaning that they could never claim that they had an interest in being Chelsea's parent. Gratefully for us, neither Helene nor Sandy ever wanted to be her parent or ever expressed any desire to claim her as their own. They had done this for us, and that was their only goal: for Dennis and I to be the sole parents of Miss Chelsea.

So we left that day with a date set for another hearing. We quickly hired two more lawyers for Sandy and Helene and then in a couple of weeks headed back to court with the requisite signed documents giving up their parental rights.

On August 11, 1994 we entered the courtroom of the Honorable John Henning and sat at our defense table waiting for his entrance. Our whole family was there including my parents and several other family members, and we had all dressed for the occasion in our Sunday best. (I guess for Dennis it would be his Saturday, Temple best.) Chelsea was adorned in a lovely crinoline floral dress with a perfect Easter bonnet for good measure. Shortly, the judge walked out with a smile attached to his face. He looked kindly down to all the parties and told us everything looked to be in order. This time that dear, sweet judge appeared more comfortable. He asked both Sandy and Helene to state in court that they were willing to give up their parental rights.

"Yes," said Sandy.

"Yes," said Helene.

"Well, then, I don't know how Chelsea's birth certificate will read, but I will allow Dennis to be the legal parent of this child."

That was it. Every base was covered, and in a few minutes it was a done deal. We loved this guy. Everyone was beaming, and we shared hugs all around. The judge suggested we get a photo for the history books, so we took pictures on the bench with the judge and the baby in, might I say, an adorable adoption ensemble. It was not official, but as far as the judge, our attorney, or anyone legal that we talked to knew; ours was the first case of a gay couple in California going for a second parent adoption when the parties were all related. Around mid-September when we received Chelsea's new birth certificate in our mailbox, it had a slash after Mother and Father and instead read: "Parent and Parent." We were legal.

That comfort was so important to us. Now if something (God forbid . . . Kinenhora[1]) should happen to me, Den would have automatic custody; and if we should have relationship problems (God forbid . . . Kinenhora . . . puh, puh, puh[2]), he would have the comfort of knowing we stood on equal ground. It was a glorious event in our lives, and as we sat down reading and re-reading her birth certificate we finally felt we were a complete, legal, and legitimate family. At least to us.

---

1. a Jewish expression that means to ward away the evil eye—I'm so yiddisheska

2. another Jewish custom to spit three times to ward off evil (they are very careful people!)

What to do on a rainy day?

Life's a Beach

Chelsea traveled well (when travel did not involve a car seat), so we jaunted all over, introducing our little darling to the world. When she was about sixteen months old, we decided to go to the Bahamas. This was the longest trip we had considered taking. First we'd need to get to Miami, then hop on a connecting flight. The longest leg was six hours and we were a little worried, but the little girl was a trooper and we touched down unscathed at the Nassau International Airport, a modest structure just a step above a corrugated metal lean-to. Since we now had proof that we were her legal parents, we'd blindly bought our tickets and hopped on a plane, not thinking twice about what issues might come up with international travel. Now, happy as clams, and prepared with lots of paperwork in hand (passport, birth certificate, feeding schedule, etc.), we waited in line to clear immigration.

When our turn came, we approached the immigration officer's station and stood, ready to be inspected, in front of a true Bahamian mama, a stout, large woman with her hair neatly braided. She seemed bored with the process as she looked at our paperwork. But when she looked up, she did a double take.

"Where's the mother?"

"She has two dads." Bahama Mama wasn't convinced.

"No, I mean, where's her mother?"

"Well, I'm Kevin and this is Dennis, and we've been in a gay relationship for eleven years. We took my sperm and Dennis' sister's egg and my cousin carried her and if you'll look on her birth certificate we are both listed as parents."

"Oooo, dear me . . . ooo, for the love of . . . . Okay, now I've heard everything . . . okay, okay, I need a break." She started to laugh, but she waved us through.

"Ooo, no, seriously, I think I have to go home . . . ooo, help me, Jesus!!"

Relieved and grateful, we moved on through before she could change her mind. While we collected our luggage, we could still hear her in the distance laughing and carrying on, calling for her supervisor to let her go home . . . but, we were in!

We hopped in a cab and, passing all the action in downtown Nassau, drove fifteen minutes to our hotel on the beach, ready to recover from jet lag and relax in our tropical paradise. Mid-day and time for lunch, we all looked forward to getting to our room, then finding some lovely restaurant to settle in and satiate ourselves.

To our dismay, as soon as we checked in the rain started. I should have recognized this as a sign, kept my little bags packed, and headed for home, but no. Not easily dissuaded, we braved puddles and downpours, lugging our little one on our hips, and found the closest hotel restaurant. The rain continued. After we ate we headed back to our room with our sixteen month old to sit, read books, and play with stuffed animals. Still it rained. It rained all day and all night, and into the next day. I thought about building an ark. We tried to break the monotony by taking a cab to a Mexican restaurant in town. When we arrived, we sat down to a table with a lovely basket of chips and salsa in the center. Chelsea wanted the salsa.

The devoutly non-overly-protective parent that I was, I followed my dad's parenting vein.

"If it won't kill her, and she wants to try it, by all means let her."

However, to hear my lovely nervous nelly partner tell it, it almost did kill her. He tried to persuade me to not let her have something spicy, but I convinced him she would be just fine. So Chelsea took one tiny dollop, and honey, did she start to scream. Honestly, you would have thought I had cut off her toe. I gathered her up and got her out of there, so the local police wouldn't come and arrest us for child abuse. It's part of the overly sensitive child scenario to not like anything picante, but I had no idea at the time. Dennis and Chelsea never let me forget what a bad, bad, Dad I was in the Bahamas, and to this day Chelsea cannot stand anything spicy.

To top it off, Chelsea was going through a developmental stage that just tore Dennis up. Every child goes through this stage, but that didn't help. I used to see it everyday: the dad playing in the park with his little one, and the child takes a tumble. The kid starts wailing for the mom. The dad tries and tries to comfort them, but to no avail. There is usually a wrestling match where the kid does their best Nadia Comaneci impression, bending and flailing to get away from their adoring dad, while the dad looks around with that, "So sorry, this really is my kid" kind of embarrassed smile.

Even after the salsa incident, Chelsea attached to me and wanted nothing to do with Dennis. I was her primary care giver and she bonded with me to the rejection of every other person on the planet, including Daddy. It's hard on both parents; I couldn't get a break, and Dennis felt the sting of her rejection. We tried and tried, but she wanted nothing to do with Mr. D.

The drama peaked one morning at breakfast. I had to use the restroom, and as I left the table Chelsea started wailing.

Poor Dennis tried to comfort her while looking like he was torturing her. Then, after I returned and got her calmed down, we returned to our room to discover that an entire troop of ants had escaped the rain and moved into my suitcase. That was it! Prepaid hotel be damned, we caught the next flight out of there and didn't look back.

Thankfully all our travels were not as dramatic as the Bahama drama. In Chelsea's first two years we flew to a wedding in Chicago, a Bar Mitzvah in Ohio, San Fran, Washington, etc. As Chelsea racked up the frequent flyer miles, we became familiar with not only the rhythm of traveling with a small child, but the comfort of being a family in many different places. We were always greeted with respect and, what surprised us the most, people all over the country were moved by our family. Many times they welled up with emotion as we told our story. We had yet to meet people who would reject a family based in love and joy, unless you count a few of our own family members.

—⟩⟨—

CHAPTER

18

I grew up as the middle child in a perfect portrait of the American family. We went to church every Sunday; my brother, Marc, was a straight-A student and a letter man in swimming and water polo; I was the performer and the ham; and my little sister, Melissa, our little darling, was the baby of the family. She was the only girl, so she received the attention reserved for the princess. Or so I thought.

I can't quite explain it, but I always felt distanced from my sister. I never quite related to her and she seemed like the "odd girl out," a puzzle piece slightly off skew. Somewhere in her teen years she split from our religious upbringing and found her spiritual home in a fundamentalist Christian church. This move widened her split with me. Our church was more of a social structure than a religion. We accepted the tenets of Christianity, but beyond weekly attendance, I never felt that we struck a chord of devotion.

When a revival-type event came to our little Methodist congregation when I was in middle school, I made a public pronouncement of accepting Jesus as my lord and savior, and I felt the elation attributed to the Holy Spirit washing over and through me, but it didn't last long. Once I objectively contemplated my future as a Christian, the numbers didn't add up. How could a God that loves us more than anything on earth condemn us to a fiery Hell? Also I knew in my heart I was homosexual, and that was, according to most church-going attendees, a most grievous sin. There was no way my heart could rationalize that, so I had a very short-lived redemption before happily continuing my sinful ways.

Because they didn't have the deep conviction of a life totally guided by Jesus, but more of a quiet "let everyone experience their own form of devotion to God" kind of experience, I had no pressure from my parents or my brother. But when my sister took a turn for the far right, joining a church that spoke in tongues and had a very hard-line approach to Christianity as the ONLY true religion, the fissure in our family grew for me.

In the beginning, Melissa was quietly devoted, but when she was eighteen and a senior in high school, and I was twenty and in the throes of The American Academy of Dramatic Arts, the first real sign of change came. She decided she could only listen to sacred music. Fine by me; she gave me all her secular albums. (An album is a large, black, vinyl disc that spins on an electric turntable. You place a diamond-tipped needle on it, and music comes out of two large black boxes.) While I enjoyed receiving all the Melissa Manchester albums, I began to wonder about my sister's religious life.

As the years passed, Melissa went to college at UC San Luis Obispo for architecture. We still had a good relationship. I even visited her at college and had a great time. But, then she decided Architecture was not for her, and she transferred to a college in San Diego to study Home Ec. While there she met her future husband, Maury, who shared her religious views. Maury, a lanky 6'3", was the shyest person I had met to date. As you approached him, he would bow his head and a cartoon bubble would float aloft, "Please don't speak to me! Please don't speak to me!"

Melissa called me once from college. She was concerned for my well being because of my gayness. I was living with Eddie at the time, and she explained that homosexuality was a sin, and she loved me so much that she wanted me to be in heaven with her when the Apocalypse came down, and not in a fiery pit with Eddie. I took her call as an honest and kind gesture, and though I doubted the threats, I still felt some fear, so I talked with Eddie about our eternal fate.

Now, Eddie had been raised on Orthodox Christianity, and together we thought that maybe my sister had a point, and we should resist the temptation, so that evening we went to bed together, but to alleviate our carnal desires, we slept in our underwear. Alas, a thin coating of cotton between us was not sufficient protection to keep the devil at bay, so once again, I continued in my path of sin and degradation.

Even my sister's argument, "I know you believe God made you this way, but that means he has the power to change you," was not strong enough for me to ignore the obvious. This is who I am. No amount of prayer, humiliation, or fear is going to change that fact. As I shook off her delusional fog of fear, I also realized that I love who I am, that every part of who I am is a gift from God. There is no reason on earth for our Divine Maker to create something and then force it to change its inherent nature. That would make no sense. From that point on, I decided I would have to find a God that was unconditionally loving, kind and non-judgmental . . . and guess what? That is the God that lives in my heart and the deity to whom I am one hundred percent devoted.

When Melissa was a junior in college and deep into her Home Ec. courses, she crossed the line once and for all. One warm afternoon, I dropped by my folks, as I often did, to check in. No one was home, so I grabbed a snack out of the fridge and looked at the mail on the kitchen counter. There was a letter from my sis, and thinking I would catch up with what was going on with her at college, I innocently opened it up. But when I read it, my blood started to boil. She'd written my parents to say that something was seriously wrong with me, and that because I was homosexual, my parents had to get the devil out of me. She added that if she had to choose between her brother and God, her dear brother was on the short list. I was enraged, not that I cared so much about what she thought of me, but how dare she try to turn my parents against me? Fortunately they weren't so easily convinced, and they wanted me to let it pass. But I wasn't ready to let it slide and called her immediately.

"Hello Melissa?" I said. "Hi, it's Kevin."

"Oh, hi," she said tentatively. I felt that she could sense something was up.

"I just want you know that, regardless of your beliefs, I think it's horrible that you would try to lobby Mom and Dad against me and put them in a position to pass judgment on their son!"

She began to break down and exclaimed, "I only care about your well-being! I don't want you to not be with all of us in heaven when judgment day comes."

"Well, I appreciate your concern for my place in eternity, but that should be between me and God, and not on your 'to do' list with the folks."

She was remorseful about causing me grief but held firm in her judgment of my heading to hell. In my sister's mind, the fundamentalist Christians are the only ones that have the correct path, and you must follow them or be doomed. I told her that was just ludicrous. Where does it leave the billions of Buddhists, Jews, Muslims and Hindus? But, if I've learned one thing over the years, it's that arguing a point on religious matters is a futile and ridiculous exercise. Everyone is entrenched in their own viewpoint. The best I could offer was to tell her that no matter what she believed, I was who I was regardless and I didn't appreciate her attempt at turning my parents against me.

Over the years my sister and I never really resolved our issues, but we did silently agree to disagree. Along the way, I discovered my own intolerance. When talking about her with my family I used to refer to her as "Sister Margaretta." I thought I was being clever, and it seemed good for a laugh, but when I knew I would be seeing her, I tried to remind myself not to say it to her face. Well, of course the first time I saw her after a long absence, I blew it.

"Hey, Sister Marga . . . ooooo," I stopped.

"Sister Margaretta, huh?" she replied. She wasn't upset, but I realized at that moment I was judging her as harshly as she was judging me, and if I wanted to live the loving life I proclaimed I did, I would have to shift.

When we were expecting Chelsea, I called Melissa to tell her the news.

"Well," she said. "I guess I'll have to love her because she is your blood." You can imagine what that did to my blood, but I let it go. Nothing could dampen the joy of our impending blessing.

It has been a rocky road with my sis. When Chelsea was about five years old, Melissa decided she wanted to host Christmas. When my mom gave us the news, Dennis and I looked at each other and sighed, the "Oh geez, that sounds like no fun at all, but for the sake of keeping the peace in the family, I guess we'll agree" sigh. As the holiday drew closer, my mom (again the bearer of news) called and said that Melissa thought that everyone had had a rough year financially, so it would be better if just the kids exchanged gifts. I took a breath and said to my mom, "Well that's interesting, because I have one kid and

Melissa has four. How is that helping my financial situation?" My mom, bless her heart, stuttered and stammered a bit.

"Don't worry, Mom," I said. "I'll call Melissa and talk to her about it. You shouldn't have to be an intermediary."

I called my sis and suggest we draw names or give family gifts, because it didn't seem like a fair exchange for us to buy four gifts while they bought one. On the call my sister told me she wouldn't be comfortable with us staying at her house, because she wouldn't know how to explain Dennis' and my relationship to her kids, who ranged in age between six and

thirteen. We would have to stay in a motel.

"Well," I said, "I've always thought that telling the truth is the best policy and also high on the list in your religious practice. I also don't really care what you say about me. You could tell them I'm the devil incarnate. Whatever you think would make you most comfortable."

"Well," she replied, "I'm not comfortable explaining your lifestyle to them." I was almost at my limit.

"Look," I said. "Why do we have to do this? Why do we have to try to merge our lives when it seems so uncomfortable? I love my life and my family, and you seem to love yours too? Why don't we just let it be and not try to get together for Christmas?" She got quiet for a minute.

"Well," she said. "I'll talk to Maury and see what he thinks."

Ten minutes later the phone rang and Melissa told me she thought it was better if we didn't come to Christmas. I was shocked. And relieved. I didn't really think she would rescind the invitation, but I was grateful we didn't have to go through the motions of pretending we were one big happy family.

I know Melissa has struggled with how to live with a gay man in her family and has sought out advice from many of her fellow devotees. When the AIDS crisis took over our country, she went to a close family friend, who was a pastor. His advice to Melissa was to make sure that she kept her four kids away from Dennis and me for fear of contracting the virus. And they say ignorance is bliss?!

I have to say that Chelsea, though, has lived up to her reputation as a "bridge for humanity." My sister softened, and I believe it has to do with Chelsea winning her heart. Melissa embraced her totally and has never given Chelsea cause to feel anything but love from her aunt. The most amazing gift, though, is that Melissa's kids have never been anything but loving to our family. I think that is because Melissa never tried to persuade them that there was anything wrong with loving their uncles and cousin. Whether she explained the details of homosexuality or just let them come to the realization on their own, I shall always be grateful to her for not influencing their opinions of us. My nephews and nieces have been nothing but a light to our family, always gracious, loving, and kind. My sister and husband have done an amazing job of raising wonderful kids. I don't know that I have been that unconditional and accepting, as Chelsea knows a lot of the struggles of my relationship with my sister. If her kids know anything, they have never let on.

My sister has her own journey, and it saddens me that it is not enough for it to be her journey alone. It must include convincing the entire world that hers is the "right" one, but having her as a sister has taught me many things about tolerance and intolerance. One thing I know for sure is that I wouldn't want to live in her shoes with her fear and struggles even for a moment.

*Chelsea at 3 just
hangin' around*

My Auntie

The Little Mermaid

*A*s I mentioned earlier, the number one question people asked when they encountered us was, "What does she call you?" We thought she would work it out and give us names, as kids often do, so the first year and a half she called us both Daddy, which worked okay, but then we ran into a problem. How would Dennis and I differentiate between ourselves when talking to other people? We realized we'd have to make a decision.

Words are very important, especially names. A choice that made one of us not seem as equal would have translated into Chelsea's experience of her dads. Our first thought was that one of us would be Daddy and one of us would be Papa, but my father was already Papa to his grandchildren. So, after going through a short list of options including Daddy Dennis and Daddy Kevin (there was no way my child was going to refer to me by my first name), we settled on Daddy and Dad. Dennis REALLY wanted to be Daddy. You know, "Daddy's little girl" and all. I had no problem being Dad, so that was that. The titles were intimate enough, and neither of us felt like we were the second-player parent.

One day when Chelsea was about three, Den took her to her swimming lesson, a task I usually handled. Chelsea's swimming teacher, Caroline, was an angel in a Speedo. A very large woman with a huge heart and a degree in child development, she used the most gentle and nurturing methods in teaching the little ones to float, paddle, and breaststroke. At each lesson Caroline gave a running dialogue of Chelsea's progress, so today, as Chelsea swam under water, Caroline said, "Look, Dad, she's swimming using her mermaid arms." Chelsea popped up out of the water and said, "He's not Dad; he's Daddy," then re-submerged to continue her mermaid arms. Other people got confused—even we did from time to time, but Chelsea was clear.

Children ask a lot of questions. However, we listened to the advice to not give kids more information than they can handle. They don't need to know everything that transpired starting from when the earth cooled; they want an answer, and the simpler, the better. So many times I had to forgo the explanation I wanted to give and just answer the question. So, at three years old (Chelsea was very busy at three), during our regular daily routine, Chels looked at me and said, "Where did I come from?"

"Well," I replied, "A tummy."

"Who's tummy?" she wanted to know.

"Sandy's."

"Oh, did she give me away?"

"Oh, no," I explained, "Daddy and I wanted to have a baby very badly, but you need a girl and a boy to do that, and Sandy loved you and us so much that she said she would help us. So, we put you in her stomach to grow until you were ready and then you came out and Daddy and I got to take you home."

"Well that's good," she said, not missing a beat, "because I always wanted a Daddy and a Dad anyway." I teared up with relief.

Apart from the normal childhood challenges, which we could look up in numerous child-rearing tomes and learn about from countless other parents, we were in uncharted territory and had no idea what Chelsea's experience would be in the two-dad scenario. We only knew of two other gay families even close to our situation, with two dads and adopted children, and Chelsea was still the oldest of those kids, so there wasn't a history with our family dynamics to draw from. However, this little talk led me to trust that she truly felt complete in her family, and at that moment I realized the situation doesn't matter so much. Whatever a child experiences becomes "normal" for them. In their heart they are complete and whole. Issues arise when there is a comparison to others and society at large or a lack of love from those closest to them. To Chelsea, two dads was normal. Of course, that didn't mean there weren't questions from other little people.

One day at the park while playing in the sandbox, Chelsea met a little girl who asked her where her mom was.

"I have two dads," Chelsea replied. But the girl was insistent.

"You have to have a mom," she said.

"Well, I don't," Chels said with perfect equanimity.

"Well you either have a mom, or she's dead."

From the mouths of babes! Chelsea looked at me and said, "Oh, Dad, she just doesn't get it!" Nothing moved Chelsea to believe there was an issue with her family.

When Chelsea reached the standard preschool age of two years and nine months, rather than hunt down a school that might guarantee her future admission into Harvard, I looked for a solution close to home. Call me selfish. The Malibu Jewish Center had a wonderful school just down the road. Given that Dennis was Jewish and was very attached to his Jewish heritage, this seemed to be the perfect solution. They welcomed us, and Dede the preschool director, bent the rules and allowed us to come one day a week rather than the required two or three. Dede, who could have been a 4'10" angel sans wings, was adorable and changed hair color regularly from auburn to "Lucy" red. She loved every one of those kids with a passion, and I knew Chelsea was in a nurturing environment. Because Chelsea was an only child, socialization seemed extremely important, and I thought she may even like the experience—if she would let me leave.

Chelsea, like many other toddlers, suffered from separation anxiety, so I created a school-day drop-off routine:

1. I would read her a book, then

2. she could pick how many kisses she wanted, and then

I would say good-bye.

Well, I'd like to say it worked beautifully, but she cried every time I left. Then, of course, the moment I walked out the door, she stopped crying and played with her friends and teachers. For three whole years.

Even though I snuck a peak and knew she was fine, I still felt the sting every time. I could take it for a couple of weeks, and then one day, I would break down on my way home and try to see the road through tears. Another instance of her childhood trauma being her childhood, my trauma.

Despite the separation anxiety, preschool was invaluable for Chels. She realized she could survive without me and that she could learn how to share and interact with other children. It also expanded her circle of safety. The more people she loved and trusted, the bigger her world grew, and the less scary new experiences became for her. Preschool also expanded our world. Before we had a baby, the extent of our social circle in Malibu was we knew a couple of checkers at the supermarket. Go have a baby, and your social world expands a thousandfold. We found an entire community of families in our hometown.

Socializing had a societal benefit as well. The kids that Chelsea grew up with have known Dennis and I since they were toddlers, so for them we are not extraordinary, just the family next door. It was a beautiful thing to watch these kids grow up and interact with us knowing it would never occur to them to think of us as odd or scary. That was our goal from even before we had a daughter: being gay should be a "No Thing," nothing special and nothing awful, but something as common and neutral as blue sky or macaroni and cheese. It shouldn't require a second look or a parental discussion. I saw that ideal come true with these kids, and it gave me hope that we were moving in the right direction.

Unfortunately, outside her regular circle, some confusion remained. In 1997, Dennis went on a business trip to Waikiki, and Chelsea and I got to tag along. Chelsea, age four, found a girl about eight years old to play with. One day while they built a sandcastle, and I sat on my towel a little ways away applying frequent doses of SPF 50, the little girl came up to me.

"She says she has two dads."

"Well, she does," I replied.

"Oh," she said, and went back to playing in the sand. Then they seemed to have a bit of a disagreement.

"No, he's not," Chelsea insisted.

"Yes, he is!" her playmate demanded.

"No, he's not."

"Yes, he is."

Back and forth it went, until Chelsea finally walked over to me.

"Dad, she says you're gay!"

"Well, honey, I am."

"Oh," she said.

I asked her if she knew what that meant.

"No."

"Oh," I said. "Well, most times a man and woman fall in love and want to be a couple, but sometimes a man and a man fall in love and want to be married, like me and Daddy; and that is called being gay."

"Oh," she said, then yelled back across the sand, "I'm sorry . . . he is gay!" and off she went to finish building the sandcastle.

Once when Chels was three, while sharing some ice cream, Chelsea started a dialogue that astounded me.

"You know, it was very cold in Sandy's tummy!"

"Really?" I said.

"Yes, it was so cold that I had to go all the way to the back and get a sweater."

I was stunned and didn't want to comment or interrupt, but it made so much sense. Sandy was such a non-emotional kind of person, I could understand that it might feel kind of cold in there, but then Chelsea continued.

"You know, I kept trying to be born. I kept trying to come out and trying to come out, but I kept slipping back in."

"Wow, honey, that's interesting." She had just described her birth. I'd heard that for the first seven years, children remain more connected to the "other side," but as they age, they start to lose the conscious memory of where they came from. I saw this as a validation of her obvious connection to the Divine . . . (the Omniscient, not the actor).

The questions came and went. We lived our seemingly regular life, and Chelsea continued to be the happy, well-adjusted daughter that we couldn't believe we were blessed enough to have. Even though we came across challenges in parenting as every family does, like learning how to discipline with love and how to deal with that insufferable separation anxiety, life got better and better. Finally, Dennis and I came out of our three-year infancy, sleep-deprivation fog.

—✳—

Shoe 'em those
pearly whites!

Celebrating with
Auntie Melanie

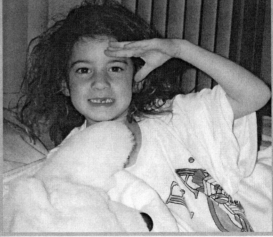

Aye, aye tooth fairy!

20

*N*ow, we all know that Karma is the law of cause and effect. What you put out there comes back to you—the good and the bad. Or, to quote one of the oldest bestsellers, "What you sow, so shall ye reap." Well, in a past life, the Montgomery-Dubans must have been Mother Theresas (but maybe with a little more compassion), because we were totally blessed this time around. God and the angels rained an endless list of gifts on us: each other, friends, abundance, and joy, all in buckets full. However, if our good fortune resulted from a stellar line of past lives, Chelsea must have been a naughty dentist or something in several of hers, for it seemed she had a wee bit of negative tooth karma.

When she was about three years old, Chelsea and I were playing at a lovely little playground near our house in Washington. The playground had intricate jungle gyms and fun concrete tunnels to explore. One day, when she was on top of one such tunnel, she slipped, fell, and hit her two front teeth. The tears and wails resounded through the park. I took one look at her mouth, saw the blood, then grabbed her and ran. I managed to get her into the car while trying to comfort her and control my own panic: What should I do? Should I go straight to the hospital? No, if

I call Den from the hospital, he'll have a heart attack! Should I go home and get him first? No she's bleeding from her mouth!

I did several donuts in the parking lot before I decided to go get Dennis (to save him needing his own ambulance) and then go to the hospital together. When we arrived home, I remembered that our neighbor was a dentist, so I called him. He told us to see how loose the teeth were. If they weren't dangling (ewww!), they should reattach themselves, and we didn't have to make any necessary medical maneuvers. We wiggled her teeth, and, glory be, they were still attached and seemed fine.

However, a few months later, the next time we went to the dentist, we received not so lovely news. The roots of her two front teeth were dead, and they would eventually turn dark grey or brown. What? We had three options:

leave them and let them be dark and ugly;
pull them, and she would have no front teeth until her permanent teeth came in; or
bond over them so that they would look white and nice until they came out.

Well, option three it was! A girl at Chelsea's preschool had her two front teeth missing, and somehow every time I looked at her I saw trailers and chitlins, which reminded me too much of my distant relatives in Appalachia. Even though hers were still little, teeth make such a huge impression, and I didn't want my daughter looking like she had a corn cob pipe in her future! Nothing against corncobs, but there was enough of that ilk in my extended family already.

We had those babies bonded, and she looked great. Her dentist worked with many young actors in Hollywood. He was such a pro and Chelsea was such a trooper, that she didn't even know she'd had a shot. She lay still for almost a half hour of dental time, before I saw one little tear fall down her cheek, but she never moved or pitched a fit.

However, apparently that wasn't quite enough karma for our little girl. Oh, no! Perhaps she'd been a maniacal dentist who ripped teeth out of people's heads with no Novocain, because this was just the beginning.

Six months later, we had another dental appointment, and after taking her x-rays, our fabulous dentist called me into the room and showed me the illuminated screen with the black and white photos of her teeth. He then proceeded to show me an extra tooth Chelsea had growing above her permanent teeth. He explained this was common and didn't mean anything about her oral health, but that it would have to be removed, because, as is sometimes the case in these situations, it was growing up towards her sinuses. Often they grow in the right direction, come down on their own, and can be pulled; but there was nothing common about our little girl.

So now we had an appointment with the oral surgeon and nerves to calm in my little three year old. When we arrived at the oral surgeon's office, we took our seats in the tiny, dark waiting room with several requisite Highlights magazines on the coffee table. Our nervous little crumb cake met the nurse who was going to prepare her for the procedure. The nurse, a calm, sweet woman with a silver bow clip in her hair, explained that she was going to give Chelsea some good tasting medicine to relax her, and when Chels felt like she was sleepy, we should let the nurse know. Well, Chelsea took the meds, then walked around the waiting room looking at the magazines and pictures, claiming she didn't feel a thing, and asking when she was supposed to feel sleepy. Then, out of the blue, she crawled up in my lap, laid her head back, raised her wee head and exclaimed, "Get her!" then passed out. Even in her drunken stupor, she was responsible.

An orderly took Chelsea in—alone. Don't these people realize we are attached like Siamese twins? After she was settled, the nurse came out to tell me that everything was going great, and they would return her to me once they were finished. I told the nurse that I needed to be there when she woke up, and she informed me that was against procedure, and I would have to go back and sit in the waiting room. But I had promised Chels I would be there, that my face would be the first thing she saw. If I broke my promise, Chelsea would never trust me again. Needless to say, I did my best pleading ("You can't have me let my daughter down; she's counting on me!"), arguing ("I don't care what your policy is, every policy can be broken!"), and negotiating ("What if I'm just across the room at the doorway, so she can see me?"). I think the last one got her. The nurse started to weaken and told me she would have to ask, but that it was definitely against procedure. Well, guess what? My face was the first thing Chelsea saw when she woke up! With a mouth full of gauze, she smiled, and in her sleepy voice said, "Daadaa." She felt wonderful! I gathered up my still sedated baby, made our way to the car, put her in the car seat, and home we went.

About five minutes into the drive, she started to pound her head on the car seat.

As we traveled down Sunset, she had a reaction to the anesthesia and she started to chant, "I want Daddy, I want Daddy."

On and on with no let up in sight. Then I remembered I had forgotten to get soft foods for her to eat, so we needed to make a stop at the market. If I could get her out of the car and into my arms, I figured she'd be comforted and could calm down. Boy was I wrong. She didn't stop for a minute. So here I was making my way through the grocery to the deli counter with a little girl pounding her head on my shoulder and screaming, "I want Daddy! I want Daddy!"

You can imagine what I thought the other shoppers on aisle ten were thinking. I knew at any minute there would be a posse of cops, guns pointed at my head, telling me to release some sweet father's little girl! I looked around. No guns. No dirty looks, even. A little scary when you think about it, but in that moment, I was grateful. I smiled at the deli attendant, and with a nod toward my wailing wonder, said, "Anesthesia . . . And a container of mashed potatoes, please."

We made it back to the car, Chelsea ranting the entire twenty-minute drive home. I carried her up to her room, put her in the bed, and asked if she would like some ice cream. Lo and behold, all tears abated, and a smile emerged.

"I would love that!"

Yet again I was left to recover from the trauma while my child slurped Cookies and Cream.

Keeping with the dental theme and jumping way ahead in our story, in middle school, we graduated from dental karma to orthodontic karma. Shortly after navigating through the some-what calm waters of braces, her new, adult dentist told her that the roots in her two permanent front teeth had died and she would need braces again. Apparently the force of her fall at age two had killed the roots in her permanent teeth years before their sched-uled appearance. When the dentist suggested a repeat round braces and also veneers, Chelsea burst into tears. She couldn't fathom going through that torture again. Plus, the dentist didn't have the best bedside manner, so I decided to find another one. I cold called a dentist I had seen on TV who'd done a lot of work on "Extreme Makeover." When in doubt, go Hollywood. It turned out to be the best decision. Dr. Dorfman was calming and wonderful, and after his examination and our explanation of the situation, he said he had a plan.

"Good news, Chelsea. No braces," he said.

The guy had her attention.

"But," he added, "You do need a crown lengthening and veneers."

"Oh, lord," I said. "What's that?"

Dr. Dorfman explained. A crown lengthening procedure would increase the part of the tooth that is visible by shortening the gums. It was used to turn "Chicklet" teeth into lovely pearly whites. Sounded good to me, so Dr. D gave us the number of his favorite oral surgeon, and we made an appointment for a consultation.

Dr. Rosenblatt, our new dentist, worked on the third floor of a very nondescript building and was the sweetest man ever to wield a drill. At our first appointment, he explained the process to us. In a heavy accent from somewhere in Europe, he told us that he would sedate Chels, then trim the gums back and stitch them in place, revealing more of her teeth for a lovely smile. All three of us, Den, me, and Chelsea agreed that it should be done. Now, Chelsea had quite the schedule at that point, and it turned out the only time available for the whole team was the very next day. Chelsea went into panic mode. Her fear of going under anesthesia and having shots was overwhelming. So we talked and talked—and talked some more. In the office; in the hall. In a box and with a fox. We called Daddy and went over the options with him. We told her she didn't have to do it, but that if she wanted it done, she might as well get it over with. As we worked our way through the fear, I randomly asked her if she remembered having her extra tooth pulled and having a bad reaction to the medication. Well, no she didn't remember it actually, but Dennis and I had told that story as dinner-time conversation so many times that Chelsea had built up a fear of anesthesia based solely on legend. She didn't have a personal experience of it at all. We'd made what we thought was a funny story into a frightening tale. Lesson learned. Be careful what you put out there for your babies to hear. They take everything in. Your cute story can be their Armageddon!

By the end of the day, Chelsea opted to have the procedure. Her dentist put on eight beautiful veneers, and today she has a million dollar smile. (Well, it wasn't quite that much, but I'll bet we paid enough to work her through all her past dental karma plus a good down payment on several lifetimes to come!)

Hiking age 4

Travelin'

Two cuties

21

*P*arenting is a set-up. You fall in love instantly and unconditionally with your new little angel. The entire first year, spent in a constant fog of sleep deprivation, you are still in awe of God's little creation (though you are oh, so tired!). Then you spend the rest of their lives disciplining them and pushing them away from you, so they can become independent, leave you, and, if you're lucky, send you a card on Father's Day. It seems convoluted and cruel.

Chelsea was truly a good-natured child. Although we'd heard horror stories about the "terrible twos," she never had tantrums or fits of defiance. I found this to be true about a lot of child rearing information. Child development is not so clear cut. Sure, there are general behaviors that prove themselves accurate in a lot of cases, but every child is different. Many things that people told us to prepare for never happened. However, other issues no one even mentioned caught us totally off guard. For example, Chelsea's sensitivity to everything from fabrics to loud noise and her separation anxiety nearly slayed us.

When Chelsea was about 14 months old I realized for the first time that she might not be 100% angelic. She picked up a very delicate music box, and when I took it away from her, my darling sweetheart sprouted claws. Quick as a cat, she reached out and tried to scratch me. I'd never seen her display any kind of aggressive behavior at all. I recoiled in horror and felt so sad that I cried. What happened to my daughter? I imagined our bleak future, me bringing her candy bars in the penitentiary, the warden telling me in his firm voice that it was closing time, and I'd have to leave. I know that every child has moments and tests the boundaries, but at the time I felt she had morphed into the devil's own spawn.

One day when Sandy was still expecting, I'd had the local news station on in the car and heard a segment on child rearing, where a parenting expert told a great story about what to do when your child starts to test the waters:

"Say you're in a basketball stadium, and you tell your daughter she can play anywhere in the seats, but that she cannot, under any circumstances, cross the line onto the court. Now of course the first thing the little munchkin will do is run down to the line, look back to make sure you're watching, and step right onto the court to see what you will do. Here's the important part: How you respond will determine if they trust you. If you don't follow through with a disciplinary action, they will never believe you or trust that you mean what you say."

Well, that made sense. Chelsea's trust was precious to me, so this became my number one rule: Once I draw a line in the sand, I can never go back. Sometimes I regretted my choice of where to draw that line, but once I had, I never wavered, and this has proven to be the most valuable parenting tip I received.

I also realized early on that parenting Chelsea couldn't be all about Kevin—what I wanted, where I wanted to go, or how much sleep I got. Each choice had to be about her well-being. Otherwise, I would be in a constant struggle to meet both of our needs, and I would resent my daughter. It is amazing how one can change a mindset. When I relinquished my desires in service to the greater good, I became happier. This doesn't mean I indulged Chelsea. Believe me, I was a hard ass. I made very strong, clear rules, and I made sure that I never wavered in them. If a line was crossed a consequence followed (with lots of love and cuddles afterwards).

I've heard friends and other parents talk about how they want to maintain a friendship with their child. One friend, who had a fifteen year old boy, said his son had come to him and wanted to smoke pot, and the father wasn't sure what to do. He didn't want to ruin the great friendship they had, so should he smoke it with him? Perhaps even help him buy some? Are you kidding me!? That wouldn't work for me at all. First of all, it's illegal, and second of all, I'm not my kid's best friend. I am the parent. There should be a dividing line in there that separates me from my child. Without it, she won't respect me and the very thing I want to experience, her love and respect, would elude me. There would be plenty of time to become friends when we are both adults.

Although you can find a book or expert to back up an infinite array of parenting styles, there are certain social boundaries that, if crossed, cause harm to the child or others. We'd met several other gay men, who'd adopted children a little after we'd started our process. One Christmas when Chelsea was not yet three, we were visiting another gay couple who had a young child. Another visiting child started to destroy the Christmas train and decorations. Her parents, the ultimate yuppie, urban gay couple in their Christmas business attire, (any suit cleverly accessorized with a hint of red) calmly sat on the sidelines continuing their conversations and sipping eggnog. While casually refilling his nog at the punchbowl, one of the dads explained that they had recently attended a parenting seminar where they learned that you should never tell your child "no," but rather let them work out their issues for themselves. Are you kidding me? I looked around for someone to stop this, but the host parents were nowhere to be seen, so to the horror of her parents, I became that child's issue. I immediately got down on the kids' level and told them that this was inappropriate for anyone to not respect someone else's property. I then sent them off in another direction and turned to the parents. As they slowly closed their dropped jaws, I shared my own parenting seminar pearl: never let another human being cross a line to harming anyone or anything that isn't their own. I was very clear. My daughter will tell you that I will parent anyone, child or adult, if I feel their behavior affects anyone else in a negative way. Somewhere in these eons of parenting history, some people thought that guidance and boundaries stunted children's creativity and freedom. My dear, if making my daughter behave with dignity, kindness, and use of the golden rule would stunt her creativity, then stunted she would be.

Kids want boundaries. They resist them, but they feel safer when boundaries are intact. They know that the world is a big scary place, and that they don't know the best thing to do in any given situation. Too much decision-making power frightens little ones. I have seen the problems caused by a child being given carte blanche: Where should we eat dinner? Do you want to go to school today? Where should we go for vacation? It overwhelms them and creates insecurities. We gave Chelsea choices, sure: Would you like the chicken or the tofu? The blue jacket or the black one?

But, as far as I was concerned, that was the extent of it. As she grew and matured, we gradually gave her more and more responsibility—but not until she proved she was ready.

Chelsea had incidents when she tested, but because I was clear about the proper behavior, she quickly seemed satisfied and understood. One day somewhere in her twos, we were playing together in a public sandbox. Another little one wandered over and started to play near us, which really upset Chelsea, because she wanted the sandbox for herself. As time wore on and she saw that the other child wasn't going anywhere quickly, she looked at me.

"I want them to cry!" she said. Oh no, return of the devil daughter.

"We have to learn to share in life," I said. I explained that if the roles were reversed, she wouldn't want to be turned away or rejected. She turned back to the bucket, filled it, and seemed to have no reaction; so I wasn't at all sure she was satisfied. However, as she grew, the guidelines I imparted, while they didn't necessarily have immediate results, seemed to get filed away in her little noggin, because at some later date I would see the fruits of what Chelsea called my "Verbal Labor." And she definitely saw it as labor. I talked and reasoned with wild abandon, having faith that with reasoning and time outs, I could get the desired outcome. When I told my dad that I didn't spank (the custom when I was growing up), he was horrified. Perhaps he thought I was questioning his parenting, which I wasn't, but what if there was another way?

I didn't rule out spanking, because you never know what situation may arise and though it was my intention to avoid all corporal punishment, I never say never. But for my daughter a non-violent approach seemed to be just fine. However, there were downfalls to the verbal tactic. On one occasion when Chels was about three, I started in about something she'd done.

"You don't understand the ramifications of your actions. If you continue to carry on in this manner, your results are going to be something that you regret ..."

She looked up at me and started to cry.

"Dad, I'm just a child!" Okay, so sometimes I went too far. I believe my lectures were like verbal spankings to her. The fear of my disapproval was one hundred times worse that any sting of a paddle on the bottom. I apologized for a lot of mistakes, because many times I didn't get it right, but I learned that if you make a bridge, no matter how deep the hole you've dug, you can redeem yourself.

One morning when Chelsea was about three, Dennis and I were having, shall we say, a heated discussion. He was trying to leave for work; I was trying to complete our so-called discussion; and Chelsea was busy putting clothes in the washer and periodically calling me.

"Dad . . . Dad . . . Dad . . . Dad . . . ," etc. On about the fifth interruption, or the twentieth "Dad," I yelled at her.

"WHAT!?"

She was crushed and started to cry. I scooped her up and told her that I had made a mistake. I was frustrated, and it had nothing to do with her. On the way to preschool I felt horrible for yelling, and I wanted to reinforce the idea that it was not about her.

"Chelsea, I'm so sorry . . ."

"Don't worry, Dad. I know you just made a mistake."

Even as little people, they understand we are human and certainly not perfect. If we admit our faults and frailties and are honest with them, they will in turn shower us with honesty and devotion.

We also learned that these little people soak up everything. I have to admit that our language was not the best. When she was little, I made the mistake of thinking she wasn't listening, so I was not cautious or wise with what came out of my mouth. One time at our home in Washington when Chelsea was three, we loaded her in the backpack and started out for an adventure in the wilds. When we were about a quarter of a mile down the road, Chelsea piped in, "Oh shit, I forgot my sunglasses."

Den and I were stunned. We looked at each other without saying a word, trying not to crack up. We weren't sure how to respond and didn't even want to acknowledge she had said it. When we got home, we discussed being more careful about the example we set. We had family members who had a bit of the "potty mouth syndrome," and apparently we were not far behind. Chelsea was going to encounter all kinds of approaches to many things in life. Rather than try to control the input, we wanted to teach her how to respond. We shouldn't (and couldn't) control what others said and did around our child, but we could control ourselves and make clear to her what we believed to be appropriate. So we strived to make ourselves the best examples possible and then, when we experienced an example of behavior we considered, shall we say, lacking in tact and decorum, we talked to her about what we thought appropriate behavior would be. I was amazed how well she understood. People around her could say and do almost anything, but she was well aware of what our family considered verboten.

Dennis and I were both big on manners. We'd seen a lot of children who, left to their own devices, were selfish, rude, and inconsiderate, and we were not going to raise our daughter like that. We believed that by being kind, polite and thoughtful to others, people seek you out and want to have you around. It is actually a selfish thing in many ways, because by being kind and thoughtful, you are treated with kindness and included rather than avoided. I always joked that Chelsea's gravestone will read:

"What do you say . . . ?"

"Thank you."

—⁂—

The Jerbeths Italy

More fun with the gang

CHAPTER

22

*T*he seeds for Chelsea's life as an activist were planted in her subconscious early on. One night, when she was still at toddler, Dennis came home and told me about a group of new people he thought we should be social with. Now, in our entire relationship this has occurred maybe three times. Dennis talked to people all day long, and usually the last thing he wanted after work was to be social. I on the other hand, spent all day in the house with a mini human and loved the idea of playing with grown ups. Plus, we are naturally different in the social arena. I'm a "let's go out" kind of guy, and Den is a "stay at home" kind of guy. So when he walked in with the idea of, "Let's make friends," I stood up and took notice.

Earlier that day, Jonathan Stoller, an artist's manager, had come into Dennis' office. He and his longtime partner, Herb Hamsher, managed the actress, Judith Light, and her actor/ screenwriter husband, Robert Desiderio. Both of them were dedicated to activism and bringing light to gay causes. Judith, Robert, Herb, and Jonathan came as a unit, like a family. (They were so tight, we later came up with a nickname for the gang:

The Jerbeths.[1]) Of the four, Dennis had only met the boys, but he liked them immediately and was convinced I would too.

Many months later, while we were in Washington state about to celebrate Chelsea's third birthday, Dennis found out the whole "gang" was in Vancouver, Canada where Judith was filming a movie. Dennis suggested that because we were so close, they should come visit us when Judith got a break from filming. Chelsea and I had not met any of them, but Den was so certain; we trusted the hand of God and fate.

It turned out that on one weekend during the filming the Jerbeths were going to celebrate Herb's birthday, and while we weren't normally social with clients, and they didn't normally agree to share a weekend (let alone a birthday weekend) with people they didn't really know, they said yes. Our motivations to bond must have been divinely inspired, because none of us were certain about why we felt moved to be together, but we followed our hearts, and like a box of Betty Crocker Brownie Mix, we simply added water and . . . voilá: instant best friends!

The entire weekend felt like putting on a favorite pair of jeans; comfortable, comforting, and easy. Because they were on the cutting edge of the gluten-free movement, I cooked a birthday dinner for Herb complete with flour-less chocolate cake. As we walked down to the beautiful rocky Washington beach and skipped some rocks with little Chels, we laughed, talked, and discovered our parallel spiritual beliefs.

After that initial meeting, we began spending time together in LA, and soon Jonathan invited us to join them on a biking trip to Italy. Well, I told him I would love to go, but I knew there was no way Dennis would agree. Dennis biking in a foreign country

---

1. Saying all four names every time they came up in conversation was time consuming, so we took a bit of each name: "J" onathan H "erb" Rob "e" rt Judi " th" . . . Jerbeths."

Biking in Italy

with people he barely knew? Not gonna happen. But I said I
would ask.

"Sure," Dennis said immediately.

You had to pick me up off the floor. Who were these people?

Now that we'd agreed to go, we had an issue: How would we
leave Chelsea for three weeks? While I knew it would be good

for her, even with Amparo staying at the house, Chelsea's separation anxiety would make this difficult.

We contacted Dr. Anne, a local child psychologist who'd spoken at Chelsea's preschool. With her quiet and thoughtful manner, Dr. Anne told us that kids at Chelsea's age don't understand time. They cannot tell the difference between three weeks and three years. They don't have a reference. She suggested we put up a clothes line in Chelsea's room with a pin on it for every day that we would be gone. That way she'd have a visual of the days shrinking until we returned. Brilliant! Also, she suggested we leave a little gift and note for Amparo to give to her each night at bedtime. So we packed little brown bags with notes attached to pens, erasers, buttons, and trinkets.

After we prepped, it was time to break the news to Chelsea. I braced myself, and one morning at breakfast, I carefully, well, spit it out.

"Honey, Daddy and I are going to go on a biking trip with the Jerbeths."

"What?" she said as her eyes welled up.

"We are going to be gone for a little while, but we love you so, so very much and you'll get to be here with Amparo and have a great time."

"I don't want you to go!"

"I know, sweetheart, but sometimes things come up that we are going to do that will have us be apart for a while, but that doesn't ever change how much we love you and that we are always there in your heart."

There. I'd said it. No fun and lots of tears, but we explained that we were always with her no matter where we were. Just like we're not in her room at night; two rooms and a hall separate us, but we're still with her. Little comfort for a three year old. The build up to us leaving was tough, so we talked about it as little as possible. Although Den and I found much comfort in the fact that Amparo was going to be with her, and we knew Chelsea would be fine, it didn't help the pain in our hearts. Our angel seemed tortured, but we thought that if we didn't give her opportunities apart, she wouldn't know she could survive without her dads.

Somehow we made it out of the house, even with Dennis running back in for three more "last" hugs, each time pretending that he "forgot his jacket" . . . or, "Oops, I think that's the phone ringing" . . . etc.

The first night we got to Italy, Dennis spent the entire night freaking out. Physical adventures were not his bag 'o nuts, and he was totally nervous and plagued by thoughts that he wouldn't be able to keep up on the bike or that he couldn't make the long distances. At breakfast the next morning he bared his soul and shed some tears.

The Jerbeths couldn't have been more wonderful. They comforted Dennis and let him know that this trip was going to work for everyone. If he ended up driving in the van and not biking at all, then so be it. Needless to say, all that worry was for nothin'. Dennis was a star; he put his bike into low gear on hills and passed us all.

Mixed in with the fun, we missed Chelsea, so we would occasionally check in and of course, hear that she was doing great. We'd made a pact to call only a couple of times, but Dennis was hilarious. One day I figured out his motivation for passing us when I found him biking ahead and hiding in the bushes to call her—one extra time, until Chelsea told him, "Daddy can you not call so much? It makes it harder." Who's raising whom?

Our relationship with the Jerbeths grew. They swooped us into their lives, and their incredible commitment to gay rights inspired us to be more proactive as well. In October of 1996, Den and I went on a business trip to Philadelphia. Herb called

Dining in Italia

us to tell us about a candlelight march on Washington where the AIDS quilt would be laid out in the National Mall. He said we should join them, so we popped into our rental car and off we went. We marched and then found ourselves in front of the steps of the Lincoln Memorial watching in awe as the likes of Elizabeth Taylor, Cher and Chastity Bono, and our new friend, Judith, spoke brilliantly. We felt proud to be friends with people who were making the world a better place.

Even in the midst of these peak experiences, our favorite moments were the quiet dinners we shared far away from the marches and benefits. We found ourselves laughing and discussing real topics of conversation: world issues, aids, poverty, the need for mentors to young gay youth, and the difference we can all make with just a small commitment. We also talked about our shared joy to travel the world and the burgeoning phenomenon of gay families like ours. We almost always brought Chelsea, and, as with every other parent, when our daughter wasn't around, I would tell the latest story of the cute thing she had done. Herb, being the trained psychologist that he was, would always ask, "Are you writing these down?"

"Well, no."

"You'll regret it, because you will never remember them." He suggested I write them to him in an email.

"I'll save them," he said. "Someday, you'll write a book of Chelsea stories, and you'll want to have these."

Thus was born "Dear Uncle Herb," which I shall be forever grateful.

We have traveled the world, marched on Washington, spoken out against prejudice, and spent family time with our dear friends, but one of the greatest gifts the Jerbeths gave us was the reminder of the small joys in life.

Dear Uncle Herb (DUH!)

Age 7

Dennis was commenting to Chelsea how nice it was that she had a dad that could teach her so many things, like swimming, music, gymnastics, and all the things she likes to do. Dennis said that he himself didn't have a talent for many things, to which Chelsea replied, "Oh, Daddy, you do have a talent. You know how to love."

—⁄⁄\—

AIDS Ride Tent City

We found a Vineyard

Robert, Kevin, and Jonathan starting the AIDS Ride

CHAPTER
23

DUH!

Age 5

This morning Chelsea said, "We don't have to go look for the meaning of life because I know what it is." Dennis said, "Really, what?" Chelsea answered, "Love!" I asked her how she knew and she replied, "I thought and thought and realized love is really special, so that must be it."

he Jerbeths had lit a fire in our bellies to help create a better world, and our life in activism began to grow. In the Fall of 1999, Dennis and I attended a fundraising Gala for the Los Angeles Gay and Lesbian Center, with all four of the Jerbeths in attendance, of course. During dinner the hosts screened a video of the "California AIDS Ride," a fundraising tool created by visionary Dan Pallotta. Upon graduating Harvard, Pallotta combined his passions of being outdoors, riding his bike, and making the world a better place, and organized his first ride, "Ride For Life," a transcontinental tour. He and thirty-eight of his classmates flew to Seattle, then rode 4,256 miles back to Boston. Their mission: to raise money and awareness for

Oxfam-America, an organization dedicated to ending poverty. Pallotta then shared his idea with the Gay and Lesbian Center as a way for them to raise money and awareness for the AIDS crisis.

By this time Dennis and I had lost literally hundreds of friends to the devastating virus, and we thanked God daily that we were together and healthy. By the time the California AIDS Ride dinner was held and I saw the video, there had been several years of AIDS rides, seven-day bike rides from San Francisco to Los Angeles.

The managerial aspect of each ride was overwhelming. The cyclists rode each day and slept in tent cities each night, quite a logistical feat. Each rider raised money by asking friends and family to sponsor them, and the monies collected went to the Los Angeles Gay and Lesbian Center. Hundreds of volunteers created food, shelter, showers, and a safe route for the thousands of people on wheels.

The Jerbeths had all participated on the first ride. "Good Morning America" following Judith the whole way; and each year since, Herb, Jonathan and Robert had joined in. As I watched the video, I was deeply moved by the dedication of so many people: teenagers, people living with AIDS, drag queens, and grannies; all willing to challenge themselves and go out of their comfort zone to help others. Tears rolled down my face, and, thinking of our beautiful family and counting my blessings, I grabbed Dennis' hand. It was time for me to give back.

I grabbed a sign up form and told everyone at the table I was "in." I felt excited and nervous, as anyone would be, thinking about the challenge of raising money, not to mention riding over 500 miles on a non-motorized contraption on two needle sized tires. I had until the first week in June to get prepared, just about ten months for me and my contraption to get acquainted. The physical challenge seemed daunting and a wee bit scary, but I was up for it. Judith and Herb would be working, so they wouldn't be on the ride this year, but Jonathan and Robert would be my teammates. I would also need to share a tent. However, I wasn't sure I wanted to share sleeping space a quarter of an inch from a total stranger. I do have limits! Robert offered to be my tent-mate, and I accepted, with relief.

Following the suggested guidelines, almost immediately on signing up, I began to train and raise money. We all went through an orientation process to get clear on what would be expected and to answer any questions about logistics and policies. Each person was required to raise at least $2,500 to participate. Plus, to prevent any catastrophes, there were very strict safety guidelines about helmets, proper equipment, and rules of the road.

Following my orientation, each morning I plopped Miss Chelsea on the back of my bike and took her to preschool. Then I rode the hills and canyons of Malibu, steadily increasing my distance. I gradually built up my time on the bike, from ten miles in the beginning to attending organized practice rides on the weekends that ranged from twenty-five to fifty miles. I was determined to be ready, so I rode daily and tried to challenge my length of ride every time I got on the bike. I would bike to Dennis' office (twenty-five miles each way) on a regular basis and then do an AidsRide organized training ride on the weekends. I love the freedom of being outside and seeing the beautiful serene nature of the Santa Monica mountains. On the flip side, it was often unnerving to navigate the Los Angeles road map of congestion. I very quickly realized why they were so adamant about safety. Cars and bikes are like oil and water— they don't mix, and when they do, it can be very messy!! But, I was determined to be in perfect shape before I rode from SF to LA. The longest day on the ride was supposed to be just over one hundred miles, so one of the suggestions of the organizers is to ride a "Century" before you do the ride. They had many organized rides and there were centuries thrown in here and there to give everyone a chance to make that accomplishment. So, a couple of months before the ride, a "Century" I did. It didn't turn out to be as daunting as I thought. My main issues were my raw butt and my sore neck from craning it in that very attractive shape so common to bike riders.

I knew I was in a position to ask many people who had the means to give generously, so I made it my mission to raise as much money as I possibly could. I sent letters to all of our clients, friends, family, and even neighbors that I had never met. One of our wonderful friends, Jeff Heinginger, the president of Softride, Inc., shipped me an incredibly expensive bike for my ride. The generosity was amazing. Love and donations were pouring in. Thinking it can never hurt to ask, I even sent a solicitation letter to billionaire mogul David Geffen, who had a home down the street. Though I did not hear back from Mr. Geffen, I had my friends, family, and many acquaintances offering to sponsor me. The response was overwhelming.

I was thrilled because I knew I had raised more money than anyone. The year before the top fundraiser had raised $26,000.00, and from what I'd heard they'd had made a huge "ta-do" about that on the ride. I'd raised over $50,000, so I knew I was destined to grace the history books as the top fundraiser and greatest AIDS rider ever! On my first trip!

The week of the ride arrived. I shipped my bike and myself to San Francisco to meet up with Robert and Jonathan and commence this journey of a lifetime. We made our way through the sign in process amidst hundreds of other riders, and my excitement and anticipation grew. I was so wrapped up in my imminent fundraising fame, I didn't even think about riding my bike.

Robert and Jonathan introduced me to all the major players. Jonathan introduced me to Tom, a handsome young gay man and the chief organizer of the ride, and told him I had raised $50,000. I smiled shyly, awaiting his applause or gold metal or whatever.

"That's wonderful," Tom said, looking at Jonathan. "Did you hear about Betsy from San Francisco? She raised $126,000." I smiled weakly.

"Wow, that's awesome," I said with a bit of an Eeyore vibe. I got a pit in my stomach and I was crushed. So much for the accolades that I craved.

I realized my fatal flaw. I had raised money not for the cause, but for an ego stroke. That was a tough reckoning to deal with right before riding 500 miles on a bike seat the size of a postage stamp. But, what a wonderful lesson! I slathered my "butt-balm" on and spent the first riding day thinking about how to manage my ego. That was a long day.[1]

The ride itself was beautiful and touching. So many folks on bikes, volunteering, and giving of themselves. Every day hundreds of smiling volunteers prepared food and drinks and offered encouragement for the riders. In the middle of nowhere, with her best drag queen wave with Miss America panache and flourish of her congratulatory wand, Glinda the Good Witch would appear on the top of a hill. Just when I wanted to complain about my sore butt, an old lady, twice my age, would ride past me crushing my ego and warming my heart. It is a week I shall always hold dear.

The last day was our shortest ride in total, but we had a long stretch of thirty miles along Pacific Coast Highway, and we rode

---

1. At the evening event on the third day—the one night we decided to skip the festivities, of course—the emcee made an announcement acknowledging my contribution. I had to laugh. The Universe made sure I got the point—but not the applause.

right past home. Since there was a lunch stop just before our house, Robert, Jonathan and I promised Dennis and Chelsea we would stop in and eat with them.

In her very first attempt to give to others and make a difference in people's lives, Chelsea wanted to do something for the cyclists, so she made her own Snapple stand and plopped herself down on the side of PCH, ready to give away Snapple to any rider who wanted it. When we rode up and saw her sweet face holding her sign, my heart skipped a beat.

"Snapple for the AIDS riders . . . . Thank You!!"

I swooped her up in my arms, and she started to cry.

"Dad, no one wants my Snapple!"

This was one of those life moments that was hard for both of us. My innocent little angel had a dose of bittersweet reality. As much as I knew they appreciated Chelsea's gesture, the riders had rested and eaten lunch less than a mile away. No one wanted to stop, and no one needed Snapple. I explained to her the situation and that I was so proud that she would want to do something so kind for the riders. She seemed a bit appeased, but the moment reaffirmed my commitment to an idea I'd read in "All I Really Need To Know I Learned In Kindergarten" by Robert Fulghum: Never pass a lemonade stand without stopping to purchase their wares. For all you know, like Chels, it could be their entry point into activism!

We pedaled to the finish line in Century City surrounded by thousands of screaming well-wishers. There is nothing like it, and I realized something very important: Joy in the heart can numb pain in the butt!

About a week after the ride ended, I received an amazingly generous check from the David Geffen Foundation. This man, who didn't know me from Adam or Eve, took the time to make sure that someone answered this letter from a stranger and sent a check as well. The entire experience solidified my commitment to giving wherever I could.

DUH!

Age 4

At the closing ceremonies of the AIDS ride, Chelsea had a hard time waiting for us to get there. She was winding up to cry, so Dennis finally took her to the Century Plaza Hotel away from the crowd. She cried the whole way until they walked in the front door, where she said, "Oh, this is nice," and it was all over.

Our Sat Kaur

24

DUH!

Age 6

Yesterday in the car Chelsea started in on how Amparo may go to Colombia this December, but they might have a civil war and could get killed, so they may not go. And that led to; "Dad, you know when I was in heaven with God, I was watching over Israel and they had a big civil war and everybody got killed except for eleven people and one bad guy. But, they put the bad guy in the snow and he melted into the ocean." Then she transitioned to; "On July first I was in heaven and I came down and saw this cute house and it said on the door, you were looking for a child. I thought, this is a good house, a cute room, and a nice family. I could live here. Dad, did you see a mist or a fog on July first? Because that was me. If you ever saw a mist or a fog, that was me looking around. Then I found Sandy and went inside and was born."

A midst all the excitement, wonder, and fabulousness of having a daughter, we were clear that raising a child was the hardest thing Dennis and I had ever done; separately or together. The lack of sleep alone was daunting. Parenting brought such angst and a constant wondering of whether or not we were doing everything (or sometimes anything) right for our child. Add to that the mental drain, the challenge of constantly entertaining a little one, and a slight anxiety in every moment caused by an awareness of the fact that we had no clue what we were doing. The whole drama was exhausting.

Because of the daily pressures of life, Dennis and I both had steam to blow off. Since we would never take it out on our darling daughter, we directed our tensions at each other. Sometimes in the simple act of getting ready to visit a relative, we found ourselves snapping at each other about forgetting something at home or not remembering how to get there. Chelsea was now three years old, and though we'd survived the hardest part of raising a child, we'd entered the most difficult period in our relationship.

At one of our lovely dinners with the Jerbeths, we shared frankly about the trials of parenting and the stress it caused us as a couple.

"You should go see Sat Kaur," Judith said.

"Sat Who?"

Judith explained that Dr. Sat Kaur Khalsa was a magnificent marriage and family therapist they had gone to see. Their recommendations were rarely off target, so Den and I took her words to heart. She warned us that Sat Kaur had a huge waiting list, and offered to call ahead in hopes that maybe we would not have to wait a year. We took the number, and later that week, we dutifully called the doctor. By some miracle, we got an appointment within a couple of weeks.

When we arrived in Dr. Sat Kaur's modest Santa Monica waiting room, a man wearing sunglasses and a baseball hat pulled down low—and who had just graced the cover of People

Magazine—came rushing out of the office. Dennis pointed out that in uptown Beverly Hills therapist's offices, there was usually one way in and another way out, so that people could keep their anonymity. The conspicuous lack of such a set up was our first clue that Dr. Khalsa was not moved by the norm or worried about what Hollywood clients thought, a good thing in our eyes. She came out of her office, a petite woman with an angelic smile, and invited us in. Her office, painted in shades of cream with orchids and crystals, created an ambience of serenity, which matched her calm, comforting manner.

Dr. Khalsa is a practicing Sikh, a peaceful religion based on dedication to God through daily rituals, meditation, and devotion to love. The founder, Guru Nanak Dev, summed it up in the fifteenth century, "Realization of Truth is higher than all else. Higher still is truthful living." Sat Kaur's lovely white clothes and her turban wrapped delicately around her head gave the illusion of an angel of truth, and that was what she was for us.

We made ourselves comfortable and dove into our story, availing her of all the gory details. Dr. Khalsa listened, jotted down notes, then sat back, took a breath, and said, "Well it's obvious that you love each other very much. You've just lost sight of why you do."

I couldn't believe she could see that: it seemed like we'd spent half the session complaining about each other. But she saw through it all. Her words reminded me of how much I did love Den and how we had let the daily stresses get in the way, and I was immediately put at ease. If she could see our love in the midst of complaints, then maybe we didn't have far to go.

Dr. Khalsa gave us a concrete plan and some simple homework. She told us to institute a weekly date night, just the two of us—with rules.

We could not talk about Chelsea.
We could not talk about family.
We could not talk about schedules.

Off we went to fulfill our mission. The first Friday after our appointment, we went to Tra di Noi, a lovely Italian restaurant in Malibu. The weather was warm, so we chose an outdoor table. Now what? Avoiding family and schedules, not too hard, but not talking about Chelsea? That was grueling. We dutifully went out every Friday and some dates we just sat and stared at each other. What a joy to do nothing at all. And, boy howdy, did it work! Our stresses melted away, and we connected on a much deeper level. I recommend date night to every couple with kids, to nuture your relationship and remember why you chose each other in the first place.

Sat Kaur gave us many assignments. After we'd been seeing her for a while, she suggested we create the feeling of getting away from everything by setting up a rendezvous at a hotel. Just the excitement of knowing that we were going to "share" (ok . . . have sex) with each other really got me in the mood. But Sat Kaur didn't just want us to share, she wanted us to get naked, sit on the bed, and stare into each other's eyes for five minutes. Umm, okey dokey. We giggled at the idea, but we are up for anything. So we excitedly took on our assignment and made a reservation at the Ritz Carlton in Marina del Rey for the next Friday.

Thinking they would add romance, I loaded a bag of every candle I could grab in the house, from half burnt vanilla candles to an old Christmas candle present from Aunt Betty. Den and I placed them all over the room, lit them, and settled on the bed for our naked-eye-stare bonding moment. About three minutes in, the candles smoke set off the fire alarm, and we ran around, dingles a-flyin', blowing out candles—which created more smoke. So we put all the candles in the bathroom trying to capture the smoke. We had visions of the hotel manager showing up at our door with the whole Westside Fire Department in tow to put out the two flaming queens.

Luckily, in what seemed like four hours later, but was probably only two minutes, the alarm stopped. As it turned out, no one came to our door. We could've been toast on the carpet. After our hearts returned to a normal pace, we cracked up and decided to go to dinner. We could save our bonding for later—in the dark.

We saw Sat Kaur every other week from the time Chelsea was three, and to this day we still go. Many times we think, "Are we done? Shouldn't we graduate?" But, the reality is, we have the healthiest relationship we can find. We believe it's because we take the time to nurture it, and a lot of that nurturing is created in a small room in Santa Monica, where Sat Kaur has been our counselor, our guide, our teacher, and our love for fifteen years.

DUH!

Age 4

After Dennis' birthday party the other night we came home and were opening his gifts. Chelsea had helped pick out a candle and a card. The card had a little puppy on the front and as he read it Chelsea explained to him. "See how the puppy has such a worried look on his face? That's like you Daddy. You always worry. You worry about your life. You worry about your family. Well, the puppy can now worry for you and you won't have to. That's my present to you."

Ron and Anne Smith and Den

Chels and Anne and butterfly

Smiths and M-Ds date night

25

DUH!

Age 2½

Dennis and Chelsea were driving down our road in Washington and stopped to park on the side so he could visit a neighbor. He had buckled Chelsea in the car seat with her stuffed animal, "Puppy," but didn't realize the seat was not attached to the car. As he parked he backed into a hole the size of Venus, and the car nearly tipped over. The next thing he knew, Chelsea was upside down dangling from her car seat and he heard her little voice pronounce, calm as ever, "I'm trapped and Puppy's hurt."

We spent most summers and Christmas holidays at our home in Anacortes, Washington. When we first bought the house there, we'd interviewed architects for a remodel. At the conclusion of our first meeting with Ron Smith, a very quiet, comfortable, and talented architect, we knew he was the one for the job. When we looked his drawings and described our dream project, he lit up. He seemed to resonate with our sense of style and mentioned we should walk down Commercial Avenue (the main drag, right out of small-town USA) to a local clothing shop and meet his wife and the owner, Anne.

We bonded instantly with Anne. She was a welcoming statuesque blonde; vivacious and wonderful. From that day, we started a lifelong friendship that has taken us on the road (sometimes in an RV, sometimes to Europe), through family milestones (weddings, Bat Mitzvah, birthdays), and into each others' homes as we shared cocktails, hors d'eouvres, and yummy dinners cooked up by Ron the chef. Those family get-togethers stand out as some of our most wonderful memories in our Washington home.

With a church on every corner, a drive-in A&W, and a bowling alley with the best breakfasts for miles around, visiting Anacortes was like eating a little slice of small-town Americana. On the night we purchased our house, we went out to the local Chinese restaurant and asked the waitress (who was almost as Chinese as I am) questions about the town. Two friends of ours, Carolyn and Kelly, whom we had followed to Washington, were there also. Carolyn was a tall, beautiful, mocha toned woman and Kelly was a singer and former Miss Indiana. I had sung with them in Vegas several years before, and they had also purchased property in Anacortes. Since they were both African-American, they asked if there were any black people in town.

"Well," said our waitress, "There might be a couple."

Then Dennis asked if there were any Jews.

"Well, how is it again that you can tell if they're Jewish?"

We all looked at each other, realizing she truly thought there were physical characteristics distinguishing Jews, besides wearing a yarmulke and payos[1]. We thought it best not to ask about gays.

---

1. traditional Jewish side curl

We didn't announce that we were gay, and I'm not sure what kind of reception we would have encountered if we had carried a sign down Commercial Ave, but we felt included and at home in our little getaway. There were so many people like the Smiths who were open and welcoming, but there were also a lot of people in the community that could be considered very conservative and right wing. As I told you before, our realtor, Phyllis and her husband Harold, had been wonderful about the news of Chelsea's impending arrival even with their conservative Christian lifestyle, but there were others in town who didn't know us as intimately and who might not take the news with such joy, so we opted for discretion.

When we got pregnant and Chelsea was on the way, the Smiths had been as excited as we were. We'd spent endless evenings together contemplating our new family dynamic. Then when Chelsea arrived, we brought her along to our dinners, and she would sit in her car seat on the kitchen island, soaking up the family atmosphere as we ate, drank, and generally had a blast. The Smiths introduced us to the more accepting and liberal side of town, so we had many friends, but it's a small town and we did hear rumblings of some who were not as open-minded about two guys raising a daughter.

The guy who owned the local car wash asked Anne one day when she was getting her car detailed what she thought of having two dads in a family, because he didn't think it was right. Of course, Anne was adamant that she thought it was not only perfectly fine, but wonderful. At our next dinner Anne relayed the story to us, so the next time we went through the car wash as we watched him suds our car, we were fascinated that he never mentioned a word about it to us.

-\'/-

As Chelsea grew up during the summers in Anacortes, nothing but acceptance and love came our way. She lived up to her moniker as a tool for change. So many people fell in love with her instantly. Then when they heard our story, they were en-rapt and moved. However, like the car wash guy, some folks didn't think it was such a good idea. We named one such fellow "Homo Bob."

Homo Bob was good friends with Anne and Ron, but a very conservative kind of chap. He let Ron know that he didn't think two men should be parents together. The whole thing was wrong. Occasionally we heard updates about Homo Bob's rantings, and we thought it was pretty funny. No one's opinion could ever dampen our joy or our sense of how utterly perfect, right, and "normal" we felt. So we listened, laughed, and almost felt sorry for people that had such instant opinions without any personal experience to draw on.

One evening at dinner Ron announced that he'd had a conversation that day with Homo Bob. Apparently HB had seen us in town with Chelsea, and he'd reported to Ron that the way we interacted with her was so wonderful that maybe it might be okay for a child to have gay parents. Well, whaddaya know?

Since that day in Anacortes, we ran into HB at casual get-togethers where we were all invited. He slowly warmed up to us and would even engage in light conversation. But, he loved Chelsea! Over time we became close enough to be invited to dine with Bob and his family, and he couldn't have been more kind and gracious. We've been to Christmas parties, Fourth of July events, and lovely dinners in his home and feel as though he is a wonderful friend. He's absolutely smitten with Chelsea!

I believe everyone's eyes can be opened. We should never write off anyone, because with the right chemistry and a chance interaction, the loving part of anyone can be accessed.

DUH!

Age 6

We are away in Washington, so Amparo took Chelsea to school yesterday. While they were waiting for the teacher to arrive, one of Chelsea's friends showed up and said, "Chelsea, you found a mom." Chelsea replied, "No, I have two dads." Then she turned to Amparo and said, "What don't they understand about this?"

—//—

Chelsea and her best buds

awww Kindergarten

26

DUH!

Age 4½

One night at dinner Dennis and I were having, how shall we say, an intense discussion. (We never have "fights.") Chelsea interrupted me and said, "Dad, when you talk like that, you're thinking only of yourself. You should think about everyone. That's the nicer way to be." Well, that took the heat out of my radiator. When we got home, she and Dennis shared some time alone and Chelsea reiterated what she'd said earlier. Dennis asked her to tell me what she had said and she replied, "No. You tell him. After it comes through me, I forget what I said."

As I've mentioned, a channel had said that Chelsea would be a bridge for humanity . . . yadda, yadda. When I first heard the prediction, I didn't know exactly what it meant, but as time marched on I began to realize my daughter's gift and God's intended direction for her. She came in with a big heart, and we received a lot of accolades for her kindness and her loving soul. John Q Public attributed her beautiful persona to our parenting, but even with the same exact parenting, siblings can be very different; so my very non-scientific experiment points to the possibility that parenting is only part of the equation, a large part, but a part nonetheless. Children come in with a basic nature.

We attended a baby gym class called "Tumble Time" and watched the children play games and interact with others. One little girl was a terror. She pushed, shoved, kicked, and pitched a fit if she didn't get her way. I, of course, glared at the mother with my best stink eye. What is wrong with this woman that she can't control her child? Then one day she happened to be standing next to me and started to weep.

"What's wrong?" I enquired.

"I don't know what to do! My first daughter was a total angel. But this one is totally out of control. I've tried everything, and I can't seem to get her to behave. I'm at my wits' end!"

At that moment I realized two things:

Not to judge (and if you're going to, wait until you have the whole story) and
every child comes in with their own agenda. As parents, we have to work with what we get.

Certainly we worked very hard at making sure Chelsea had good guidance, but I we can't take credit for who she is, and from where I stood, who she was was making a big difference in the world. I believed that in order for her to fulfill God's plan as a bridge for humanity, she had to be unusual and extraordinary, because if she'd been average in nature people might have glanced up at a couple of dads raising a girl and then gone back to writing their grocery list. But, since Chelsea won people over so profoundly, everyone stood up and took notice of our unique situation. So her nature transformed people's opinions of gay parenting.

—∗—

It's very hard to determine how your child is going to function in society until they start to interact with others. Chelsea was very shy during her preschool days, and because of her attachment to us and her separation anxiety, it was hard to predict how she would interact in the real world. When she entered kindergarten, we received very positive feedback, mostly from adults, about what a kind, sweet, funny, and engaging little girl she was. Her Kindergarten teacher immediately adored Chelsea. She took Chels under her wing and made sure she was nurtured. The teacher was so taken by her, that she wanted them to have a play date outside of school, to take her out to tea, and even thought it would be fun to have a sleepover. I know she sounds like a kid, but she was just a sweet kindergarten teacher.

With other parents Chels also seemed to be winning friends and influencing people while she was still only knee-high to a grasshopper. For Dennis and me it was a glorious time. Not only did parenting become a blast, because she was now old enough to begin to interact on a more mature level, but we saw that the hard work we had put in, trying to give her positive guidelines, was paying off. Chelsea was a polite and kind little girl, and as I had told her, people wanted to be around her. Every day we stood on the sidelines, breathed a sigh of relief, and quietly took the accolades—as our buttons burst.

Amparo also did a great job making sure Chelsea socialized. On the days they played in the park, Amparo connected with other families and set up play-dates. Before Chelsea started Kindergarten, she had two best friends, Christina and Tarin. Christina, with long brown hair and intense brown eyes, even at that age was recognized as the "kid in charge." Tarin, a little pixie with masses of long blond curly hair, was more soft spoken.

Though not the "kid in charge," in her own quiet way she was a tough cookie.

Chelsea loved her time with them, and they were registered to attend the same elementary school. But a triad often presents the problem of someone getting left out and hurt, and in the "C,C, and T triad," Chelsea usually ended up playing third wheel. They teased her, as children will do, but Chelsea felt the worst when as a power play they would stop talking to her. It was painful to watch. I realized that while boys get mad, hit each other, then get on with the game; girls play mind games.

Chelsea learned this at a very young age. Better at five than at twenty-five. But she spent a lot of time crying and not understanding why they would want to hurt her. Young children believe everything is their fault. Of course the girls' behavior was not personal, but that is a very hard lesson to learn in kindergarten. At that age everything is personal. If it rains on your birthday, it's personal; if a puppy goes to your friend first, etc. Learning detachment takes time. I counseled her to move on, that if they weren't being nice, she could find others to play with. This is easier said than done for an adult, let alone a five year old. Chelsea chose to be a loyal friend, hoping the situation would change.

Chelsea also had a friend named Stephanie whom she met the first day of kindergarten. Stephanie, an angelic-looking child, was fiercely smart and had the confidence of a thirty year old. Once you got to know her, it was easy to see why. In Stephanie's family, being the best was the name of the game—at any cost. So maybe her confidence came from fear of failure, but she was as hard as nails. From soccer games to math tests, Steph would point out how she was better "at it all" than Chelsea. This prompted a conversation with our daughter about competition.

"Chelsea, the most important thing is not if you win or lose, but that you do your best."

"But, Dad," she responded, "it doesn't feel good not to win, or if someone else wins!"

"Well, sweetheart," I plowed on, "First of all, no one wins every time. And it takes many losses to get a win, so every loss brings you closer to your win. Besides baby doll, it's most important that you tried your best, not where you finished. As long as you are working as hard as you can, that is the only "win" that counts."

"Ok, Dad."

"Besides baby, don't you want everyone to celebrate when you win?"

"Of course."

"Well then," I told her, "you have to be happy no matter who wins, so that everyone gets to celebrate every time."

It took a lot more talking.

With Chelsea's friends, having two dads was never the issue. In the forefront, and far more challenging for her, were the normal growing-up issues that all kids go through. We were the family next door, but of course our next door was decorated to a "T."

DUH!

Age 4

When I was reading an astrology book on birthdays I told Chelsea she was ruled by the moon. "No, I'm not," was her reply, "I'm ruled by God."

*Photo shoot with my
baby girl*

"I'm not sure I trust you Dad!"

27

DUH!

Age 5

Chelsea was teaching me to play a ball game, but whatever I did, it was not quite right, so she comforted me and said,"Don't worry Dad, the process is long, but the minutes are short."

don't pretend to know a lot about parenting, but what I know, I know. Mostly, what I know is that parenting requires a lot of research, a multitude of questions, infinite patience, and a willingness to learn from being wrong.

As a parent I was tested everyday. With every move, I second guessed myself, concerned that I might be doing the wrong thing. It is such an unfortunate circumstance of human nature, but it seemed my default was to believe that I did it wrong. As a parent, we don't usually get immediate feedback. The child rebels and struggles with any and all forms of discipline, and the parent has no idea until much later whether or not a positive impact has been made. It was usually months (if not years) before I saw Chelsea make a new choice in a situation where we had had an issue, and let me tell you, my heart exploded with pride and gratitude with every realization that she understood. But, for heaven's sake, why does it have to take so darn long? I felt like a wet dishrag most of the time, worn out by the stress that my child was going to grow up deranged and end up in jail, with no conclusive proof otherwise, until some miraculous event occurred where my precious baby redeemed herself in a new situation.

With all my grandstanding about parenting, I've made my share of mistakes. Like every other lesson, I learned more from what I did wrong than from what I did right. And every time I botched it, I was painfully aware of my impact on this little being.

One day, overwhelmed and stressed about who knows what, I was driving Chelsea to elementary school. I think she was in the first grade. She was going on about what she wanted and what she needed done for her, and I don't remember the exact question, but I asked her if she could do me a favor (probably along the lines of staying later at school, because I had something I needed to do). Well, Miss Chelsea pitched a fit and I lost it. I started screaming about how it's always about her, and she can't even do one little favor for me. I staged an entire, outraged pity party in about ten minutes, melodramatics and all. I was pissed, and according to both Den and Chels, when I'm pissed I am one frightening dude. Although I do think a certain amount of fear and trepidation from your kids is essential for them to think about consequences, a screaming lunatic does not a good parent make. I ranted and raged, until I saw Chelsea huddled in the back seat sobbing. I'd frightened my six year old little girl. I was immediately consumed with guilt and fear, so sorry for my outburst and afraid I had permanently damaged my little angel. Regardless of the situation, she didn't deserve this. On the outside, I started apologizing. On the inside, I agonized about how

I would make it right. When we arrived at school, I opened the back door to the car, but she still cowered.

"Dad, I'm afraid of you."

That crushed me. I wasn't sure what to do, but I realized someone else was going to have to comfort her. I asked if she wanted to call Daddy, and she weakly said, "yes," so I got Den on the phone and laid out my transgression. I could see she was listening. Den had a gift for getting Chels to come back to center and feel secure again. How blessed we were to have each other in times of crisis.

Chelsea calmed down and even let me hold her hand as we walked into class. On the way, I apologized again and told her that we all make mistakes and that I was heartsick that I had caused her so much grief and fear. She seemed to take it in. I promised I would make it up to her with some wonderful cozy time later that evening.

I learned that day about the dangers of letting my emotions run my parental mind. I vowed never to repeat that again. Although I have "lost it" many times before and since, this was the only time I let myself get to the point where my daughter was afraid of her own Dad.

I continued to be a strong disciplinarian, which proved to be an important element to raising a confident, grateful, polite, and caring child. But I am still learning every day about listening, not reacting, and expressing my frustrations and anger sans fire and venom.

I did a series of Kabbalah classes a few years ago. Kabbalah, the mystical side of Judaism, gives lessons in karma, overcoming ego, and tools for creating the life you want rather than letting life "happen" to you. It is wonderful information and I found that it followed what I knew from my studies to be the way the energies in the universe worked. I found these studies helpful in managing my emotions while parenting, because Kabbalah teaches us to not live in the ego, especially when dealing with children. Kabbalah says that if you are angry, state that you are angry, but do not add emotional fuel to the mix. Instead talk about what needs to happen, and the children will understand. [1]

DUH!

4 ½

During a particularly hard day for Chelsea, she said, "I don't want you to be my Dad anymore." I told her that was okay, and I would always love her. That night she told me, "Dad, this is the deal. No matter what, I will always love you. Even if you do something terrible. Even if the police come and take you to jail. I will always love you." I appreciated the sentiment even if the jail part had me stumped.

—>|<—

---

1. This will save them lifelong pain and unlimited reasons to spend years at the therapist, which saves you money.

DUH!

Age 6

This weekend, as we drove to Laguna for a synagogue retreat Dennis would be attending, Chelsea announced, "I think God is the luckiest woman on earth, and because I'm a part of God, I must be the luckiest girl on earth."

*Y*ou don't realize how much you rely on your partner until you are unable to ask their advice. And you can't ask their advice when the object in question is a surprise for them!

Dennis and I started late in the parenting business. When Chelsea arrived, I was thirty-seven and Dennis was forty-two, and although we tried to keep up our youthful figures, there was no getting around aging. Dennis was about to turn fifty, and we needed to celebrate such a huge milestone in style—hopefully as a surprise.

One day while running, I thought I'd better make a decision about this, and soon. It takes time to put such things together.

May as well start right away, so I began agonizing about the following:

> *Should I give him surprise party?*
> *How could I pull it off?*
> *Since all the bills went through his office and across his desk, how would I pay for it?*

It felt like standing at the edge of a cliff. As I ran, I weighed the options, but every time I got close to a decision, I panicked. Instinctively, I wanted to call Den to ask his advice, which of course was silly, but we always made joint decisions as a team. Reminded of what a wonderful partnership we had, the stark contrast made me feel like an island. This would have to be a solo affair, so I took a deep breath (difficult because I was running) and decided to don my party-planning hat, get on with it, and order up one big fiesta for my sweetheart.

Unsure where to turn first, I decided to solicit the help of Carol Rosen, the wonderful no-nonsense party planner who had done an amazing job with Helene's wedding. A well organized, caring, and very put together Jewish mother from the Valley; I was sure she could help me with this screaming adventure. When I got home, I called her, she jumped on board and we were off!

Next step: choose the venue. I wanted somewhere unusual and elegant and immediately thought of The Athenaeum at Caltech in Pasadena, a stately and beautiful place on the campus of Caltech, with the charm of a grand mansion from yesteryear. It seemed perfect. Plus, I had the perfect ruse to get Den there; my parents belonged the club, so I could tell him it was a party for them.

Carol, my parents, and I toured the space. Because of the size of the party, we had some logistical challenges. The main room held about 150 people, and we planned to invite 250. Hmmm.

Thank God for Carol. She took me to King Dahl Productions, the preeminent party designer in LA. A vibrant showman, Dahl had the energy of twenty people. Hands flying with descriptions of linens and lighting, etc.; he immediately started throwing out ideas and concepts. Based on how many guests we were going to have, we would need three rooms with a huge screen in each streaming videos of what was occurring at the party. This way no room would feel left out. It was an inspired concept, and I loved the idea—until Dahl gave me the estimate, and I saw why they called him "King."

After I fainted, I signed my name. I didn't have any idea how I would pull off the payments or the planning, but I kept breathing and moving forward.

Now to get the guest list and invitations in order, then figure out what lie I'd tell Dennis to get him there. Since my father had recently retired, I decided to pretend the party was for him. The only way to make sure Dennis bought the ruse would be to send a "real" invitation for the fake retirement party, so I put that in order as well.

Now, Chelsea was only seven and I wasn't sure whether I should clue her in or not. On one hand, she was a mature little girl. On the other hand, she might blow it, and I'd invested a lot in this little shindig. After chewing on it for about a month I decided to take the risk and planned a special lunch to wrangle in my partner in crime.

"Honey, it's Daddy's 50th birthday coming up," I began. "I think we should throw him a surprise party. But, we have to make it a huge secret and can't let on at all. Do you think you can do it?"

"Of course, Dad," she came back. "It will be easy! Do you think I could do a special dance?"

"Absolutely, honey. Daddy would love that!"

I then asked Chels if she wanted to arrive at the party with Den and I or get there ahead of time and wait with the rest of the guests. She wanted to get all dressed up and yell "Surprise!" so she opted for choice B. This posed a minor problem. It meant she couldn't be invited to my dad's fake retirement party. So, I sent the phony invitation to just Den and myself. On the day the invite arrived in the mail, Den opened the envelope, Chelsea asked if she was invited, and I held my breath.

Dennis glanced at the names on the invitation and sheepishly told our little dear that no, she wasn't invited. Right on cue, Chelsea burst into tears, then ran and buried her head in my legs. I was shocked at how well Chelsea pulled this off! As he stomped upstairs, Den gave me a grimace and grumbled.

"I have no idea why they couldn't invite children to celebrate their own grandparent!"

When Den was safely upstairs, Chelsea smiled up at me.

"How did I do?"

I beamed at her. I knew at that point I had a little actress on my hands. (It must be in the genes.) Of course, I was also a little frightened at how easily she was able to fib!

While Den worked at the office, we plowed full steam ahead. I bought a post office box for the replies. Chelsea and her dance teacher started choreographing a special dance for her Daddy. I ordered the cake and hired a band. We ordered a martini-bar ice sculpture where the martini would pour through the ice into a waiting glass, and I hired a magician to entertain guests while they awaited our arrival. King Dahl and I chose a different décor and lighting for each room, I culled through movies and photos to come up with a "This is Your Life" montage. Totally schizophrenic, I played the role of party central during the day, and at night pretended I had a boring day dusting (I'm kidding; I don't dust).

It's official, He's 50!

Den's surprise birthday party

The RSVP's started coming in. We were going to have a packed house, and everyone seemed to have kept the secret. To keep Dennis thinking I was doing something for his birthday, I told him we were having a birthday party for him the day after my dad's party. So he wouldn't ask anyone about the party (just in case they thought he was talking about the real party, and then blow it), I told him we were going to surprise him with who was coming. I tried to think of everything! I'm surprised I could keep anything straight at that point. Videos and Chelsea dance rehearsals . . . food tastings and décor approvals . . . it was non-stop party mania!

When the big day arrived, I ran Chelsea over to get her hair done and then dropped her off at Auntie Helene's. When I arrived home, Den met me at the front door. "Honey," he told me, "I took my ring to the jewelers for tomorrow. I told them they could keep it overnight. I don't need it until then."

"Great!" I said to him . . . "Holy Crap," I said to me! Of course. He wanted his ring beautiful for his party and didn't feel he needed it for my dad's event! I made up some excuse about picking up dry cleaning, ran to the jeweler, and told them to give me the ring because I know he'll be royally upset if he doesn't have it at the party he doesn't know he's having. Then, because he wanted to get a really nice shave for the birthday party he thought he was having the next day, he didn't shave . . . oy vey! To top it off, he says to me, "Hey, this party tonight isn't a surprise birthday party for me, is it?"

Before I could answer and then faint, he giggled, then went on.

"Oh, right, we got that formal invitation . . . you would never send a fake invitation."

I smiled sheepishly and said a secret thank you to whatever angel had saved my keister.

So, off we went to the party—with Dennis' razor and wedding ring safely in my pocket. I'd calculated our drive time to the minute and had arranged to tip off our guests with a phone

Dancing with his baby girl

call. The phrase, "a check for $10," was my the cue that we were ten minutes away. As we exited the Old Pasadena freeway, I told Dennis I needed to call my friend about a PTA check. Then I put on my actor hat, dialed the number, and gave the shortest and sweetest performance of my career.

"Oh, hey, Carol . . . I didn't want to forget to tell you we need a check for $10 for the playground monitor on Monday" . . . Whew! Done.

Ten minutes later, we pulled up to the club. It was gorgeous! King Dahl had lit the entire outside of the building, and it was a wash of spectacular color. I wanted to appreciate the beauty, but my heart was in my throat with love and nerves. The valet took our keys, and I prayed everyone was in place and wouldn't be arriving just as we got there.

We climbed the steps and opened the mammoth, Italian, carved-wood doors. The moment we entered, the Happy Birthday song rang out. Den stood paralyzed, and Chelsea ran to hug him. It couldn't have come off better! Friends and family had flown in from all over the country. There were so many people it took us forty-five minutes to get out of the front hall. Each room with it's special lighting, linens, and floral masterpieces looked beautiful. A five tiered cake with our birthday boy's name graced the center of the patio. It felt like being in the most exclusive gentleman's club awaiting your gin and tonic. We had the setting of a lifetime, and we began one of the best nights of our lives together. The love of our family and friends was palpable and the joy of our blessings, overwhelming.

However, not all went as planned. Chelsea got stage fright and decided not to dance, which was okay. The worst part was when Sandy approached me and I asked her to dance. This proved to be a turning point in our relationship.

DUH!

Age 6

The other evening, as I was laying with Chelsea, before she drifted off to sleep, she said in her little voice,

"Dad, Jason is really mad at me."

"Why?" I asked.

"I just scooted him over a little, because he was too close. And he really irritates me. He never listens, and then asks me what we have to do."

Well, I said, "Maybe you should have asked him if he would move, before you moved him yourself? And maybe you could tell him to ask the teacher if he doesn't know what to do? Why did you move him? Do you not have enough room?"

She replied, "He's just too close, and I don't want him there. And my teacher told us we would have to work it out."

"Did he tell the teacher?" I asked.

"No, I told the teacher that he was in my way, and then he said that I pushed him." "Well," I replied, "Maybe if you talk about it with him you can get an agreement on where your area is and his area is?"

"Well," she came back with, "I just scooted him, it was really nothing."

"Well," I said, "I think that this is something you have to work out with him."

"I don't want him to be mad at me," she said.

"Did you apologize for moving him?" I inquired.

"Kind of."

"Well, maybe you should tell him you're sorry for moving him without permission?"

"Okay," she said sleepily as she was just about to drift off. A moment later I barely heard her say, "I didn't mean for him to fall off the chair!"

CHAPTER
29

DUH!

Age 4½

Dennis and Chelsea sat down to meditate for the first time together. After lighting the candles and gathering the crystals together Dennis said let's say a prayer. Do you want me to go first? "No," said Chelsea, "I'll go." "Dear God, I miss you so much, but I'm so glad to be here with Daddy and Dad. Every night when I go to sleep I come to see you. I love you so much and then before I wake up I come back in my body and I'm so glad to be back with Daddy and Dad. I love you so much."

My relationship with my cousin Sandy is complicated. Obviously. When she was twenty-one and moved out to California, we were best friends. At age eleven, I was the totally devoted little cousin and loved being with her every minute I could. As I got older and she moved back to Oklahoma, we remained close. Although she wasn't a big communicator, and we saw each other rarely, when we did it was wonderful and fun. We sailed through my coming out and her second marriage, but, with Chelsea's birth our story became immensely complicated.

When Sandy said she was willing to carry our child, Dennis and I were overwhelmed with joy and gratitude. The thought of her loving sacrifice was beyond our comprehension. But, as I mentioned before, the journey through the pregnancy and the effort for Sandy and Alex to adjust to their new life in California while Sandy was pregnant caused some ups and downs. After Chelsea was born, things seemed to even out for a while, and Sandy and Alex seemed to be doing well.

Now, we had signed contracts with Sandy. We paid her quite a sum of money and also paid for all of her expenses while she was pregnant. Dennis also gave her a job with a good salary plus a very extensive health insurance policy to cover her costs. He bought her a complete maternity wardrobe and paid for everything over that, which was only fair.

A couple months after Chelsea was born and Sandy no longer had doctor's appointments, Den and I had decided it was time to bring Sandy's payout to market value levels. We kept her salary at the number we had agreed upon while she was pregnant, but reduced her insurance coverage to what everyone else in the firm received. Although we hadn't specified in her contract how long the benefits would continue, which was obviously a mistake, we thought that she would understand that we couldn't maintain that level of insurance, but quickly learned that, no matter who is involved or how close you feel you are, you must put everything in writing.

One Sunday afternoon she called and said she wanted to come over to talk. She did not understand why we'd cut her benefits. In quite an emotional state, she explained to me that her ex husband had once asked her to tell him whom she loved the most. To my astonishment she'd included me at the top of the list, right alongside her girls—and before her hubby. I was shocked. I had miscalculated our relationship. We'd barely talked over the years, and I had no idea that, outside of her daughters, I still held the number one spot. She said she saw me as the one man in her life who would never hurt her, that would love her always, that would never be an asshole, which was a big compliment from Sandy. (Her screen saver on her computer read, "All men are shit." Either I was not a man, or I was on a pedestal. Either way, I was screwed.)

I never wanted to hurt her. I will always love her, but I was in a horrible position. No longer that eleven year old who idolized her and spent every waking moment with her, I saw no way to live up to her ideal. I had a husband and now, thanks to her generosity, a child. I couldn't be her one and only.

That day on our deck, after Sandy left, Dennis and I decided to agree to whatever she wanted, not only to appease her, but because we could, and because she'd given us a gift we could never repay.

After this incident, we tried to include Sandy in our lives. However, she never once called us. When I told her I wanted to have a relationship, but that it had to be a two way street, she said, "Oh, I don't call anyone. Even my girls have to call me."

I rarely saw her and only caught up on what was going on with her through news at the office from Dennis. Every once in a while, she would walk into his office and tell him how much she loved her work. Which would floor us both; other than these sporadic reports, she never gave a clue that she was doing anything but tolerating being there. She also made no attempt to have a relationship with Chelsea, and while Chelsea had no animosity toward her, with no effort or warmth on Sandy's part, Chelsea seemed content to have her just be "Cousin Sandy."

Then came the night of Dennis' fiftieth.

After we showed the video montage and were well into the festivities, I was on cloud nine. I swooped Sandy up and started to dance, and she whispered in my ear.

"Where was I?"

"What?" I replied.

"Where was I in that video?" she said again.

"You were there. Didn't you see?"

"I wasn't there. Don't I mean anything to you?"

I was dumbfounded! Of course she was in the montage. I knew there was at least one shot of her five months pregnant with Chelsea, and also family pictures with Alex. But this was fifty years of Dennis' life, so maybe they got lost in the shuffle? There weren't a lot of pictures of her, but she didn't lend herself to getting her picture taken, and her only real part in Dennis' life, outside of work was carrying Chels. Once Chelsea was born, she wasn't really in our personal lives at all. I realized she was upset with me and had a lot of unresolved anger, but there was no way I was going to handle this at a birthday party. She left soon after our dance, and I went back to enjoying the party, but it haunted me, and I couldn't put her words out of my mind.

Two days later I sought out Sandy at the office. She felt badly about bringing up her issues at the party and apologized for her timing. I told her it was okay, but she knew it wasn't. I told her I loved her and we could work anything out, but she has never come to me to talk about it. We continued on as if nothing happened. I'm sure she was still hurt, but without communication, I saw no way I could help.

When Sandy retired from the firm in 2007, I put together a beautiful party with her friends and the entire office staff. I gave her a tribute book and numerous gifts with personal meaning for each one. At the end of the night, she said, "Will you come to Oklahoma? You're REAL in Oklahoma."

"You mean I'm not real here??"

"Yes!" she said. I was shocked. How was I not real? How had I betrayed her love and friendship? Because I could never get her to talk, I couldn't unravel her anger or frustration with me. Every time I tried to make amends, she would not respond or she clammed up. I saw nowhere to go with this.

Every time I tell the story of how Chelsea came to be, the comments I hear the most are about how amazing Sandy and Helene were, and mostly about what a sacrifice Sandy made to be pregnant and give birth at forty-six. I agree. I cannot imagine what it takes for a woman to give birth. Usually she has the blessing of a child as her hard-earned reward, but in the case of a surrogate, the effort is for someone else's bundle of joy. I will forever remain grateful to Sandy for giving herself in a way that goes beyond my understanding.

I'd not imagined the impact our adventure would have on my relationship with my cousin. I've battled over and over about my part in its deterioration. Was it enough that we took care of her, brought her to a new life, and tried to include her in ours; or should we and could we have done more? I may come up on the wrong side of public opinion on this one, but I can only tell you that I gave it my all.

Sandy has now retired and moved back to Oklahoma to be with her girls and their families. I believe she is happy, but I haven't heard from her, and she did not leave me her number. Although I still have my Polyanna cheer and hope for the future, I have agonized for years about my relationship with this woman who has played such a huge role in my life.

DUH!

Age 6

One night Chelsea was lighting candles creating a ceremony of some sort. I wrote it down as we went be cause I wanted to remember it exactly. First, we would each hold a candle and say the Pledge of Allegiance. Then she spoke extemporaneously: "You see, I know a lot. You have to think to know this much. Thinking is the key to everything. Love is the other key. Give life your heart and soul to passion for another soul. To give others your world. At night, I say my prayers and speak directly to God and into the future. To my next life. Let life take on your next birthday. Let the whole world share, never litter, and go forward with good manners!!"

DUH!

Age 4½

Today Chelsea grabbed a volume of the Zohar[1] off the shelf and said "Let's study some Hebrew." She then made up some Hebrew from the page, which I repeated. Then she would translate. "Dad, this means that God is all around us. All the love and joy. Every heart is connected. When people die, their spirit is still with you and you feel them connected in your heart."

After second grade, Christina, one of Chelsea's best friends and one third of Chelsea's "close friends triad," moved to Cheyenne, Wyoming. The news was very abrupt and shocking not only for Chelsea, but Christina too. It appeared her parents gave her no warning. The family had gone on their yearly jaunt to a summer home in Cheyenne and called to say that they wouldn't be returning and they hoped we could visit. Christina found out when her parents took her to register for school.

---

1. the teachings of Kabbalah in Hebrew

Change is hard for all of us, and Chelsea was particularly challenged by shifts in her life. But we made a plan. Although the girls had a difficult friendship at best, they had vowed to make sure it continued. They would keep in touch by phone, and they would visit each other. Christina would come to us when she could, and Chelsea in turn would go to Wyoming.

When Chelsea was eight years old, it was her turn to make the trek. Even though she still suffered from separation anxiety, we'd always sought out opportunities for her to realize she could be safe and happy with and without us, and this was not her first plane trip alone. We'd begun when she was five, booking her as an unaccompanied minor on a thirty-minute flight from Los Angeles to Palm Springs to visit Den's folks. I figured it was a short enough flight for a trial, and all went well. Before boarding Chelsea was a little anxious, but the flight crew let me accompany her on the plane and get her settled in her seat. That, plus the many hugs and kisses and attention from the flight attendant, and Chelsea was fine. Her dad was another story.

I'd waited until I saw her plane take off, then I started to bawl. As I wept, the rational part of me hovered above my body and thought, "Oh, dear God, Kevin, you are making a fool of yourself!" But I couldn't help it; I hadn't expected the separation to leave a big fat hole in my heart. Then, a short half hour later, I received word from the grandparents. Chelsea had arrived safe and sound, and had not only done well; she'd had a blast. She told Dennis' folks she felt like a princess sitting at the front of the plane. After one night there, they drove her back to us, and everyone agreed that our trial big adventure had gone off perfectly. (With some extra cuddles and a bowl of ice cream, I survived too. Thanks for asking.)

Now for the real test . . . . Seattle to Cheyenne.

On the days leading up to the Cheyenne trip, our girl had many moments of thinking she wouldn't be able to do it. Several times we talked it through, and several times she calmed down—for a while. Then she got worked up again. The day of the departure arrived, and Den, Chels, and I made our way to the airport. On the drive, Chels battled her anxiety. When we checked in, the attendant told us the flight had been delayed, so we sat in the airport, waiting for the repair crew to fix the problem and calling Wyoming with mechanical updates. As the day wore on, Chelsea was not only anxious, but exhausted from the waiting. We all were.

Six hours later, as we waved from the terminal, Chelsea tearfully made her way down the ramp and onto the plane. We breathed a sigh of relief that she was finally under way, and the ordeal would soon be over.

Den and I decided to stop for dinner on the way home. It was a beautiful little restaurant with a romantic atmosphere, a lovely little home that had been converted to a restaurant. Seated in the quaint, former living room by a lovely fireplace, we went over what a process it had been to get Chels on the plane, but how exciting that it had all worked out and she was on her way. We felt relieved and elated! Then, just before we ordered, we received a call from Christina's mom, Carol, saying the plane had mechanical difficulty and had had to land.

"Okay," I said. "Where is she?" Carol explained that they weren't exactly sure where it was, but it was on the ground.

"What!?"

Carol, God love her, had reached over the counter and told the agent that they'd better find out where the plane was, because there were unaccompanied minors on that flight, and we would not rest—therefore they would not rest—until we knew exactly what was going on.

I immediately got up from the dinner table, walked outside, and started a series of calls to the airline, trying to find out the location of our child. As I paced across the manicured lawn, I asked the customer service agent if she had kids.

"I do . . ." she replied.

"Do you know where they are?" I asked.

"I do . . ."

"Well, I don't know where my daughter is! Think about how that might feel."

After I brought her to tears, I made my way through the entire on-duty airline staff, and when I didn't get the answer I wanted, I asked to speak to the airline's President. Well, that didn't happen, but they clearly got from my relentless pursuit for answers, phone calls, and demands that they find my daughter; that I was not giving up until I knew exactly what was going on. After an hour and a half, they let us know that the plane had landed in Spokane, and that Chelsea was fine and with the flight attendant. Of course I wanted to speak to her, but they said that she wasn't somewhere where there was a phone. Are you kidding me?! I told them to find a phone with a long cord, and now! That was before eight year olds had cell phones.

After another twenty minutes of haranguing the airline employees, I got the gate agent near where they had Chelsea sequestered at the airport.

"My daughter was on the flight that had an emergency landing there and they tell me she is close to your gate. I just need to talk to her to make sure she's okay," I pleaded.

"Sir, I'm in the middle of getting a flight boarded; there is nothing I can do," she replied.

"But I just need to know she's okay and not scared, and help her decide what to do," I begged. "Is there anyone that can get a her to a phone?"

"Sir, I can't deal with this right now!" Then she hung up on me.

Well! You can imagine how well that set in my craw! I started a barrage of calls to customer service, who gave me boiler-plate answers about standard operating procedure and their inability to help me.

"My daughter was entrusted to your care, and your care was not provided. You didn't even know where she was for the first hour and a half, and then when she was found, I was told there was no way to communicate with her because you had other passengers to help. What could be more important than caring for an eight-year-old girl who is alone, scared, and doesn't have the comfort of her parents?"

"I'm sorry, sir," they said repeatedly, "but we have no control over the situation, and we can't get a phone to her."

"How can that be possible? You can run a muti-million dollar airline with three-ton flying tubes hurtling through space, but you can't provide a phone? If I'm not mistaken there are phones at every gate? No?"

"I'm sorry, sir, but that is just not possible right now."

"Well, when might that be possible?" I replied.

"I'm not sure, sir. We'll see what we can do."

Over and over again, there seemed to be no one willing to find a way to comfort a child and alleviate the anxiety of her parents.

After the seventeenth "I'm sorry sir," by the grace of God, I finally got some information. I was told that she could spend the night in a motel with a flight attendant or take a bus through the night to Cheyenne with other passengers. And then, miracle of miracles, I was able to talk to our little girl. I held myself together and remained calm for our baby. Considering the circumstances, she was doing okay and sounded better than I did.

"Dad, I'm not sure what to do."

"Are you feeling okay?" I asked.

"Yes, I'm okay. I just don't know if I should spend the night or take the bus."

I was relieved that she was such a trooper and was just worrying about logistics.

I told her I thought she should get on the bus. At least she would be moving. Plus, she would get to Cheyenne sooner. I also told her that if I could, I would happily drive, charter a plane, or do anything else to get to her, but by the time I did any of these things she would already be with Christina. After many tears, she agreed to get on the bus. She'd met a lovely lady on the plane and sat next to her during the bus trip. This woman kindly took good care of Chelsea, who was so distraught she threw up on the ride.

We were told the ride from Spokane to Cheyenne would take about five hours. It was now almost 10:00 P.M. I had spent our entire dinner and more on the phone pacing up and down the yard . . . in and out of the restaurant, giving Dennis sporadic updates. The lovely people at the restaurant, including all the diners, were riveted with our drama. Each time I came back in and gave Den the latest, he shared the news with the other patrons, and they would commiserate, until the next bit of news. Eventually all the diners went home, and as Dennis and I had lost our appetites, the sweet couple who ran the restaurant packed up our food, and Den and I headed home to await word on Chelsea's progress. We tried to sleep, but it was impossible knowing that Chelsea was out there scared to death. Finally the call came in at 3 AM that Carol had her, safe and sound. We both broke down and cried.

The rest of the five-day visit went well. We were in constant contact with Chels and also Christina's mom, but after her harrowing experience I don't think Chelsea really recovered. She seemed fine on the phone, but very reserved and not her usual talkative self.

I convinced the airline that they had to fly Dennis and me to Cheyenne to pick her up. There was no way we'd put her on a plane alone again. When we arrived in Wyoming, we all three ran to each other and grabbed on so tight, we couldn't breathe. The relief of holding our baby again riddled our cheeks with tears.

The next day, as we approached the airport to fly home, Chelsea quietly held onto my hand and started to cry. I asked her what was wrong. We were with her now, but she still had a strong fear that something might go wrong. We spent the entire wait for our flight talking her down. When we boarded the plane, I thought she would relax, but no. Instead she fidgeted in her seat and couldn't sit still. Her face was scrunched with a furrowed brow of concern, she continually looked out the window, asking where we were in the flight and how much further we had to go.

About twenty minutes into the flight, Chelsea asked me, for the twentieth time where we were in the journey. I told her we were over Washington State, past Spokane. Immediately she relaxed and un-furrowed her brow. Apparently once she had passed over the city that had been her Armaggedon, all was well. At that moment Spokane became that city in eastern Washington known to the Montgomery-Dubans now as "Spo-Can't."

DUH!

Age 8

When she was trying to get a good night's rest before her trip to visit her friend in Cheyenne alone on an airplane, Chelsea woke up very concerned that the flight attendant would forget her on the plane. She became pretty anxious, so we decided to

Happy to be home from "Spokant"

get up and give her a hot bath to relax. As she bathed, I told her she never had to worry because God and her guardian angels were always with her and would take care of her. As I told her, she said, "Look Dad, there's a heart in the bubbles in the tub!" Sure enough, there was a heart-shaped glob of Mr. Bubble. We agreed that it was a sign of confirmation of all things unseen.

2005 Tour of Italy with guide extraordinaire Uncle Paolo

Venice with the Smiths

DUH!

Age 5

One day Chelsea asked if she was Jewish and I said, "Yes." The she asked if I was Jewish and I said ,"No." "So what are you?" "Scotch, Irish, French, Dutch, Cherokee, English and German. And so are you." "Well," she said, "Thank God I'm Dutch. I've always wonted to be Dutch."

During the Fall of 2004, when Chelsea was eleven, Anne and Ron, our dear friends from Washington, came down to Malibu and paid us a visit. Early one afternoon we decided to throw together a lunch. Chelsea and Anne got to work chopping peppers and onions, and Ron, the only real chef in the bunch, guided Den and me through cooking pasta while he grilled some London Broil.

When the five of us sat down to enjoy our creation, Ron mentioned that he and Anne were thinking about taking a big trip that summer to Europe, and if we had any interest in going? Well, all three of us lit up like fireflies. It sounded like a great adventure. Den and I told them we had been thinking about taking Chelsea to Italy, because at eleven she was old enough to appreciate it.

We threw ideas around over pasta. We wanted to concentrate on one country at a time, while Ron wanted to start in Austria, but would love to include Italy in their plans. We agreed that it would be fun to meet at Cinque Terra, the fabled five cities that perch cliff-side on the Italian Riviera. Spontaneity and excitement abounded as Ron and Den grabbed their laptops and began searches for maps, hotels, sights, and plane fares.

Everyone pitched in ideas, and for the next several months, plans progressed. Ron, our quiet, dry-witted friend, and Den were the meticulous planners; and Anne, Chels, and I, being chatters (and an enthusiastic peanut gallery), became the cheerleaders.

We gathered our frequent flyer miles together and booked plane reservations. Den spent hours with Roz Wolpert, our Superwoman travel agent, who was able to book everything from B&B's to yacht charters in a single bound; as well as arrange cars, sight-seeing adventures, dinners, and hotels. We planned to meet Anne and Ron in Cinque Terre where we would spend several days before our little family drove up to the Leaning Tower of Pisa. Then, we would land at our rented villa for the week, after which we would part company with Anne and Ron while they continued on to Vienna. We would then drive to Venice, stop in Milan and Lake Como, stay over in Perugia; and then on to Rome and a quick trip to Pompeii . . . a tour de force of Europe's great boot! I couldn't wait to embark on our dream vacation!

Our flight from LAX to Europe included a layover in London, and poor Chels drank so much tea on the plane that she didn't sleep a wink the entire ten hour flight. Jet lag is awful. I felt so bad . . . for her and for myself. While a rare occurrence, what a cranky little soul she was! Then I remembered the poor kid had only traveled on short-term flights before. After the longest ten hours I could remember, with crying and moaning about how miserable she was, she survived (and so did I!) and we made it on to the next flight to Turin, Italy. A car met us at the airport for an hour and a half ride to Cinque Terre, where at about 10:00 pm local time, after a total of about twenty hours of travel door to door; the three of us, bedraggled and exhausted, arrived in the beautiful town. It was totally charming with it's picturesque, cobblestone, no-car-zone pathways and the added bonus of the view over looking the aqua blue Mediterranean.

I could have slept on the sidewalk, but when we met up with Anne and Ron, a renewed vigor coursed through all three of us. The only possible explanation could have been it was morning in LA. Such a beautiful night, and we were all so excited to be in Italy together! After a midnight celebratory drink over the bay in Monterosso, the first and biggest of the five towns with red tile roofs and ancient stone houses; we fell into our respective beds with Chelsea in a lovely cot in our room for a sorely needed night of blissful slumber before the next morning's hiking trek to Vernazza. Before I could settle into a good snore, I heard a long whistle followed by an explosion, then another, and another; the signature sound of fireworks. I got out of bed to see the sky lit up and our room filled with celebratory snaps and bangs. For what, we had no idea. I think the Italians celebrate National Cheese Day, Italian Independence, and every day in between—with fireworks. Chelsea tried to settle in and nod off, but, as tired as we all were, sleep was out of the question. So we sat and cuddled on the edge of the bed till late, watching the fireworks and barely slept at all.

The next morning, the three of us pulled our weary selves out of bed, determined to get on Italian time. We met Anne and Ron (both of them radiant with that warm, cheery glow reserved for people who sleep) for breakfast then headed out on the sheep trails. These narrow dirt pathways connect the five towns and at times hung on the edge of the cliff. I can't tell you how wonderful hiking was, because it was not! Italy was experiencing a 100-year heat wave, and even having donned as few clothes as possible, we dripped and drooped.

As we reached the crest and looked down at the idyllic town of Vernazza, the heat seemed to wane, and as I looked down on the gorgeous town below I felt like I'd walked into a movie. The village below seeming unreal, a mirage of what a mystical Italian village would look like . . . small stone and red tile roofed buildings stacked together, with no seeming rhyme or reason, connected by ancient stone pathways. We'd walked into a picture postcard.

When we reached the quaint town square, situated on a beautiful harbor sprinkled with small boats, we plopped at the nearest outdoor café and ate lunch. Amazing what a little shade, pasta, and sparkling water can do to cheer the soul. Once we completed our micro journey through the other beautiful towns, we took the train back to our hotel, grateful for a wonderful day . . . HOT, but wonderful.

We left Cinque Terre for our extended adventure. The villa turned out to be quite a bit smaller than the wide-angle lens travel photos had promised; but our host, Monica, was an angel and welcomed us as her own family. Over dinner on our first evening there, we casually mentioned we were here for my birthday.

"Why you no tell me?" Monica exclaimed. "Why you no tell me?"

On Monday we made our first foray into Florence. This was a bit of a disaster. After a forty-five minute drive into town, we found out our guided tour of the Uffizi was not possible. The touring company had failed to mention that all museums are closed on Monday. Our driver felt so horrible that they had made such a blunder, that he contacted his girlfriend, a tour guide. Maria agreed to meet us the next day in what would be the best museum experience I have ever had. She was delightful and told us that she was only going to show us ten paintings. This seemed a bit light, seeing as the museum held thousands of the most well known pieces of art in the world. She started at one end of the building under one of the portraits of the Medici family and told the rich history of the family and their influence over medieval Florence. Like a spine-tingling novel she held us captivated, painting her own picture of the rich history of the region. She then moved to a painting from just before the Romantic period and described how the figures were two dimensional and flat, as was the style of the day. Then, she had us slowly turn around and look across the room at "The Birth of Venus" by Boticelli. The painting jumped out at us almost as if it was in 3D. The whole tour, a lesson in painting, history, and civilization; read like a page turner.

The rest of the week was every bit as wonderful! Monica sent us off to sample a restaurant, part of the "Slow Food" network that relishes the time honored (and time-honoring) tradition of savoring and appreciating your food in a "slow" and pleasurable way. We went in the back room surrounded by cured hams and cheeses. The very large proprietor (who by his girth obviously loved his own creations) brought amazing food out by the truckload, and we appreciated every morsel.

We included a trip to the Palio in Sienna during 103 degree weather, and Chelsea continued to surprise me as she endured the heat and the crowds better than I did. A pleasure to be with, she was cheery and enthusiastic long after I would have preferred a nap and a fan.

As our week at the villa wore down, we prepared to part ways with Anne and Ron and go to Venice to celebrate Chelsea's twelfth birthday, while they headed back to Vienna. Chelsea loves everyone being together and hates good byes, and at the last minute, she begged Anne and Ron to delay their return to Austria and join us in Venice. They hemmed and hawed with the idea of changing travel arrangements, then spontaneously decided to join us. Thrilled, we packed up two cars, said good-bye to the lovely Monica, and headed out for the city of canals. Den, Chelsea, and I piled into the front car with a professional driver, and Ron followed with Anne in a rental.

Now, our driver was a bit of a speed demon (did I mention we were in Italy?). As much as I pleaded with him to ease up a bit, he kept Ron on a harrowing chase. Then, halfway there, we discovered that Chelsea had left all of her best dresses in the armoire at Monica's. Too late to turn around, we called Monica on our cell, and she said she would ship them back to the States. In the meantime, we would have to take Chelsea on a little shopping spree. So sad!!

We arrived in Venice several hours later, and Ron and Anne, after barely tailing us, pulled up totally frazzled. Anne got out, and our driver told Ron where to park. Off Ron went to find a spot, while we waited, and waited, and waited. Anne, usually calm, was up in arms. Ron must have been lost. In the meantime, Chelsea, so excited to be in Venice on her birthday, stood on the edge of the canals, mesmerized by the skyline.

"Anne!" Chelsea exclaimed. "Look at the water taxis and canals!"

To which Anne responded, "I've seen them before."

From ten yards away I could see that Chelsea was crushed, and being a papa bear, I stepped in.

"It's her birthday," I said to Anne. "Can you get over your worry for a second and share her excitement?"

Anne immediately got on board, walked to the dock with Chelsea, and appeared to enjoy the amazing panorama. From that point on Anne was a trooper, listening while Chelsea pointed out the exciting highlights, even when she was worried Ron had ended up in Yugoslavia.

A few minutes later Ron showed up, and off we went on our water taxi to greet Venice. We arrived at their hotel, which our travel agent described as the last room available in the city. I saw the place as a hovel I would never ask anyone to live in for $400 a night, but no complaining from Anne and Ron. I am so grateful for good friends. The rest of Chelsea's birthday was magnificent. We found some beautiful clothes for her, and Dennis arranged for a gondola ride with a second gondola (for the singer) to follow. It was magical. Afterwards we sat on the dining deck of our hotel restaurant and watched the sunset.

The rest of our Italian extravaganza progressed sans Ron and Anne, but continued to be a grand adventure for our family of three. We had three wonderful days exploring the grandeur of the Lakes and the Alps, and hired a guide to take us shopping in Milan to find Chelsea her Bat Mitzvah dress. (What girl doesn't want to say she found her dress in Milan?)

We arranged for a personal shopper to pick us up and drive the half hour to Milan. However, once we got there, we found out he didn't have a clue where to go for an adolescent girl's evening gown and was far more interested in finding a present for his mom (again, did I mention we were in Italy?). So we kept suggesting well-known stores: Gucci, Yves St. Laurent, etc., and then, if they didn't have a suitable dress, we asked the sales staff where we might go to find an evening gown that Chelsea could wear. After about an hour and a half and upwards of ten stores, we discovered a local boutique. Den and I pored through the wares, but Chelsea said she would know it when she saw it. After agreeing to try on half a dozen gowns that Den and I loved, she spotted a beautiful yellow chiffon number. When she came out of the dressing room, all three of us nearly burst into tears. Our little girl looked so beautiful and sophisticated. Despite a few frowns, "tsk tsks," and disapproving looks from some Italian women; we made the purchase. It was perfect for her Bat Mitzvah party. Mission accomplished; we headed south to our Perugia resort, our travel agent's words ringing in my ears:

"Go there. You just have to trust me on this one."

She was not wrong. High on a hill overlooking the countryside sat a beautifully refurbished country manor with grand and beautifully decorated rooms, French doors on every wall overlooking the gorgeous country side, and the best food we had had in Italy . . . which is saying something! We dined on the veranda where we met fellow travelers from all parts of the world. One couple from England asked us about our family and were so enchanted with our story they asked Chelsea to give them a fashion show of her new yellow gown. They applauded as she came down the stone staircase and descended into the garden terrace. Magic!

After three relaxing and magical days, we set off for Rome, for both mine and Chelsea's first time. We named our new driver and tour guide "Uncle Paolo" a wonderful, young, gay man who even though we begged him to eat with us every meal, maintained a proper distance. As much as we tried, he wouldn't dare cross the line into familiarity. He knew every detail of the history of Italy and took us on a "magical, mystery tour" of all the Roman sights. In addition, he spoke English, relieving us of the broken Italian and crazy hand signals we had been attempting throughout our journey.

A client of Dennis' who lived in Rome asked us to go see Madam Butterfly at the Baths of Caracalla. The ruins of an ancient bathhouse that formed a series of stone wall fragments, creating an amazing stage and outdoor setting for the show.

As the lights lit the stone walls and tunnels, the artists entered through magnificent archways and descended thousand year old steps. We sat under the stars listening to fabulous music in a transcendent setting, a once in a lifetime experience.

Back in our car and still glowing, Chelsea realized she had left her best purse in the bathroom. I jumped out of the van and ran back to the baths like a salmon headed upstream, passing thousands of audience members, the whole time thinking it was surely gone. This was Rome for heaven's sake; the purse was gone before she put it down. But as I approached the ladies' room, to my surprise and joy, I saw a group of ushers looking at the purse. They didn't ask me why it didn't match my outfit, but they did want some form of identifying proof. I told them what Chelsea carried in her purse, which was next to nothing, but I remembered and described an identifying picture we had looked at recently, and they promptly handed it over. That act forever reminded me to refrain from generalizing or falling prey to rumors about regions and areas. I'm good most of the time. Not so good in Arkansas.

After a lovely trip to Pompeii, we headed back to pack up for our flight to the States—and reality. Once on the plane, we filled out the standard immigration forms. A flight attendant had told us all persons living under the same roof could be on one form, so we put the three of us together as usual. When we disembarked at LAX, we stood in an Immigration line. The officer who manned our line, a middle age curmudgeon, had a gruff look and gave the impression that to utter a few words might burden him beyond repair. After twenty hours of flying, seeing him did not make my day. He barely looked up from his screen, and ushered people through the process in a very abrupt manner. When it was our turn, all three of us toddled on up to his counter with our sweet faces. This stick in the mud held out his hand for our forms like it was a big pain that he had to interact with us at all. Dennis presented our form, repeating what the flight attendant had told him. The officer gave us a look and said the attendant was mistaken.

"Where's her mother?" he added.

We went into our normal banter and presented her birth certificate, but that didn't appease the beast.

"The two of you need to fill out separate forms."

"What about our daughter?" I asked.

"She can go on one of them."

This was the first time Chelsea had been in the position of seeing us have to choose which one of us would be her parent. Apparently straight unmarried couples with children can go on one form as long as they have the same address, but as we were not married at the time, he made the arbitrary decision that we would have to pick one of her parents to be considered her family. Though not exactly Sophie's Choice, Chelsea was stressed; concerned that the decision to have us place her name on one form would invalidate her other dad. She didn't want to hurt anyone's feelings. We were all uncomfortable! We hated that she was put in this heart-wrenching position. It's nerve wracking to go through those militaristic type screenings, but then to be judged as not a proper family was beyond horrible. We had no ego about who was picked as parent, we just didn't want her to have to feel like she didn't have a family like everyone else. Dennis puffed up his adorable 5' 7" frame and argued for a bit with Grumpy, but it soon became clear he wasn't going to budge.

Chelsea teared up, but we started redoing our paperwork. Out of the blue, Chelsea's nose began to bleed. Mr. Grump got flustered, stamped what paperwork we had, and sent us past his station. The incident deeply affected our girl, and from that moment on and all the way home, she kept increasing her cries for us to tie the knot. It was not only the negativity that bothered her; she immediately started to talk about the injustice of this kind of prejudice and vowed to do whatever she could to change minds and expose bigotry. First and foremost she wanted us to make it official, so there could never be a question about the validity of her family.

In spite of the little challenges, Den and I realized that we loved traveling with our girl. We enjoyed the magic of discovering the world together: Den was our meticulous planner and navigator; I was the implementer and detail man; and Chelsea charmed everyone along the way (well, anyone that could be charmed!).

On the way home, Den turned to me.

"Honey, how did we end up so blessed? How did we end up with such an amazing girl?"

"I'm stumped too," I responded. "We must have been saints in another life!"

DUH!

Age 8

Chelsea was about eight when she told Den what our respective roles were.

"Daddy, you bring home the bacon; Dad cooks it; and I eat it."

Our Sugar Plum Fairy!!!

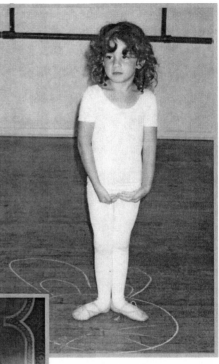

The beginning of her dance craze

Just an understated Mother Ginger . . . girls?
What girls??

32

DUH!

Age 2½

Dennis was reading a certain book to Chelsea for his first time. She and I had read it numerous times before. As he read he would misread little words, here and there and each time Chelsea would correct him. After the third time Chelsea looked at him very seriously and said, "Do you need a flashlight?"

One sunny afternoon, when Chels was about two and a half, she and I went for a stroll. We had been at our local playground in the Malibu Country Mart, and I decided to do a little window shopping. Chels followed along holding my hand. When we walked past the dance studio, we peeked in the large picture window and saw the grand room complete with ballet barres and a bevy of little five year olds, all dressed in pink tights and tutus, skipping around it's polished wood floor. Chelsea stopped, riveted. I asked her if she wanted to go in and watch, and she nodded, so we walked up to the viewing window inside, where my little dear did not move for a solid twenty minutes. Now, if you don't have (or have never had) a two year old, you may not realize how long twenty minutes is to them. It's about the span of an ice age. Chelsea was captivated by the music, the "big" girls dancing and skipping, and the beautiful ballet teacher, with her graceful arms and elegant bun, smiling and guiding the little ones through their valiant attempt at dance. I immediately enrolled the two of us in Mommy and Me classes.

I have been accused (for some odd reason I cannot fathom) of steering her toward dance, the arts, and musical theater, but I'm here to tell you it was all her doing. We did our level best to make sure Chelsea had every opportunity to experience any avenue available to her. She had lessons in art, flute, piano, horseback riding, soccer, ice skating, skiing, roller blading, gymnastics, and even Cotillion; but she always came back to dance. Performing, and dance in particular, moved her soul and is what she was drawn to from the time she could remember. Whenever soccer practice interfered with dance rehearsal, I always asked which she would like to go to. It was always dance. So much so that everything else eventually fell by the wayside, and dance became a seven day a week routine.

We started at Ballet by the Sea with the formidable Joanna Jarvis. Joanna, classically trained, ran a very tight ship. The picture of a Ballet Mistress, she was tall, erect, non-smiling, a no nonsense teacher with a very serious approach to dance. Her performing years were far behind her, and her studio was her baby. For her, dance was serious business. She taught classical ballet and hired other teachers to teach jazz. Joanna had formed a wonderful non-profit organization, The Malibu Ballet and Performing Arts Society, which had four companies under their wing: Malibu Civic Ballet, Concert Dancers, and two jazz companies, Dance Asylum and DGen. The four of them together did a yearly concert in the spring and a wonderful production of the "Nutcracker" at Christmas. It was a great dance experience for the girls. The Society provided outreach to children that didn't get to experience the arts, either because of health or societal issues. Each year a "Make a Wish" child would be featured in the "Nutcracker," and the girls learned about giving back.

In Chelsea's first big recital, her show-biz genes showed! At five years old, she was chosen to be the line leader and guide her group on stage to curtsy at the feet of the princess, then sit down. Well, on the night of the performance, here comes the line of kindergartners, but no Chelsea! My heart jumped. My stomach turned. Then, lo and behold, after all of the other girls were onstage, here she comes trailing after them, completes her curtsy, and calmly sits in her place on stage. Such calm. Such grace. Such talent. At intermission I ran backstage to congratulate her and my star ballerina was in tears.

"Dad, I was waiting for them to come get me, and no one was there, and they didn't see me, so they went on without me; so I had to go at the end of the line, and I wanted to do my part and . . ." She ran out of breath and broke down.

I told her that there is always something that goes wrong in the theater.

"It's not about being perfect," I said. "You did what you had to do and carried on. Good job! You went on stage, even at the wrong time, and never let on there was a problem. That is the mark of a professional!"

While Joanna didn't have the requisite stick and bad accent of a Russian dominatrix, she was tough. She subscribed to the Royal Academy of Dance (RAD) curriculum and wanted even the very young girls to go through the RAD exams once a year. It is a tough exam where the girls dance before a panel of judges and perform a set of exercises. Their performance is scrutinized and given a fail, pass, pass with merit, pass with extreme merit, exceptional merit, or "my god, she's Anna Pavlova!"

The following year Chelsea was old enough to participate in the RAD exams, and Joanna approached me, but I refused. Why add judgment to something she loves so much? We are already judged so much in our lives. Well, Joanna was not happy. But the next year Chelsea asked if she go. All of her friends were doing it, and she wanted to be a part of the gang. Because it was her choice, I relented.

The preparation was nerve wracking for Chels. It took many hours of class to learn every exact move and exercise to be performed before the adjudicators. She was very quiet on the way to the test, and anxious about finding the right building and dance studio.

"Are you sure it's here, Dad?"

"Yes, baby this is the address."

"But, is it in this building?"

"Yes, honey, this is the place."

Sure enough, we were in the right place, and she got through it okay. She came out smiling and told me she was relieved it was over. There was a bit of competition between the girls about how they did, but it wasn't an overwhelmingly upsetting experience, so I let Chelsea continue the path of Joanna and exams.

One summer day when Chels was seven, as she waited for ballet class to begin, Diane the musical theater teacher, talked her into joining her performing class . . . just to try it out. Diane is a master recruiter, and after one rehearsal Chelsea was hooked. She became a part of Diane's performing company, "Center Stage," participating in two shows a year, with songs from every show ever on the boards. Performing arts had officially taken over her life.

Diane was amazing with little kids. She gave them voice lessons and built their performing confidence. She wanted everyone to have a part. No matter how long you had to sit in the theater, everyone had a bit of a song. In Chelsea's first show, "Lily at the Carnival" ("Carnival" in it's Broadway incarnation), we sat through a three hour performance in a small, hot, local theater to see Chelsea sing three lines of "Frere Jacques," but she loved it. For each production, Diane chose a title close to the original musical, but when she was done, the show looked nothing like the original. In her rendition of "Into the Woods" (or I think she called it "Princesses in the Forest"), Chelsea played Princess Belle (no Belle in the original) opposite an amazingly talented young man with a stunning voice as the Beast. I watched her fly down the aisle, dance around the Beast, and then sing her part, and I thought, "This girl has a spark!" While I may be delusional, I believe I'm objective about talent . . . even when it is my own daughter. I always look from the audience's perspective, and I can feel when we're losing them. Some people grab you, and while they may not be the most intrinsically talented, you can't stop watching them. I call it, the "it" factor . . . and in the eyes of her dear ol' dad, Chelsea had "it" in spades. People were drawn to watching her.

During the first act of "Princesses in the Forest," we all heard a loud crash coming from back stage. Then Chelsea's entrance came up, but no Chelsea. The cast covered for her and moved on, but after a couple of dance numbers went by, numbers I was sure Chelsea was in, I realized something was wrong. Den and I sat there and panicked but the show continued, so we had to wait to find out what was up. At intermission, I left Den to find Diane and see what was going on. I charged backstage and found our girl sitting with her arm on a pillow. She had tripped on a cable and fallen. We wiggled the fingers and moved her arm around. It seemed okay, so I asked her if she wanted to stop or continue with the play.

"Dad, it's a show!"

Okay. I was convinced it was just a bruise anyway and felt confident she was fine, so we watched her finish. Her arm dangled at her side the rest of the show. However, at the curtain call, when her cast-mate grabbed her arm for a bow, the anguish and little tears streaming down her face should have clued me in, but no; I'm a show must go on kind of a guy, so I stood up and applauded with the crowd.

The next day we left for our house in Washington, Chelsea's arm still very sore. She slept with it resting on a pillow, and a couple of days later, while playing The Game of Life on the living room floor, I noticed she seemed to be nursing it a lot. I told her she needed to move it somewhat to get it back in shape.

"If you baby it," I said, "it won't get the exercise it needs. It's just a sprain. Come on honey, spin the dial."

"Owww, Dad," she replied.

"Hmmm . . . it IS a little blue." We spoke to Helene, who was insistent we needed to get it checked out. Although I was still reluctant, I said okay, if she thought it was necessary. So off to the emergency room we went.

Well, this very polite and sweet local Washingtonian doctor approached us in her green scrubs, took one look at Chelsea's arm, and scooted her off to a room for an x-ray. After about forty minutes, she came back out to our room and said, "You guys are awfully cheerful for having a daughter with a broken arm."

I shrunk to the size of a pea and I was sure they were going to revoke my Dad card! I'd grown up with a dad who lived on a ranch and lived by the creed that you fixed everything yourself and never babied bumps and bruises. I felt horrible and learned that day that a little babying once in awhile might not be a bad idea.

Chelsea's arm healed and her passion for dance and performing continued. The "Nutcracker" was always a huge event in Malibu. Joanna put on quite the production, and the balle-rinas looked forward to playing all of the parts in turn, from their humble beginnings as Gingersnaps all the way to "Sugar Plum Fairy," and every part in between. The production required many additional volunteers, so in Chelsea's first year Joanna approached me to be one of the adult party guests. Of course I agreed, and then, when she told me that she needed a "Mother Ginger" (always a man in drag with little gingers coming out from under "her" dress), it sounded right up my alley! That show started Chels's and my history of performing together, some-thing that warmed my heart and remains one of the best experi-ences of my life.

Now, you have to know that I'm a shameless ham onstage. I lose my mind and have to make sure the audience is entertained every moment. Well, my first go-around at Mother Ginger, I worked that audience, and they responded in kind! The little dears made their entrance from under my mammoth pink satin dress that they had to lower over my head from the rafters while I balanced on my stilts. Once the kids exited my dress they chas-sed, pliéed, and curtsied their little hearts out in front of me, while I madly upstaged them with my Joan Crawford on Crack makeup and Dolly Parton wig; doing my best vaudeville clown act. The audience clapped and yelled, and the girls were thrilled. After the act, Chelsea hugged me.

"Dad, they loved us!" she said.

"Yes, they did, honey! They certainly did."

I was making such a hoopla as MG, I'm not sure the audi-ence even knew there were girls onstage, but I never told Chels this. Every year, as a new set of gingers packed themselves under my skirts, my character became grander in her performance, and my beauty mark grew larger to accommodate my hammi-ness. I waited for a parent to scream at me about stealing the attention, but I think they loved that fact that it was the most fun moment in the show (though I'm sure many "Sugar Plums" would disagree), and the parents felt their girls were part of it.

When Chelsea was about ten, she and all her friends auditioned successfully for the Junior Ballet Company, "Concert Dancers." She was thrilled. In this new production of the "Nutcracker," they got to be "Candy Canes," who were always played by the junior company of "Concert Dancers." While a royal pain for the parents (who had to sew yards of red satin stripes on to white unitards), this was a great honor for the girls. After two years of being in the junior company, the forward progression continued, and the Concert Dancers were allowed to wear pointe shoes; those horrible but oh, so classic satin slippers in which no human foot was ever designed to stand, but which look so graceful in the eye of the beholder. After learning the impossible—how to balance and dance en pointe, the dancers auditioned for the senior company, Malibu Civic Ballet . . . the big time!

Because of our schedules, Den had less time with Chelsea, so we had planned a three day vacation for the two of them to get away. After we'd prepaid the hotel reservation, I found out the auditions for Civic were at the same time. I didn't want to have to change travel plans, and I was sure it would all work out just fine, so after Den and Chels returned I called Joanna and asked if Chelsea could audition.

"Absolutely not," Joanna's replied. "There is no way I can put the people together again to judge her."

I was shocked. Chelsea would be heartbroken if all her friends moved up to Civic, and she was left behind. I felt horrible. I told Joanna that I would facilitate getting all the parties together for the audition, and it wouldn't be hard to take a few moments out of everyone's day. As Joanna and I went around and around about this, I finally got that her answer was an unequivocal, "No." Not one to give up, I explained that it was my fault, and if I thought that it was a cut and dried kind of deal, I would have never let them go away for the weekend. I had seen Joanna play favorites, giving certain girls the best parts or a break if they couldn't make a rehearsal, while the others were expected to follow strict rules. I even heard her tell one girl, in front of all the other girls, what a special dancer she was and how she would pay special attention to her. So in my mind, Joanna's rules could bend, but she wouldn't budge.

We had a huge row with many unsavory words exchanged, and I believe one of us hung up on the other. Then, she called me back a while later and offered a solution.

"When the girls audition for the "Nutcracker" later this year," she said. "I will consider this Chelsea's audition for Civic."

It seemed like an okay compromise for now, so I accepted, hoping that it would lead to letting her ultimately join her friends in Civic.

Needless to say, Chelsea was devastated that she couldn't audition. I never told her about Joanna's and my dispute, but Chelsea took it well and seemed okay with the compromise. I was so proud of her. Some of her girlfriends who were the most competitive with her got into Civic, while she stayed in Concert Dancers, but she held her head up and marched on. Peer competition is brutal for a ten year old, but my baby seemed to have the courage to withstand the pressure.

At times Chelsea asked if she could maybe try to go to professional auditions to be a child actor, but we refused. I knew the pain of rejection from my own career, and I didn't want her to go through that. I also told her that I didn't see many examples of child actors who made it to adulthood unscathed. From what I could see, they either ended up on drugs or homeless. The life of a performer brings too much attention for a young person to endure. I added that, to want to be a child actor, your motivation is either the money or the fame; and both are empty goals. I wanted her to know that if you really have a passion to perform, there are many avenues that aren't professional and that will give you the satisfaction of giving to an audience without the baggage of money or fame. If this was truly her passion, and if she still wanted to pursue theater after she graduated college, we would do everything in our power to help her, but until then her career would be limited to local performances for the sake of the craft.

In early October, the "Nutcracker" auditions began. We drove over to the studio and waited outside for the good news, but five minutes later Chelsea came out and told us she didn't have to audition. All of the Candy Canes would be played by Concert Dancers; no audition required. What!? I marched right back in there and confronted Joanna, but she claimed that she thought it would be good for Chelsea to be in CD one more year, be the best in that company, and then audition for Civic next year. I was dumbfounded! If Chels hadn't said that she was fine and really just wanted to dance with her friends, I would have pulled her out. I never wanted to taint Chelsea's experience, so I didn't let her know. I was cordial to Joanna for the next couple of years for Chelsea's sake, but I cringed every time I had to see her or interact with her. I continued to volunteer and do the "Nutcracker" for the good of the production and the community, but I had a hard time letting go of my resentment, and seeing Joanna weekly was a stomach-churning experience.

Chelsea never wavered in her love of dance and performing. It has given her a confidence and a beautiful carriage that will carry her far in life, and for that I am grateful to all of her teachers, even the ones I choose not to invite for tea.

DUH!

Age 5

Chelsea said, "Dad do you know who I love the most and is most important?" I expectantly said, "No." Thinking I did. Her answer . . . . "God."

So proud of our
Bat Mitzvah girl!

PARTY!!! Soaking up
the joy!

Her surprise tribute. Never so proud!

DUH!

Age 6

Chelsea was having a play date with a friend and Dennis overheard their conversation and Chelsea exclaimed, "Oh, if you only had a daddy and a dad you would be so happy!!!"

While Dennis and I were on the same page when it came to our spirituality, we came from and practiced very different religions, and this presented an unexpected bump in the road from the very beginning.

When it came to dating, I'd never followed specific religious or ethnicity guidelines. The gender issue was enough to deal with! My first love, Eddie, was a first-generation Palestinian Arab, and through the years I'd dated Peruvian Catholics, Irish-Protestant WASPs, Black Southern Baptists, agnostics, and an occasional Buddhist. I looked at the person, not the trappings. You might say I was an equal-opportunity dater. When I worked at a movie theater, my manager said she would never date anyone who wasn't Jewish, and I thought that was crazy. What if she fell in love with a Hindu? I didn't want to limit myself, and, as long as he was a good and loving person, it wasn't important to me how my lover worshipped.

When Dennis and I first started seeing each other, the religion thing never came up. Dennis, a practicing Jew, went to the High Holidays, Rosh Hoshana and Yom Kipper, with his family. We also celebrated Passover with his folks. I attended the services and dinner and enjoyed learning more about Judaism, which seemed to be the most open and loving of religions, not trying to convert or convince anyone that it was the only religion and founded on basic tenets about being loving and living a moral life. I had no issues whatsoever with that, so religion was never an issue with us—until we had Chelsea.

Having a child forced us to be clear and reevaluate all of our beliefs and behaviors. When Sandy was close to her second trimester, Den and I began discussing religion. Den said he wanted Chelsea to be raised Jewish. I had no problem with that, because I wanted her to have a spiritual foundation, and I liked Judaism. Den clarified that he really just wanted her to be Bat Mitzvah'd, and then she could decide for herself which path she wanted to follow. Sounded good to me.

A Bat Mitzvah is a Jewish girl's rite of passage into adulthood. She prepares by learning to read Hebrew and studying about what it means to be a Jew. Then, at thirteen years of age, she participates in a beautiful ceremony where she reads aloud from the Torah (the holy scriptures written in Hebrew on a big, beautiful scroll) and makes a speech based on the portion she has read. She is then handed a symbolic torch of adulthood and its accompanying responsibility. She is given a tallit, a beautifully decorated, fringed prayer shawl that symbolizes a small tent to hold her and enhance her prayers. The fringe is to remind her of God's commandments. It is a very moving and wonderful event for the girl's family and friends. I was totally on board. Besides, the ceremony is followed by a huge party.

As Chelsea approached the age of seven, we realized that if she was going to be Bat Mitzvah'd, we needed a place for her to study Hebrew for the next six years. This meant we would need to become members of a Temple and enroll her in religious school. We had generally gone to Den's folks' Synagogue for services, but that was in the desert, and Chels needed to attend two days a week, so we looked nearby. Of course our first choice was just down the street, at the Malibu Jewish Center and Synagogue, where Chelsea had attended preschool since she was three, and (apart from crying every time I left) thrived. However, before we joined, we decided to meet with the rabbi to get a sense of how we might be received as a gay couple.

We made an appointment with Rabbi Judith. When she had first been hired, we'd heard she was a strong charismatic woman from Santa Fe, New Mexico, and that she had been involved in their rich cultural theater community, so I was looking forward to meeting her.

We showed up at her office a bit nervous and wondered what her response might be. As gays there always is a trepidation when showing up to be included in a practice that may not have many gay people involved. We wanted to be sure our sexual orientation would have no negative impact on our daughter. Rabbi Judith brushed away every concern for us and Chelsea's welfare. She marched around her desk and swooped us into her arms and her temple, and when we expressed our concerns, she told us that if any of the congregants had a problem with us, that would be their problem. She would not allow any kind of discrimination on her watch. We joined the synagogue on the spot and enrolled Chelsea to begin studies at the start of the next Hebrew School year, then left the meeting feeling loved and appreciated. This was the place for our family.

⁓∖∕⁓

While Chelsea studied away at her Hebrew, Den, and Sat Kaur, and I had many discussions about our family and religion. During our therapy sessions, we would sit on her cushy sofas, holding hands and discussing our universal spiritual philosophies. Both Den and I had exactly the same general feelings about God, love, and prayer, but as we talked about Judaism, I felt my Christian history evaporating, and as we moved closer to the Bat Mitzvah, I felt unsettled. My family heritage and history as a Christian was somehow getting lost. Although I had no desire for Chelsea to be Christian,[1] I wanted my daughter to understand my history. I wanted her to know how I was raised, and a significant amount of my early life took place at church.

Den didn't understand. In his eyes, it made no sense that I felt put out. We had decided as a team that she was to be raised Jewish; I didn't subscribe to one religion; and I certainly wasn't a practicing Christian. But I wanted my history honored. As we sat in the good doctor's office week after week, we discovered and peeled away the many layers of this onion. I came to understand that the pull for both Den and myself was not so much the religion as the cultural heritage. As parents, we both wanted to identify our child as coming from our roots, our stock.

It seems to be a very powerful draw for all families to identify strongly with their sense of history. It didn't seem to be as intense for WASP-y types, including me, because we are such a mixture and hodgepodge of races. For Jewish families it seems inherent in being Jewish to identify with ethnic, old-world roots,

---

1. I'd taken her to a church service once. After five minutes she put her head in my lap, tried to go to sleep, and told me afterward that she felt they were trying to make people be a certain way and she didn't like it. She was five!

and is particularly potent. The Christians who feel strongly about their religion are generally focused on the religious aspect more than the cultural history, but the Jews place importance on the cultural identity of being Jewish. There are many, many people that identify as Jews, but that are not necessarily religious. As we waded through the religious waters (which for some can be holy, but for us began to feel a bit tumultuous), we gained clarity about each of Chelsea's parent's "take" on religion and how we would clarify our beliefs and spiritual base individually and as a family. As parents, the most important point was to be united.

One of the many reasons I love my husband is that when he looks at himself and his issues, if he gets the reasoning behind someone else's point, he makes an instant shift. I'm not so easy. When I asked him what he wanted for his daughter, he of course said, "joy and happiness."

"So, Den," I said, "if she feels that Judaism is not what brings her joy and happiness, would you still want her to identify as Jewish?"

He paused, then said, "I get it."

From that point on, we were both clear about our motives. Neither of us wanted to let go of a portion of "who we are." Chelsea would be raised Jewish, but we would both honor our own and each other's upbringing and history. I don't think the months of therapeutic chats changed anything about how we proceeded with the Bat Mitzvah, but I felt Dennis and I were closer, and from there on, it was smooth sailing to Bat Heaven, well, for us anyway.

No child loves Hebrew school, and Chelsea balked with the best of them, but she went every week, managed to do well, and in addition, took dance class every day. As we came closer to her Bat Mitzvah year, the Malibu Jewish Center hired a wonderful teacher who made it fun for the kids. Michal related well with the children, taught them to ask questions, and brought them to the realization that no one is a cookie-cutter kid. She encouraged each child to approach life on their own terms, and her approach helped prepare Chelsea to make her way into adulthood.

We did an over-the-top, lavish event from soup to nuts. If there was ever a little girl who deserved it, it was Chelsea. With her abundant childhood, she'd had continuous opportunities to be a spoiled brat, but she never took that path. While we certainly spoiled her, she seemed to be spoiled good, not rotten. I always felt it was our job not to take her out of the lifestyle she was born into, but to teach her how to handle it with grace, love, and appreciation; and she proved over and over again to be a kind-hearted soul full of gratitude.

When the day arrived, a beautiful July 1st Saturday morning, everything was in place. We drove with excitement, nervousness, and anticipation, and walked into a temple packed to the rafters with family and friends, songs and prayers. My Methodist parents presented Chelsea with her Tallit (a beautiful demonstration of this temple's open nature), and Den's parents gave a prayer and blessing. We passed the Torah down from Rabbi, to grandparents, to parents. Then Chelsea accepted the Torah and read Hebrew like an angel. She then stepped up to the podium and delivered her speech, speaking eloquently about justified rebellions, based on the Torah portion she just read. She masterfully tied the rebellions for independence, civil rights, and women's rights to the important rebellion for gay rights today. She delivered her speech with charisma and confidence. She was magnificent.

Then it was my turn. I got to speak about her, but it was very difficult. I was so overcome with love and emotion for my daughter, I couldn't get two words out without breaking down in tears. When Den got up to make his comments, he broke the ice, telling everyone how thankful we were for the Gentiles, because they filled the place, unlike a lot of the Jewish families who skip the ceremony and meet up at the party. As he gave tribute to our girl, he also took many pauses to collect himself.

It was a glorious, magical event. Rabbi Judith has a mystical way of making each Bar or Bat Mitzvah a special ceremony tailored to the honoree. She took a pause to say a special blessing for Chelsea, and as she held her hand on Chelsea's head, she crowned her a miracle. Cantor Marcelo, with his beautiful voice, extreme wit, and open heart, enveloped the room with joy. All the family had played a part. Several of our Christian guests said, "if this is what Judaism is about, I just might have to convert!" My heart was so full, I forgot about the party—almost.

Following the service, we hosted lunch on the veranda next to the sanctuary, where everyone shared about the love and emotions that had been so present at the ceremony. Then while we all took a break to prepare for the evening celebration, Chelsea and I ran off to get her hair and make up done. We both were on cloud 9. Chelsea, partly because her job was done and over, and partly because of the incredible response. We giggled and talked through every moment of the ceremony, then set our sights on the party. If we had stopped there, I would have been fulfilled. The incredible love and pride I felt for my daughter filled my soul, and I was complete . . . but, I'm not one to pass up a good party!

Later, Dennis met at the hotel next door to Universal Studios. Given that Chelsea loved to perform, we'd thought a Hollywood theme would be appropriate, so we'd rented a sound stage. Chelsea, in a limo, arrived to hired paparazzi, screaming friends, and hired fans. We'd hired a mock "Joan Rivers" to work the red carpet and interview the guests. The sound stage itself was turned into an elegant "Club Chelsea," reminiscent of a forties feature film. On the walls hung huge George Hurrell style black and white glamour shots that I had a professional photographer take of Chelsea, and we blew them up into portraits. Inside there was a club section and a dinner section with a fifteen piece band and dance floor.

Our biggest challenge was Chelsea's entrance. We had a set of stairs at the back of the room, hidden by a huge feather fan. Her Uncle Robert Desiderio introduced her, and the bright pink, twelve foot tall feather fan lifted to the ceiling. As Chelsea stepped down each stair, it lit in a beautiful pink glow. Then, in her gorgeous yellow gown we'd picked out in Milan the year before, Chelsea crossed the room to the dance floor. The applause was deafening, and she carried herself like a princess. What can I say? She has two gay dads!

Other than the beautiful tribute that Chelsea made to her friends and family, the most touching part of the evening was when Chelsea took the floor and did a ballet, choreographed by her dance teacher, as a surprise for Den and me. She danced to "For Good" from the stage production "Wicked," and there wasn't a dry eye in the house (or soundstage). It was spectacular. I'd had no idea what a performer she was. I'd seen her spark at dance recitals, but I'd never had the chance to see her carry an entire number and astound and en-rapt an audience. It was stunning. I knew at that moment that, while this had been my career path earlier in my life, my true calling was to guide my girl to her dreams and sit back and applaud with the rest of the world.

The unique opportunity of being a family in a Bat Mitzvah is seeing your child, as a mature person, stand up in front of hundreds of people and show their gifts and attributes. I don't think many cultures give their kids that challenge or reward. On that gorgeous Saturday in 2006, right before our eyes and embraced by the entire community, we saw Chelsea as a magnificent young woman.

I will never forget the end-of-evening topper. As the crew packed the sets and lighting and broke down the equipment, the drummer, a very large and imposing, cool dude from the band, approached me to tell me he was inspired by our family. He had never seen a family like ours, not only a gay couple with a daughter; he said he had never seen so much love generated by three beings, and all he wanted to do was get home so that he could hug and appreciate his own family.

DUH!

Age 6

Chelsea asked, "Dad are you good at math?" And I said, "No, that really isn't my best subject, but I know someone who is really wonderful at math." She said, "I know, I know, Auntie's brother." I laughed and laughed and she slipped in, "Got ya on that one!"

High School Graduation 2011

Chels and her high school besties

34

DUH!

Age 4

Chelsea and Dennis went to Las Vegas when she was about four. They went to a restaurant on their way to the new Cirque du Soleil show, "Ka." Chelsea was worried about clowns and weird characters. They both agreed that their bus boy was the most beautiful man they had ever seen. He had seen "Ka" and assured Chelsea that there were no strange or scary characters in the show. As he left the table, Chelsea turned to Den and said, "He is cute, hot, and full of information."

*D*ennis and I kept waiting for the rebellion. It was coming; of that we were sure. We had been told since Chels was born that she was going to come to a point in her life when she would realize that:

1. Having two dads was not normal, and

2. Every child comes to a point in their tween years when they HAVE to rebel against their parents, and that is normal.

When she realized these two things, she would unleash the hounds on us. Warned in advance and convinced it was coming, Den and I waited, watched, and held our breath.

She had attended the public school in Malibu, Webster Elementary, a wonderful place. Malibu is a very small town. Granted it's a neighborhood with a world wide reputation (and an ocean), but still not a lot of people lived here full time, so it was truly a small community. Before Chelsea came along, we hadn't really met anyone from the area. But go and have a kid or a dog, and all of a sudden you're Pattie Popular. Everyone wants to talk to you and meet and pet the little tyke (hopefully they pet the dogs, not the tykes), and you start to become part of the neighborhood.

We loved our fellow Malibu-ean families and enjoyed the community, but it became extremely clear to us that Malibu High was not where we wanted our daughter to go for Middle and High school. The school had a reputation (like most schools these days) of partying and nonsense, and we wanted to give our girl the best opportunity to make it through those rebellious years with as few scars and bad habits as we could manage.

We started looking into private schools and asked a lot of questions of families whose kids had already graduated. We even got the advice of a school consultant trained to help parents navigate the decision-making. Through our not so scientific process, it seemed that an all-girls institution was the safest and best option for Chelsea. At first, thinking back to my youth, I opposed the idea. If I'd had to go to an all boys school, I would have killed myself. I didn't have anything in common with straight boys. All my friends were girls. We had so much in common . . . knitting, musicals, clothes—and boys! But, then I realized I am not my daughter, and she might thrive in an all-girls school. The rationale is that, especially during early puberty, as both girls and boys are developing their bodies and their interest in each other, girls get very self conscious and too keen on impressing the boys. They give up their own self esteem to try to get attention, so they don't participate the same in class, and they don't develop their own sense of self. We did not want that for our girl.

We looked at all types of schools, and two stood out in the crowd: Marlborough Girls School and The Archer School For Girls. As we investigated, we found Marlborough was very academic, like every girl was trying to get into Harvard or die. I could feel the threat of my kindergarten nightmares returning. Archer was more balanced in art and academics and seemed to have a more relaxed approach.

When we toured Archer, Chelsea was immediately drawn to the school. It was located in a beautiful, historic Spanish Colonial Revival building from the 1930s that had been used in the filming of the movie "Chinatown." There was a unique sense of pride that permeated the walls, and as we passed through the halls, every single girl smiled or greeted us warmly. It felt like coming home. Chels got very excited, so we decided to only apply to Archer, and if that didn't work out, we'd take our chances at Malibu Middle School.

Chelsea was nervous during the interview process.

She came out and said, "I blew it!"

"Why do you think that, honey?" I asked.

"Well during the interview the lady corrected a word I used. She said I hadn't used it properly." She thought she was done for.

When the envelope from Archer came, it was promisingly big, but Den and I had to wait for Chels to get home from school to open it. We were like little kids. As soon as she came through the door, we both handed her the package and waited while she gently tore back the seal and read quietly for a few seconds, then burst into tears.

Fun times

Dear Friends

"I got in!" She was ecstatic.

Den and I were surprised. Since the interview, Chels had given no indication she was even interested in going there. But after the tears, a few jumps, and shouts of joy, we realized how much she'd wanted Archer all along.

On the first day of school, as I drove our eleven year old to the bus stop for her first day of sixth grade, Chelsea started telling me how nervous she was to start at a new school. I told her I understood, because so was I. Every time she was in a new situation, be it dance classes, soccer, or a new school, Dear Ol' Dad also started with a whole new group of people too. Until I got past the initial meet and greet and bonded with some of the new people, each situation was a challenge. I told her it was a fact of life. If we're lucky, we continually start new experiences with new people our whole life, and although it's challenging, the sooner

Graduation day at Archer

It's all about stripes!!

we accept it, take a breath, and start meeting new friends, the sooner the new turns into the familiar.

Chelsea took my words and ran with them. She knew a couple of girls who had come from her elementary school, but she bonded with a whole new group and settled into a happy time. She loved her teachers, and her teachers reciprocated. The school taught her how to study, how to write a good paper, and how to be a life-long learner. Although most of Chels' social life was outside of school, with dance and theater, she had a great group of girls at Archer. Den and I could see things were too good and prepared for the rebellion we knew was coming. Every one of our friends who'd survived teenage kids guaranteed us it was going to come.

Eventually . . . cricket . . . cricket . . . cricket . . . nothing. Even when I volunteered at Chelsea's school and saw her during the day, she would yell, "DAD!" and come running over for a hug, right in front of her friends. In middle school. She seemed so proud of us. We relished in the joy of having our girl enjoy her family so much and so publicly. But, of course it was about to end. We knew because everyone told us!

Middle school flew by, a flurry of school, dance classes, and fun. Life was good, but toward the end of her seventh year, Chelsea began to have issues with the friend group. One girl in particular, with no explanation, stopped speaking to her. Maybe jealousy of some sort. Maybe Chelsea hurt her feelings about something. We never found out. I asked Chels what it could possibly be, but the girl refused to talk directly to her about what was going on. This made it uncomfortable for Chelsea to hang with that group, and as she advanced to high school, she shifted to another group of girls and seemed much happier. Still, Chels noticed a distance between her and her friends. She didn't have the same interests. She didn't want to party or find a boy to fool around with. While she would have loved a boyfriend, it seemed that mostly the girls were "hooking up," not creating relationships. So she increasingly hung out with teachers and didn't really have close bonds with her classmates. She thrived as a student and received numerous awards and recognitions from the administration and faculty, but more and more she seemed to be more alone in her friend group. Okay, here comes the rebellion, right? Uncomfortable at school, she'll take that pain out on her parents. Nope. Never happened. The more she felt isolated at school, the more she loved being with her family.

On May 21, 2011 Chelsea walked down the aisle of the graduation tent in a beautiful white dress, as was the tradition at Archer. She was happy to graduate and move on to college and a new adventure. All four grandparents, many aunts, uncles, and cousins attended the ceremony, so very proud of our girl. To our delight, she was proud of us too. The rebellion never happened. Sometimes, everyone is wrong.

DUH!

Age 6

Dennis and I had a slight disagreement and Chelsea quickly took Dennis aside and counseled him. "I do not like this fighting and if it continues I am going to take my sleeping bag outside and sleep in the garden. It's like I'm the parent and you are like the child." She then found me and repeated the same advice, but continued on, "If you don't stop, there is someone we should talk to and her name is Dr. Toni Grant." I asked Amparo if they listened to Dr. Grant and she said ,"Oh yes." And when she suggested that it was enough radio talk, Chelsea said, "No, I love listening to her. She's teaching me how to be with people."

—,ı~

Our innocent girl

CHAPTER

35

DUH!

Age 6

At a restaurant Chelsea was having a personal problem involving itching in private areas. So we tried to soothe it with cool water in the bathroom and seemed to cause her great grief. I wasn't sure how bad it really was and if it wasn't just a reaction to being bored and not getting enough attention. Eventually I took her on a walk to a store for some ice cream. On the way she said, "I'm so sorry Dad I don't want you to have to do this I know it's a lot of trouble," I replied, "Honey I don't mind at all if you really are having trouble I would go to the ends of the earth for you." She quipped, "How could you? It doesn't end."

SEX! The best non-secret, secret in the world. Every commodity is sold with sex. But we pretend we don't notice. Every relationship is driven and sparked by sex, but we pretend that it's romance, affection; anything but the S word. What keeps this life-producing, energizing force under pseudonyms, fancy disguises, and politically correct wraps? Shame.

Most parents have such a dirty, dark, guilt about sex that they can't even talk about it with their own children. In America, we are still run by the thoughts of our Puritan forefathers. One would think we have boards carefully stacked between couples in their marital beds to ensure any activity outside of procreation is not attempted. I vowed that this would not be the case in our family.

Dennis and I agreed that we would answer any of our child's questions about sex openly and honestly, and that we would present sexuality in the most positive and becoming light we could. We asked for tools from a psychologist friend, and she recommended several great books, including "Where Do I Come From?" with cartoon pictures that gently describe the sexual process, and "My Period Book," which provided us with much needed information about girls going through puberty.

Before Chels was able to walk, I bought these treasures and put them away for the big moment. And, of course, the fateful day arrived.

Chels was seven. She came home from school one day and said her friends were talking about kissing, sex, and having babies.

"Oh, honey," I inquired. "What did they say?"

"Well, dad, if you kiss very long and something about sex and your belly button then you can have a baby."

"Wow, really?" I replied. "Do you have questions about sex and having babies?"

"Oh, yes, Dad . . . a lot!"

This was it! The moment I was prepared for. If you are a parent, you know that being prepared for anything is cause for celebration! I told Den to grab the books and meet me in Chelsea's room. Den however did not match my enthusiasm.

"Really, honey . . . ?" he said.

"Yes, really, honey! This is it! The talk!"

All grown up

So we all convened on Chelsea's bed with books in hand and started "the talk."

I explained that couples who love each other and also want children must go through a process. We went page by page through "Where Do I Come From?" where it gently described the physical process of a man and a woman having sex. About half way through the book, Chelsea looked at us.

"Okay, that's enough, but can I keep the book?"

Apparently she'd reached the limit of what she could take in front of her dads, but she wanted the info nonetheless. We didn't go into the gay process or what the differences were, thinking we would let her ask for that when she was ready. We also gave her the period book and told her that this was about how her body would transform into adulthood and how the woman's body prepared to carry babies. She eagerly grabbed the books and threw them in a drawer, and we all went on to watch Animal Planet.

Den and I thought for sure that she would now have many questions about her own birth. She already knew she came from her cousin, Sandy, that you needed a boy and a girl, and that there was a necessary physical process. Surely she would begin to wonder how we'd done this. But, it didn't come up. There were other questions; instead words would come up, some slang, some not.

"Dad, what's cunnilingus?" What? Man, what kids pick up on a playground!

Well, I didn't pull any punches. I took a deep breath and explained it as simply as I could, all the while trying to keep my face in neutral. Chelsea's face was another story. She scrunched it up like a prune as I spoke, then said, "Thanks, Dad," and promptly escaped outside; I assume to either assimilate the definition or make a lifelong promise to herself to stop asking me questions.

Talking about sex was a tricky process. While I wanted her to have the most positive view of sex and making love, I also wanted to make sure she knew the gravity of the subject at hand. Not only could you end up with a baby; in this day and age, you could end up dead. I wanted her fully prepared and protected.

For the longest time she never asked about the genetics of her own birth, and Dennis and I wondered when it would come up. We decided that if she didn't ask about it by her tenth birthday, we would bring it up ourselves. Lo and behold, just weeks before Chels hit double digits, it happened. We were sitting in a private tatami room at our favorite restaurant in Hawaii, and Chelsea piped up.

"Hey guys, can I ask you a question?"

"Well, of course, sweetie," Dennis responded.

"Who helped Sandy have me?"

"Oh, my gosh, honey!" I spouted. "We are so excited. We have been waiting and hoping you would ask!"

We went through the entire tale from beginning to end, and as we described the process, her little face lit up like a beacon, obviously ecstatic!

"I am so happy," she said. "I feel like I fit right in between the two of you. I belong right in the middle!" We were thrilled at her glee!

"I had been wondering for such a long time," she continued. "I didn't know if I was Sandy and her husband's child, or worse: that Dad, you, and Sandy had had sex! That would have just been wrong!"

We'd had no idea she had been thinking about this for so long or what interesting solutions she'd invented to solve her puzzle.

After lunch, the three of us walked hand in hand down the street basking in pure joy. We stopped at a local ice cream parlor to celebrate with hot fudge Sundays, and Chelsea called her Auntie Helene to let her know that she was so happy that she had given us the egg and that they had a special connection. She had always felt it, but now it was confirmed. Helene was relieved; she hadn't been sure how Chelsea would react and thought maybe Chels would have bad feelings that either she or Sandy had given her up. Of course, it was just the opposite. No one had given her up. People loved her and helped to give her the parents she adored: her two dads!

Chelsea navigated her sexual coming of age the same way she navigated so much of life: with grace, honesty and lots of information. Whether we were having discussions about boys and dating or menstruation, we were always frank and honest, so when she finally did start her period, she felt prepared. It came as a surprise at a pool in Hawaii. She quietly went to the bathroom, bought her products, and discreetly called it a day. I asked if she was okay and if she needed any help, but she didn't want to discuss it and said she was fine. And that was it. She wasn't always up for a discussion, but sometimes I pushed, just to make sure. I called her Auntie Helene to ask if she could swim with her period. Chels wasn't too pleased that I talked to Auntie, but she thanked me later for the information.

Chels didn't date a lot, but I made sure that we discussed being prepared for anything, not being afraid to ask questions of me or any trusted adult, and to not wonder about life; always find out!

I constantly bombarded her with information about every taboo subject. From teenage boys (walking hormones with one thing on their minds), to every kind of sexually transmitted disease ("Always protect yourself").

While this can be an edgy subject for both parents and children, I believe because of Den's and my relentless commitment to honesty and information, Chelsea has had the tools necessary to navigate the awkward and hazardous sexual waters with preparedness—and as much comfort as can be expected.

DUH!

Age 7

On one of our numerous trips to Hawaii, Chelsea decided that she should go down to the restaurant in the mornings and get Dennis and me some complimentary coffee before the breakfast buffet was open. Well, she was great! Every morning she'd go down and deliver us two cups of hot coffee in bed. (Now, this is why I think I really had a child) On our last day she was adjusting to Hawaii time and sleeping a little later than usual. Well, I heard her start to stir and try to wake up and casually I said, "Now, where is my coffee?' Well, without missing a beat, she threw the covers back and said, indignantly, "Well, for crying out loud!!!!" Daddy and I were on the floor in stitches!

Chelsea speaking for the Human
Rights Campaign in Washington
DC before 3000 guests

Our No H8 portrait
we adore

Chelsea charming "what's his face"

CHAPTER

36

DUH!

Age 7

Chelsea's Father's Day Poem

"Faith has brought us here for Father's Day. Oh, God has blessed us from year to year. Here is a song from me to you:

I love you! So much. From Day to Day. So give me your gladness year to year."

When Dennis and I finally tied the knot on October 11, 2008, we didn't realize the depth of the connection we would feel. As I said at the beginning of the book, my Dennis, who is not one to be sentimental, woke up the day after the wedding, looked over from his pillow and said to his Husband (ME!!), "Honey, I didn't really know how this would feel, but I feel more connected and bonded than ever before!"

After the big nuptials, we were a changed family. Everything was brighter and . . . more gay! Most importantly, Chelsea felt the relief that came with our formal legitimacy. The responses from our family and friends kept us glowing for weeks, everyone moved by our inherent love and devotion, and we in turn, buoyed by their loving support. After so many years, we were delighted that we could be legally united. It was a magical time, a time between the worlds. This momentary miracle lasted all of twenty-four days.

We'd been so excited by the idea of electing Barack Obama as President. Not just because he was African-American; because he was brilliant. I felt moved every time he spoke. After eight long years of feeling persecuted by an administration with a religious agenda, the possibility of real hope in our future made me very excited. While George W. Bush was President, we'd become increasingly frightened that the laws could, at a moment's notice, change so drastically that we might lose our daughter. It did not matter that she was biologically and legally ours; we had watched cases of biological children taken away from gay parents, because someone decided that same sex parents were unfit. In 1993 a state judge in Richmond, Virginia awarded custody of a two year old boy to his grandmother taking him away from his biological mom declaring her an unfit parent just because she was a lesbian.

"In the decision, Judge Buford M. Parsons Jr. of Henrico County Circuit Court, upheld an earlier finding by the Henrico County Juvenile Court that custody of the two-year-old child, Tyler Doustou, should be taken from his mother, Sharon Bottoms, and turned over to his grandmother, Kay Bottoms. Judge Parsons called Sharon Bottoms an unfit parent."[1] Because of cases like this one, we were really scared of what was happening in our country.

In 2004, when Bush Jr. was elected for a second term, Den and I thought, for the first and only time, that we needed an

1. http://www.salon.com/2013/05/23/judge_tells_lesbian_couple_to_separate_or_lose_kids/; http://www.nytimes.com/1993/09/09/us/judge-s-decision-in-custody-case-raises-concerns.html

escape plan from the States. As I reflected on the possibilities that lay before us, I understood the need for civil disobedience. Dennis and I were both products of the sixties and had watched in awe as Rosa Parks, college students at a lunch counter, and Dr. Martin Luther King Jr. led the peaceful charge to change unjust laws. This courage and determination not to let prejudice, legal or otherwise, rule our world was where we found inspiration as we faced for the issues that haunted us. No one was going to take our daughter away, and if we had to go "on the lamb," then we would. The thought made us heartsick. We loved our country. We loved Malibu. We loved the life we'd created here. But when it came to Chelsea, we would have left heaven if it meant we could stay together. We made certain she knew that nothing could ever come between us, even if we had to do something illegal.

Even though Barack Obama wasn't in favor of gay marriage, his heart leaned toward "justice" as opposed to "just us." At the same time, we were very nervous about the possibility that Prop 8 would prevail, banning same-sex marriage in California, and our marriage would go down in defeat. With just weeks left before the election, and polls too close to call, we were nervous, but we couldn't bear to imagine that justice would not prevail on this one.

On November 4, 2008, Chelsea and I sat in our den glued to CNN and watched the polls close across the country. Dennis was in the bedroom working at his desk, within shouting range, so I would deliver each new result. We all three grew more excited as each new state turned blue on the screen, and it became increasingly clear that we might have a Democratic president. At 8pm Pacific Standard Time, the polls closed in California; and seconds later Wolf Blitzer announced that Barack Obama was declared the victor. I savored this moment. Our country had progressed so far, and President Obama's victory was such an affirmation.

When you travel a long road, even though it may often times look bleak, if you keep focused on the truth and on what is right, ultimately justice will prevail. We watched President-elect Obama and his family take the stage to fireworks and a tearful Oprah in Chicago, and our hearts soared.

But what about Prop 8? When the polls closed, the vote was too close to call, so we went to bed not knowing the fate of LGBT families and marriages in California—including ours. I was so anxious I couldn't sleep. I got up repeatedly during the night to see if there was a result, but it was to no avail. Watching the pot did not make it boil. Early the next morning, I dragged myself out of bed and turned on the early morning news. Prop 8, although only by a slim margin, had passed. In California? How could this be? Our hearts sank. With the election of Barack Obama and the passing of this horrendous piece of legislation, I felt both ecstasy and agony.

Dennis and I worried about our fifteen year old Chelsea. We didn't want the election results to discourage her. We didn't want her to think that a majority of people thought that our family was less than any other. That morning, before leaving for work, Dennis talked to her. He assured her that we would be all right. It didn't matter what the election results were, he told her. Our family would be just fine.

"Daddy, I know we will be fine," she said, "but what about all the other families? They won't be fine, and it's not fair."

Out of tragedy there can be a glimmer of hope. If we had this girl and her generation coming up, there definitely was hope for our world.

Right away Chelsea wanted to do something to help open hearts and change minds. So many of our friends and family had commented on her speech at our wedding, saying that if only people could see who she was, know how she felt about her dads, and hear her tearful plea, they couldn't possibly deny that every family should be honored.

Months later, I had the idea of using YouTube as a way to reach as many people as possible. Based on the fact that so many friends and family had commented on Chelsea's speech at our wedding, it seemed like a good option to get Chelsea's message out to the masses. If the world could get a glimpse of her passion as a daughter of two gay men and how much her family meant to her, hearts could be moved.

Chelsea and Dennis thought this was a great plan, so when we got the footage back from the wedding, I took her speech, edited it, and posted it. We had no idea what to expect. The first day we received four, then ten, then twenty views. No big deal. We'd had that many people in our kitchen. But then something happened. I came home one day and looked at the views. After only one week's time, and within hours, our number of views had jumped by thousands. I watched with awe. We tried to figure out how this viral phenomenon had happened and discovered that an online magazine in the UK called "Pink News" had found Chelsea's speech and written an article about it.

The article was published on September 17, 2009.[2] That was the catalyst. Once their piece hit the e-stands, Chelsea's link went around the world at the speed of Internet. Then Perez Hilton, a gay blogger who borders on being a Pink TMZ, tweeted it; and the rest is history. Her YouTube page went up by thousands of views each day. We watched as so many people viewed, then commented on what a beautiful message this was of love and acceptance. Chelsea got so many comments from gay youth who now felt hopeful that they too could have a family and raise children.

---

2. http://www.pinknews.co.uk/2009/09/17/video-teenage-girls-plea-for-gay-marriage/

Before, all they'd felt was judgment by society and, sadly, their own families. We'd started the process of changing minds on a global scale. Some of the comments:

poozybear

This was just beautiful. Your two dads raised a daughter to be proud of. I wish them another 26 years of happiness. Maybe by then the world will start to realize that love exists between two PEOPLE— not straight, gay, black, white—just people. Props to Perez Hilton for sharing this video on Twitter. I've added it to my favorites. Wishing you all the best. :)

snowy p

i'm a straight girl and i just can say: WOW . . . your speech made me cry, coz you said the only truth: love is all that matters!! and everyone can realize, that the things you say came from your heart whether homo or hetero or bi!!! the best of luck to you and your daddys!!! may they be together for ever!!!!

kalekarel

Congratulations! :D In time all of the US and the rest of the world (well, some may need more time than others . . .) will join our still growing group of countries where people of the same sex can marry! We were the first some 10 years ago, and believe me, it has had NO negative effect on straight marriages or society. It only made more people happy, plus extra revenue for party places, bakeries etc etc ;-) Hope your dads will live happy together! Best wishes from Rotterdam, The Netherlands :-)

    The reviews were not all charming. As we'd warned Chelsea when we posted, that her piece also brought out the ire of the religious right and the bigots:

monez14

Sucks to be her with dual fags for dads. Just because they couldn't get married doesn't mean they couldn't be together. Typical bleeding heart lib.

TRE4RERE

so both of their sperm created her? if love, protection and devotion makes a family i guess i have more people in my family then my blood-line suggest. lol dont post videos on youtube glorifying lab babies like they are a creation of god. its an abomination. she knew people would react this way when she put it on here. fuck off you pathetic need for acceptance by other people-if its about love, be happy with each other and stop trying to force others to accept it. its a union, not a marriage.

And so forth. Despite the occasional venomous comment, the support, as it had always been for us, was overwhelming.

Back in the summer of 2008, before our wedding, and when the Prop 8 campaign had started in earnest, Chelsea, at age 15, had witnessed for the first time a demonstration of hatred against her family. Up until that point, we had lived in our own world. Almost all of the people we came in contact with not only loved our story, but felt inspired by it. I believe we inspired two ideas:

Love is the only ingredient that mattered in any family,
and
Anything is possible.

I'd seen Chelsea melt the hearts of even seemingly right-winged people, so when the "Yes on 8" campaigners started show-ing up on street corners waving hateful signs such as, "God Hates Fags" and "It's Adam and Eve, not Adam and Steve," Chelsea's heart hurt. She didn't understand why someone she had never met would want to say that her family was wrong, bad, or going to hell. I specifically remember driving through Pasadena on the way home from a ballroom lesson with her. Beside a small church, a group of parishioners were gathered, holding their signs in the air. Most disturbing was seeing the young children, no older than seven or eight, holding signs that said, "Yes on 8" and "Marriage is between and a Man and a Woman." Chelsea turned to me and said, "Dad, why do they hate us? They don't even know us. How can those kids know what they are protesting. I feel so violated!"

I told her, "That's why we have to speak out. They don't know us. Maybe if they did, it would change their minds. They are fighting an idea that they have been told is wrong. It's not about loving each other, but about following a doctrine that has been fed to them which they feel is crucial to fight, or society will die."

Instead of taking her down, the campaign motivated Chelsea to make a difference. She used this energy to inspire her to let the world know that her family was just as loving, important, and caring as any traditional family. Within a month of seeing the protesters, we decided to post Chelsea's speech. With that action, she started the adventure of showing the world a more loving and accepting perspective.

Dennis and I had been involved for many years with the Human Rights Campaign, the largest gay rights organization in the United States. The HRC lobbies on behalf of LGBT people, not only to change minds but also to get legislation passed to protect and defend all marginalized population in this country. When Chelsea was nine, we started bringing her to the black tie Gala event in Los Angeles. We all loved to dress up. Dennis, always the natty dresser, looked like a movie star of the 1930's. He dresses within precision and style. I on the other hand am a bit more wild, with my pseudo tails and animal print lined tux.

I was sure the program would nearly put Chelsea to sleep, but Chelsea always loved going, transfixed by both the pomp and pageantry of a black tie event and the speeches. I, on the other hand, slept through many a presentation, as all political functions seem to have that knack on me.

Several of the board members were friends of ours, and after Chelsea's YouTube went big time, I got a call on my cell one day on my way to pick Chelsea up from school. They asked if Chelsea would like to speak on behalf of gay families at the Los Angeles Gala in March 2010. The guy barely got his words out before I told him she would love to. Of course, I hadn't asked her yet, but I was confident of her response. Chelsea was thrilled! We called Den, and he too was excited. This was a huge honor. She would be speaking before a thousand supporters of HRC. She thought that this would be the next step in promoting love for all families. (Plus, what performer doesn't like getting applause?) This was a big deal, but fortunately, we received the invite only three days before the event, so she didn't have a lot of time to get nervous.

We talked to Chris Speron, the Development Director of HRC, who produces the Galas all over the country, and he called Chelsea the day before to get an idea of how to craft the speech. Chris is calm and super cool, and immediately made Chelsea feel at ease. He thought it would be great to have Chelsea make the donations plea for the Federal Club, their sustaining fundraising tier, so he had specific things she needed to say, but he also wanted her to tell her story.

We arranged for hair and make up and arrived early for her to practice with the tele-prompters and become accustomed to the venue. She wore her beautiful Nikolaki gown from our wedding and had her hair up and looked so stunning that Chris said he hoped they would know she was only sixteen! Everyone was gracious and kind and tried to allay her nerves, which, up to this point, had been slight, a bit of nervous laughter and palm sweat, but as she got made up and dressed, the jitters started to take over. She kept pacing and going over her speech in the hotel room.

As we took our table in the room of 1,000, the enormity of her task must have dawned on our girl. She stopped talking and became very, very quiet. She had performed a lot, but I'd never seen her like this. She held her head down and could not speak. Chris had told us that they would come and get her when it was her time, but I could see, based on her catatonic state, that she needed some help. I gently put my hand on her shoulder and asked if she was okay.

"No!" she replied.

I asked if it would help if I found out exactly when she was going to speak, and she nodded gently. So I got up from our table, found Chris, and asked for the exact rundown. He told me that when I heard the announcer introduce California Senator Barbara Boxer (oh yeah, she was speaking right after our United States Senator), to take Chelsea to stage left. So, as Sen. Boxer took the stage, I took Chelsea's hand and led her to the wings.

She's never going to be able to do this! I thought. She was just too nervous. As we reached the side of the stage, an assistant told me that the stage manager would take her from there, and I could go meet her on the other side of the stage after her speech. I left her like a pool of water on the floor, praying she could get through the ordeal without throwing up.

Then, after a lovely introduction, this confident, beautiful creature emerged from stage left. I was astounded! What happened to that pool of stage fright I'd left a moment before? She was perfectly composed, said her welcome, and started in giving a powerful speech and plea for HRC support.[3] Joe Solmonese, the President of HRC, came and whispered in my ear.

"She's a superstar!" I was never so proud.

Chelsea had the audience members in the palm of her hand. She made them laugh, and she made them cry. She moved them, and they opened their pocket books for this wonderful organization. It was surreal! When she finished bowing, after thunderous applause, she turned toward stage right where I stood, and beamed at me. I couldn't tell which of us was glowing brighter. As we left the stage, Portia De Rossi, who was being honored that evening, jumped up from her seat and came over.

"How am I going to follow that?" she said.

The whole evening Chelsea found out what it was to be appreciated on a whole new level. Never had she felt the attention and adoration of so many people she had never met. She received offers for jobs and to speak at numerous events. She was in heaven. Many people told her, "I don't know many adults that could get up if front of 1,000 people, let alone a sixteen year old, and with such poise!" Dennis and I relished the joy of being the proudest parents in the world.

Chelsea now had the opportunity to reach thousands of people and make a difference. HRC took her "on the road." Within two month's time, she spoke in Los Angeles, San Francisco, and Las Vegas. Then in October of 2010, she spoke before 3,000 people at the National HRC Gala in Washington DC. She also spoke at a PFLAG (Parents and Friends of Lesbians and Gays) event and at Toyota for their Pride Month.[4] Everywhere she went, she had an impact, opening the eyes of

---

3. https://www.youtube.com/watch?v=v1mOgwKTDm0

4. We love the companies that honor every faction of their company. Toyota, with many LGBT employees, had led the charge and, for several years, celebrated a pride month.

not only those who had never met a person with gay dads, but also those within our own community. At the Toyota event, after Chelsea finished her speech, one gay gentleman in his late thirties approached her. As Chelsea gathered up her things, he very respectfully introduced himself and told her that he did not approve of gay families parading their daughter around as a poster child for same-sex families; but he had come to see what she was going to say, and after she'd spoken he was so moved. He said he realized her words came from her heart, and that she was not only inspiring, but an outstanding child who and changed his mind about children speaking out.

In addition to her live appearances, Chelsea has also had numerous articles written about her on the web and in print, including a couple of pieces on The Huffington Post.[5]

In September of 2010, Chelsea was honored by "Frontiers Magazine" as one of the top fifteen LGBT activists in Los Angeles. She has never wavered from her ideal of reaching everyone she can, to let them know that all families deserve the respect and rights that only some families are given freely. As I write this, the tide is turning. At the time of writing this book, thirty-one states[6] and the District of Columbia have legalized same sex marriage. Prop 8 was ruled unconstitutional by the Federal Court in California, in June of 2013. Things are changing and I know that a lot of that has to do with the brave straight allies like Chelsea, who have spoken out when they decided that unless everyone is equal, no one is. That's my girl!

---

5. http://www.thenextfamily.com/2010/04/life-with-my-dads/;
    http://www.thenextfamily.com/2010/04/life-with-my-dads/;
    http://www.tampabay.com/features/humaninterest/word-for-word-gay-marriage-means-the-world-to-a-teen-daughter/1041063;
    http://www.huffingtonpost.com/chelsea-montgomeryduban/post_908_b_736443.html?ref=fb&src=sp

6. http://gaymarriage.procon.org/view.resource.php?resourceID=004857

DUH!

Age 7½

Dennis and Chelsea were having an in depth conversation about life and Chelsea announced, "I know what my gift from God is. It's spiritual. It's very special. God sends me messages in my brain and then I can tell people."

━✢━

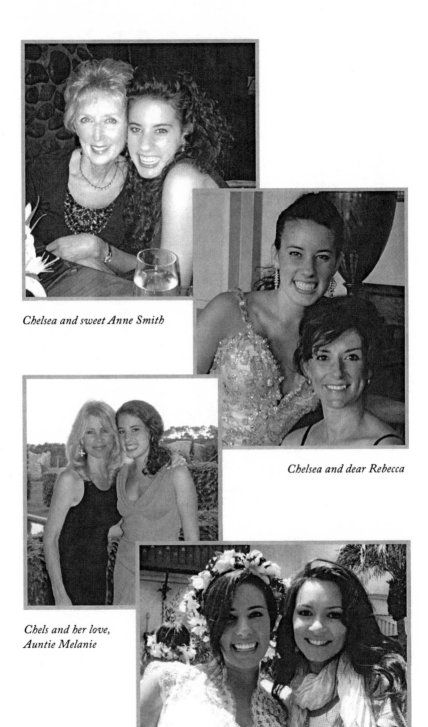

Chelsea and sweet Anne Smith

Chelsea and dear Rebecca

Chels and her love,
Auntie Melanie

Chels and her bestie Adriana

37

DUH!

Age 8

I met a girlfriend of Chelsea's that lives across the street from Amparo the other day. This child was probably 9 and so inquisitive. She started with criticism of my hair and ended with Chelsea can't possibly have two dads. "Well," I said, "That's not really true." She came back with, "A man and a woman have to have sex to have a baby, so who had sex?" So, I said, "That's not necessarily true." And she responded then, "Who made her?" And before I could say anything, Chelsea piped in and said, "God made me!"

Though Chelsea had struggled to create close "best-friend" relationships with peers her whole life, the adults in her life, especially teachers, seemed to adore her. As an only child, she'd gone everywhere with us, so she'd been interacting with adults her whole life and seemed to feel more comfortable with them. Throughout her middle and high school years, Chels had been continually awarded honors. Twice she received the Archer Arrow Award, given to the girl who most exemplifies the school's prized tenets of honesty, respect, and responsibility. In her junior year she also received the Bryn Mawr Book Award, given by the college to an exceptional student. We burst our buttons with each new recognition of our girl. In return, Chelsea loved her teachers, and her strong bonds with them lifted her up when she had hard times with her friends.

One of her closest allies was our friend Anne Smith from Washington. I would never be so crass as to reveal a woman's age (did I mention she got mail from AARP?). Anne took Chelsea on wonderful adventures, from buying expeditions for her Women's and Men's clothing store, to train trips to Vancouver and RV trips with her and her husband, Ron. The close bond with Anne filled Chelsea's need for a best friend.

Also, as miracles would have it, Chelsea and I started taking tap dance together with Rebecca Brancato Barragan, a firecracker of a woman and an angel of a soul. A curly, dark haired beauty who had danced professionally for years, Rebecca, and her husband, Raphael, had moved out to California from New York for him to pursue his acting career. I lovingly referred to Rebecca as Mother Theresa in tap shoes. She only saw the best in everyone and inspired me to be much more loving. Chelsea and I fell in love with her. Rebecca taught Chelsea to tap within about a month; a tribute to them both. Within two months, Rebecca decided that Chelsea and I should perform together at the yearly recital, setting the stage (literally) for one of the most magical moments of my life.

As the curtain went up, and my girl and I made our first flaps on the stage, I looked over, and my heart swelled with a wonderful thought. I am performing with my daughter! Twenty years ago, who would have thought I would ever even have a daughter, and here I was onstage tappin' away with my girl! It was surreal.

In addition to fulfilling my own impossible dream, Rebecca bonded with Chelsea, becoming another friend and confidante and giving Chels one more positive resource. As close as our family was, there were still times when she needed someone else to talk to, and preferably a woman. When we met Rebecca's adorable husband, Raphael, a dark handsome guy with a smile and personality that warmed your heart, together they became part of our family.

Chelsea's beautiful ballet teacher, Adriana, also came with a heart the size of the moon. She, too, took Chelsea under her wing and provided a wonderful shoulder to cry and lean on (all the while making sure she pointed her toes)! All of these women added depth and support, helping to balance out Chelsea's "She has two dads" world.

I am certain all of these women were sent by angels, but my favorite story is how Chels bonded with Auntie Melanie, one of our closest friends. While visiting a manor in Yorkshire, England, Melanie and Chelsea happened to both be wandering at the same time in a bucolic pasture full of livestock. They began to talk and wander together, until suddenly, a rogue bull decided to chase them; at which point, the two of them took off like the Road Runner cartoons. They made it safely behind a tree, laughing, breathing, and relieved to be alive; and from that moment they were bonded in a way unique to those who've shared a death-defying experience. Melanie had been in our lives for years, but one magical afternoon (in a pasture with a bull) brought her and Chels together in a way that they never saw coming (literally!). Melanie became a rock for our girl, and by the end of her junior year, Chelsea relaxed into her extended family of mentors.

Even with these wonderful women, Chelsea still longed for close peers. I felt certain college would provide the opportunity to find like-minded friends her own age, and as she swung into her junior year in high school, she started the application process. She'd always had a clear vision of where she wanted to go, be, do, and have. Her ideal was to have a career performing as a dancer, preferably on Broadway, but she realized through the years that, because it is so physical and hard on your body, a dancer's career is short-lived. By age thirty it's basically over. But she had a backup plan.

Chels decided to go for a life in musical theater, where one can work up into the hinter years and beyond. There are always character actors of all ages to play in musicals on the boards. I had to admire her forethought! Although dancing was her strong suit, she also had a beautiful voice and was quite the little actress, so I thought this was a great idea. A triple threat is hard to beat, and a dancer who can sing will always find work.

Chelsea started looking for colleges that offered a Bachelor of Fine Arts degree in Musical Theater, a specialized, conservatory kind of program. We soon found out it was easier to get into med school than musical theater. In hindsight we would have strategized very differently, but we blindly started the search for the top BFA musical theater programs across the country. Oh, and btw (I know how to text!), my daughter was quite the mature girl. She knew she was so attached to her dads that if she didn't go to a college far enough away to make weekend visits prohibitive, she would never learn how to be independent. She was way more mature than I ever was and made the self-imposed choice to only apply on the east coast, right away narrowing the options. She applied to six BFA programs, one semi-back-up school called Muhlenberg College, and also, just for fun, the University of Hawaii.

Touring colleges gave us a wake up call of epic proportions. We found out that at colleges like Carnegie Mellon (the number one musical theater BFA program in the country), 2,000 kids apply for twenty-two spots. Are you kidding me!? The odds were not in our favor, and competition was steep. "Glee" had just become a number one hit on TV, and it seemed that every kid in the country wanted a BFA in the Performing Arts. To add fuel to the fire, the girl applicants outnumbered the boys by 2:1. I wanted to be supportive of my girl, but even looking at an 8x10 head-shot brought back all the pain of my own rejection-riddled career, which I then projected onto my daughter. I was so anxious about our baby and the beginning of what could be a landslide of pain that I called Dennis in a panic from Philadelphia.

"Hi, Sweetheart!" I said, trying to sound positive.

"How's it going?" he replied.

"We're screwed," I said, abandoning positive for authentic.

Dennis calmed me down and reminded me that this was her path, we didn't have any control over it, and she had to go for what she wanted; so I took a lot of deep breaths and kept on going.

Our last campus on the tour agenda was in Allentown, PA. As we drove up to the Muhlenberg College campus, I fell in love (I fall in love a lot!). Set in a beautiful neighborhood, the campus was gorgeous, small, and very friendly. Chelsea found out at our info session that although she'd thought it was a BFA program, this was not an audition school for theater. The best she could do for a Bachelor of the Arts degree was double major in Theater and Dance. Well, when she found that out, she was over Muhlenberg; but I thought with the auditions looming for the other schools it may be our only option, so she interviewed at the school anyway. I could tell they loved her, and in my mind I relaxed just a bit, because I knew this could be a great place for Chels—if she gave it a chance.

We headed home, and throughout the summer and the beginning of Fall, in addition to preparing to apply to college, which for some is overwhelming in and of itself; Chelsea also prepared to audition for the BFA programs. Her last two years in high school nearly put both her and me in early graves. (Okay, probably more me than her, but only because I was statistically closer to pushing up a headstone.) Between studying for SATs, writing applications for each school (including essays for all), keeping her grades up, dancing seven days a week, rehearsing for the role of "The Sugar Plum Fairy" in the yearly "Nutcracker," and preparing auditions; Chelsea was stressed to her limit. I've never seen a kid work harder, and it took a toll. She was exhausted and close to breaking down every day. We talked about changing the strategy of her major or colleges, but she wouldn't have it. As is true in most cases, our dear girl would not back down, so we forged ahead.

Preparing for the auditions was particularly hard. Each school wanted a different format. Some wanted two songs: one uptempo, one ballad; some wanted three. Some thirty-two bars, some sixteen; some wanted two monologues, some three; some two minutes long, some three; some wanted them from a classical play, some only contemporary, but one serious and one funny. It was insane! Some of the kids had been working on their material for three years, so from the get go, we were a year behind.

A few months before the auditions, Chelsea pleaded with me to find an acting coach to help with her monologues. I called Chelsea's Auntie Judith, the amazing actress Judith Light, to see if she could recommend an acting coach. She told me of a coach she loved whom she was sure would be perfect. So I called the famous Ivana Chubbuck, who'd coached not only Judith, but Charlize Theron, and Halle Berry. She picked up the phone! I thought no one in Hollywood answered their phone, unless you're on a pre-approved list, and here I was on the line with a famous coach! I heard a dark, sultry, accented voice say, "Hullo."

I recovered from my shock and offered a chipper response.

"Hi there!" I said. "My daughter is auditioning for colleges and she needs a coach and I got your name from Judith Light, so I was wondering if you could help us?"

"I don't coach beginners."

"Oh."

My heart sank, but then a mini miracle occurred. Ms. Chubbuck said she had other coaches that could help us, and one in particular, Yonda Davis, had helped Ivana's own daughter get into NYU. Awesome! I thanked her, dialed Yonda's number, and explained my predicament.

Yonda was kind and encouraging, and as the conversation ensued, my current mini miracle grew bigger and brighter. Yonda asked me all about Chelsea, what we needed, and where Chelsea went to school.

"The Archer School For Girls," I said proudly.

"Really?"

"Yes, why?" Yonda then told me her daughter also went to Archer.

"Who's your daughter?" I asked.

"Ronesha Davis."

"OMG . . . I love Ronesha, and . . . wait a minute . . . I know who you are!"

We'd met at several parent functions, but out of context, I hadn't put the face to the name. Yonda told me not to worry, that she and her sweet partner, Deb, would take Chelsea under their wings and get her auditions together. I exhaled for the first time in a year and a half. What a relief to have that load lifted off of Chelsea—and me.

For the next several weeks, Chelsea met with Yonda and Deb, had voice lessons at the Colburn School of Music with Mike Stevens, her fabulous vocal coach, still managed to dance seven days a week, and pull straight A's. I would have never had the spunk, drive, determination, or desire to do what Chelsea was up against. But somehow she plodded on in grand style. I could only look at her with awe and admiration.

Then the audition process started. I took a deep breath, ignored my own audition-rejection anxiety ("OMG shoot me in the head I don't want to go through this"), and took her for the auditions. Chelsea amazed me. She actually enjoyed the audition process! For the first and only time, I wondered if she was my daughter. I didn't tell her this of course. I simply told her that she was in the right career, because 90% of an entertainer's life is auditioning. You probably work only 10 % of the time, so if you hate auditions (like moi), you are going to be miserable 90% of the time (even I can do that math). We went to all the required auditions. Chelsea thought some of them went well and others not so much, but she did enjoy herself.

Now came the toughest part—waiting for the answers. At this point Chelsea's number one choice was Syracuse University. When we'd visited the campus, she loved the school and had bonded with some of the kids. She wasn't crazy about Carnegie Mellon, because on our visit there they seemed to have an attitude that if you went anywhere else, you were so much a second-class performer. Forget that. Though the school had earned their top-ranking status, it was off-putting for them to wear it on their sleeve.

We started to get responses, and it wasn't going just as we had hoped. University of Hawaii wanted her as a dance major and even gave her a scholarship; which was nice, but not where she wanted to go. Ithaca turned her down, which wasn't too bad, because it also wasn't top on the list. However, Muhlenberg loved her and awarded her two academic scholarships. Although, it was not a BFA and still not Chelsea's first choice. Then came the day we lovingly refer to as Black Friday.

It all began when Chelsea checked her status online for Elon University in North Carolina, a BFA program and a school we really liked. The listing said she was accepted and under major read, "Musical Theater." We were ecstatic! Even if it wasn't her absolute first choice, she'd made it into a BFA program. However, at some point during our screams and palpitations, Chelsea had a question.

"Dad, you don't think that this is just an acceptance into the college, but not the major, do you?"

"Of course not," I replied. "It says, "Accepted," and right next to that, it says your major is Musical Theater."

Thus we were all convinced and spent a glorious night celebrating and feeling relief. All of her hard work had been worth it. The next day Chelsea called me from school.

"Dad, my friends don't think Elon has listed who got into Musical Theater yet. They think I was only accepted to the school."

"Okay, don't panic," I said, " I'll call them and find out."

Well, I found out. Her friends were right. The polite lady in admissions explained that they give two different notices, one for the college and one for the program, and the program notices would go out on Friday. Well, did she ever get an earful from me! How could they list the major and "accepted" on the same line and not mean the student was accepted in that major?! She curtly replied that our interviewers had told us at the info session that there would be two different notices.

Oh great! We only did fifty info sessions at fifty colleges and didn't quite remember every detail. In my best Papa Bear voice I told her this was cruel punishment, and she needed to let me know right now if Chelsea got in the BFA or not because it would be torture to have to wait a week, especially after we'd spent the night thinking she was in. Another week not knowing could give me a coronary, not to mention our daughter would be tortured, and I couldn't have that!

Well, despite my excellent (if slightly dramatic) appeal, she would not relent and said we had to wait the week like everyone else. Of course I didn't die, but I felt like I had, and Chelsea was a walking zombie.[1] And now, may I introduce Black Friday.

On Friday, April 22, 2011, Chelsea called me from Archer saying she'd gotten an email from Syracuse saying she hadn't been accepted.

"Are you okay?" I asked her.

"Yeah, I'm okay," she replied. "I just want to get out of school and hug you." I picked her up and she cried a bit, but as is her way, by the time we were half way home she had come to acceptance, and she was going to be fine. I was so proud! As a family we always make an effort to believe that everything happens for the best, but when the dream you have wished for for so long seems to fizzle, it can be very hard to remember that all will work out perfectly.

As we arrived home, I casually got the mail out of the mailbox and saw that there was an envelope from Elon—a very small envelope. Oh, no. As Chelsea opened it, her eyes filled with tears. The stress of the last several months hit her full force, and she fell apart. It was just too much rejection, pressure, and heartache for our little girl; and she ran to her room and cried.

After several minutes, I went up and witnessed a scene a parent never wants to see. My daughter looked at me and said,

---

1. I did walk away with a minor victory. When we checked Chelsea's status again on the Elon website, they had taken down the major. The line now read simply said, "Accepted."Thanks, Elon!

"What is wrong with me? No one wants me. I must be terrible."

I felt horrible, helpless, and heartbroken. It was a black day for our family. Chelsea had worked so hard and long, and the pain and rejection took more than a few hours or days for any of us to recover from.

About a week later, Chelsea recovered enough to once again begin to consider her options. She had only to hear from Carnegie Mellon, which she wasn't really interested in going to, but if it meant a BFA, then she would be happy. Attitude be damned, it was still the number one BFA program in the country. But, as the time wore on, Chelsea wanted more to feel settled and know what her future held, so she started leaning toward Muhlenberg, if for no other reason than to be done with it.

I loved Muhlenberg. I loved the feel of it, the people there, and the beautiful campus. I thought it would be the perfect fit for Chels, but she didn't want to feel like she had to go there because she wasn't accepted as a performer in any of the other institutions. However, Muhlenberg wanted Chelsea. They had given her two academic scholarships and were very much courting her to be part of their family. So, with Chelsea leaning towards accepting Muhlenberg, we went on a Spring Break trip to get away from it all.

By the time we returned, Chelsea was feeling very settled about going to Muhlenberg, so when we got home and found a very large envelope from Carnegie Mellon, we nearly busted a gizzard. Chelsea was on the priority waiting list at the number one BFA, Musical Theater program in the country. We were astounded, overjoyed, and stunned! This was just what the doctor ordered! The notice buoyed our baby girl and gave her an affirmation that she was part of a small, select group and that she was recognized for her talent, which not only took the sting out of so much rejection, but also clarified how she wanted to proceed. Although she remained on the waiting list at CM for a while, she now felt she had a choice in the matter and realized she wanted to go to Muhlenberg after all. She ordered her Muhlenberg sweatshirt, wore it proudly at Archer, and took her first steps toward being a college co-ed.

As we bonded with the Muhlenberg family, we began to face a high quality problem. Our daughter, our sweetheart, our baby girl, was about to leave her dads and head into the big world—on the other side of the country!

Chelsea seemed to be handling the transition fairly well. While there were many moments of fear and frightening anticipation, overall she seemed to process the thoughts of her future with a mature, level-headed calm. Den was another story.

Dennis suffered greatly with the thought that Chels would not be home, in her room, at dinner every night, and available for a daily kiss and hug. I was with her more, but Den was at work every day, and he constantly had the gut feeling that he just didn't have enough Chelsea time. With college on the horizon, the ache in his gut became acute.

At one point I had to take him aside and tell him, "Honey, you have to try to not be so emotional and cry at movies and commercials, weeping and grabbing Chelsea's hand. It's startin' to freak her out." He loved his little girl so much, and as cliché as it is . . . it all went so fast. In the blink of an eye. So much parenting advice we'd received was not true, but one idiom rang like a gong: You turn around, and all of sudden they're gone.

I refer to this period as the "Agony and the Ecstasy" phase. We were so proud of Chelsea. She was a light, speaking out to the world and changing hearts and minds. She was a stellar student. She was recognized by her college as a student they desired greatly and awarded with scholarships. She was a beautiful performer. But, more than anything, she was a kind, sweet, and compassionate soul who carried joy into every room she entered. DD and I were awestruck and humbled by the amazing young woman that we had and the phenomenal life we three shared. This was the ecstasy. However, after the recently traveled journey of rejection and pain of the college process, our pride and joy to was about to leave us. This was the agony.

We sat in tears with our families at Chelsea's high school graduation. As she entered the arena with her classmates, all in white with her head adorned in the Archer traditional flower wreath, our girl looked stunning. When the master of ceremonies announced the surprise honoree of the Honestas Award, (for demonstration of character and moral conviction), we were overwhelmed with joy and pride as she called Chelsea Montgomery-Duban to be honored at the podium. I can't say we were surprised.

Most of this journey had been a surprise to us. A surprise inspired by others' comments that we should be parents. A surprise that we actually followed through and brought forth a child. A surprise in the incredible love and sacrifice that Sandy and Helene made to make our dream a reality. A surprise, at the glorious creature who was our daughter. And a total surprise, that we could love this deeply and experience the astounding joy that Chelsea Austin Montgomery-Duban had brought to our hearts. We reveled daily in our blessings and kneeled humbly at our Maker who saw fit that two gay guys should be worthy enough to receive the gift of parenthood and the blessing of a child from the angels. Everything else paled . . . there are no words.

DUH!

Age 8½

Dennis had to go to Hawaii and I went my own separate way to a spa for the weekend . . . typical! Chelsea was very distraught that we both would be gone at the same time. Lots of tears and discussions about it. I felt some twangs of guilt as Lance massaged my poor muscles . . . some! So, I called home when I got in the room. Chelsea seemed very uninterested to talk to me. I kept trying and finally she said, "Dad, I gotta get on with my life!"

Our angel and our light!

Epilogue

We had one weekend to move Chelsea into her room at Muhlenberg College. We hired a dorm-moving service, Chelsea found a compatible roommate online through the miracle of modern technology, and we prepared for our little family trip; planning to get there three days early, organize and acclimate ourselves, and shop for any last minute items that a new coed might just "have to have." "Nervous" and "excited" summed up all three of us. It was such huge move, and although Chelsea had chosen to plant herself 3,000 miles away from her dear old dads, I believe we all wondered how we were going to get through this.

As Friday, the appointed move in day, approached, the bile in our tummies gradually edged closer to the surface, even while we put on our best happy faces and tried to remain calm. Then on a call with her new roommate, Ariana, Chelsea casually mentioned that we were leaving on Monday, after we spent the weekend getting Chelsea settled, Ariana corrected her.

"Oh, no," she said. "I think your parents have to leave on Friday." What? No!

We had worked this out. We would move everything in on Friday and then have dinner, maybe even lunch on Saturday.

Then on Sunday, a nice going away dinner, maybe with a few new friends. Then, and only then, on Monday the two dads would happily leave Pennsylvania and jet contentedly back to LA LA land—and their empty nest.

Dennis immediately called the college and let them know we needed the weekend to adjust. After all we were coming all the way from California. We couldn't possibly just drop and go. It simply wasn't in the cards.

Well, apparently, we had a totally different deck of cards than Muhlenberg. They were even more adamant than we were. On Friday, after move in and lunch, Chelsea would attend her first meeting of her RJ Fellows scholarship group,[1] and we would head in the exact opposite direction to a parent meeting; where they would promptly escort us to our cars with clear instructions to get in, start the car, point it toward home, and don't turn back. We were crushed. But we were nothing if not dutiful and resilient, so a change in plans was made. We changed our flights, adjusted to life on life's terms, and toddled off to bed for a very sleepless night.

On Friday morning, with renewed vigor, we promptly headed for our seven am arrival at Chelsea's new home. The college was extremely organized. Hives of happy little helpers swarmed our car and unloaded Chelsea's stuff in what seemed like minutes. After we unpacked her, we met her roommate and family and looked up to find out it was already time for lunch. In the dining hall, we met so many nice families, but our heads spun with anxiety. It was almost time. Lunch concluded fifteen minutes before we had to go to our respective

---

1. The RJ Fellows Scholarship was established by a Muhl Board of Trustees member Joseph Scheller and his wife, Rita, and awarded to students that can change the world through their chosen field.

Our sweet co-ed

meetings, and we reluctantly looked for the building where Chelsea needed to go. Finally, at three minutes to 1:00, we started our good byes. I hugged and hugged her, she started to cry, and Dennis teared up as he gave her one more last hug. The clock struck the fateful hour and Eric, a student Chelsea had just met, swooped by, scooped up our little darling, and led her away. As they left, we heard Eric sweetly exclaim, "It's like a band aid; you just gotta rip it off!"

Den and I headed in the other direction.

"My hug wasn't long enough," he said. "I didn't have enough time," to which I sweetly replied, "Don't look back, dear. Just keep f###ing walking."

Turns out, college knows best. Lingering would have been too painful. We got texts and calls from Chels all day about the wonderful friends she met and how well she was doing. Den and I felt giddy that she seemed to be acclimating and on the road to total adjustment. We walked around beautiful Bethlehem, PA that night; holding hands and feeling celebratory. Our little girl was grown and on her way to independence. We had done our job. We had done it well. You never stop being a parent, and your work is never done; but the main goal is to send them into the world as capable, strong, independent, and hopefully loving beings. We'd done all of those things: check, check, check, and double check!

Dennis has never been a demonstrative person. He's not warm and fuzzy by nature. But that had changed a lot with Chelsea. He couldn't get enough hugs, handholds, and kisses from our girl. I could not create the same desire in him. Quite honestly, sometimes I was a bit jealous that she was able to spark that in him. I know he loves me, but I didn't always get the same show of affection. Late that night, after we had been asleep for hours, I awoke as Dennis reached over, grabbed my hand, and held on tight.

"It's me," I alerted him.

He dreamily moved in and said, "I know."

End.

-/ı\-

Postscript

know that at times our story, with its Pollyanna-like quality, seems almost impossible to believe. Sometimes it's so good, even I don't buy it. But trust me; we have our challenges. As I write this, my dear, sweet husband is serving twenty-four months in a federal prison camp (think Martha Stewart) for tax fraud. We believe this is a terrible miscarriage of justice, but it is the hand we have been dealt. Our rain has fallen, and as we don our umbrellas and galoshes, we strive to be Gene Kelly-esque and dance amid the drops. We know that we will survive because of our deep love and devotion for each other, and our family, and the tremendous amount of support we receive from our friends and loved ones. Although we have felt betrayed and dismayed, we believe this challenge will result in some goodness. But we'll discover that in our next chapter . . .

—\⁄—

DUH!

Age 8

I was talking to Chelsea about the recent devastation of 911 and why someone would want to cause such pain. We talked about hou much pain the instigators must be in to do such a horrible thing and there was one person, it seemed that is the backbone of the whole event. She didn't even pause to think and said, "Oh, it's got to be something to do with his mother!"

―ᐱ―

About the Author

*K*evin Montgomery was born and raised in Pasadena California, so it was no surprise that he had dreams of being Rose Parade Queen . . . well, it was a bit of a surprise to his parents until he "came out" at 21. He pursued his thirst to perform until he realized rejection really sucks and ending up in a "bad lounge act" in Vegas was not his destiny. So, he returned to Los Angeles to his loving partner, Dennis of 10 years and started a family . . . well, it's a little more complicated than that, so that's why you got to read the book!!

Kevin, being blessed with a beautiful daughter became a full time parent and dove into that arena. He has served on the School Board for the Malibu Jewish Center and Synagogue; Treasurer and President of the Webster Elementary PTA; Financial Secretary and President of The Archer School For Girls Parent Association. Kevin has seen the positive impact that has been made on the children, adolescents and parents by being a role model as gay man intimately involved in the day-to-day aspects of their educational life.

Kevin and Dennis have been together 33 years, legally married for 8 years and have an amazing 22 year old daughter, Chelsea. The Montgomery-Dubans live in Malibu, CA.

CPSIA information can be obtained
at www.ICGtesting.com
Printed in the USA
FSOW02n1313291015
12775FS

9 780996 218009